MW00604217

OUR HOLY FAITH
A RELIGION SERIES for THE ELEMENTARY SCHOOLS

COURSE of STUDY and
TEACHER'S MANUAL for

My Father and Mother
on Earth and in Heaven

✝

Sister M. Alphonsine, S.S.J., M.A.
Sister M. Aquin, S.C., B.A.
Sister M. Joan, O.S.U., M.A.
Sister Jane Francis, C.S.J., M.A.
Sister M. Roch, H.H.M., M.A.
Sister M. Ronald, O.P., M.A.

Large Print Edition

ST. AUGUSTINE ACADEMY PRESS
HOMER GLEN, ILLINOIS

UNDER THE DIRECTION OF

Rt. Rev. Msgr. Clarence E. Elwell, Ph.D.
Superintendent of Schools

WITH THE COLLABORATION OF

Rt. Rev. Msgr. Joseph Moriarty, M.A.
Department of Religion
St. John College, Cleveland, Ohio

Nihil obstat:
    JOHN F. MURPHY, S.T.D.
    Censor librorum

Imprimatur:
    + WILLIAM E. COUSINS
    Archbishop of Milwaukee

    August 7, 1961

This book was originally published in 1961
by Bruce Publishing, Milwaukee.

This reprinted edition ©2017 by St. Augustine Academy Press
Compressed Edition ISBN: 978-1-64051-017-3
Large Print Edition ISBN: 978-1-64051-048-7

Contents

LITURGICAL FEASTS:

ADDITIONAL UNITS FOR FIRST HOLY COMMUNION

BIBLIOGRAPHY:

Introduction for the Teacher

GRADE ONE RELIGION COURSE
Theme: My Father and Mother on Earth and in Heaven

The unifying theme of religion in Grade One is God's love for us. He is our heavenly Father, who watches over us all the days of our life. From all eternity He has loved us, and it is His will that we live with His own life and share in His happiness. His love is the reason why He sent us His divine Son, Jesus Christ, to redeem us from sin and to found His Church, the Mystical Body of which Christ is head and we are members. We frequently call the Church "Our Holy Mother Church," and it is to the Church as Mother of Christ's faithful that the title refers. Because He loves us, God has given us the Holy Spirit, to enlighten our minds and warm our hearts and to dwell with us as Protector and Paraclete. Love again is the reason for the graces God showered upon Mary, and for the good things we have — parents, school, our priests and teachers. This love demands a return of love from us.

The doctrinal content of Grade One is centered on the Apostles' Creed. Within the framework of the Creed young children can be introduced to the basic truths of our faith, namely, the existence of one God in three divine Persons, Christ's work of redemption and the founding of His Church, and the role of the Holy Spirit in giving life to that Church and in uniting its members through the bonds of faith, hope, and charity.

This subject matter is divided into ten units. Along with the doctrinal content, these units suggest virtues to be practiced, fundamental prayers to be learned, and devotional practices. In addition, each unit concludes with lessons devoted to special feasts of the Church in order to acquaint the children with some of the more important saints and the way the Church remembers them in the Church year.

All the lessons in this course of study are treated as development lessons. The teacher, however, will provide review as the need arises. She will also evaluate pupil progress from time to time through questioning and by administering simple oral and written tests.

Each of the lessons in this text consists of the following parts: (1) objectives; (2) approach; (3) presentation; (4) organization; and (5) virtues and practices. The objectives and approach given for each lesson are self-explanatory. The presentation is the heart of the lesson. The teacher will take the concepts offered and adapt them to the vocabulary and understanding of a first-grade class.

After presenting the central core of the lesson, the teacher should, with her pupils, summarize this material. This can best be accomplished by having the children answer orally the questions listed under "Organization." Each religion lesson, in addition, should seek to show the children how the religious truths discussed apply in daily life. To foster this application the teacher should choose one or two of the suggestions given in the section titled "Virtues and Practices," encouraging the children to make some practical resolutions for everyday life.

Each lesson concludes with suggestions for correlated activities and teacher reference materials.

Units of Study and Approximate Time Allotments

FIRST SEMESTER

Unit One	The Church	3 weeks
Unit Two	God Our Heavenly Father	6 weeks
Unit Three	The Lord's Prayer	3 weeks
Unit Four	God's Goodness in Sending His Son to Us	2 weeks
Unit Five	The Childhood of Jesus	4 weeks

SECOND SEMESTER

Unit Six	The Public Life of Our Lord	4 weeks
Unit Seven	The Greatest Proof of Jesus' Love — His Passion and Death	5 weeks
Unit Eight	The Resurrection and Ascension of Jesus	2 weeks
Unit Nine	God the Father and God the Son Show Their Love by Sending the Holy Spirit	2 weeks
Unit Ten	Mary Our Heavenly Mother	5 weeks

If the teacher is to prepare the class for First Holy Communion, certain lessons could be omitted or compressed in order to lessen the teaching load. For example, the lessons on the feast days at the end of each unit could be omitted, and the following lessons could easily be compressed:

1. Lessons 63 through 71, on the Life of Christ, can easily be compressed into two or three lessons or, if necessary, omitted;

2. Lessons 77 through 88, on the miracles of Christ;

3. Lessons 102 through 115, on the Stations of the Cross;

4. Lessons 136 through 150, on the mysteries of the Rosary.

The suggested learning activities indicate the variety which *may* be used not only in the religion class, but also in language, music, art, reading, etc. Pictures, charts, and reading references are suggested for the all-important informational background of the teacher.

The books listed below are essential to the successful teaching of this religion program (cf. Bibliography, p. 303 ff.).

Dennerle, George, *Leading the Little Ones to Christ*, Bruce

Marguerite, Sister Mary, *Their Hearts Are His Garden*, St. Anthony Guild

Mary, Sister, *et al.*, *The Catholic Mother's Helper*, St. Anthony Guild

Fitzpatrick, E. A., ed., *Religion in Life Curriculum, First Grade Manual*, Bruce

S.N.D., *Religious Teaching of Young Children*, Newman Bookshop

Belger, Sister Mary Josita, *Sing a Song of Holy Things*, Tower Press, 5701 W. Washington Blvd., Milwaukee, Wis.

Weiser, Francis X., *Religious Customs in the Family*, Liturgical Press, Collegeville, Minn.

NOTE: See Bibliography, p. 303 ff., for complete list and information.

GENERAL OBJECTIVES FOR THE YEAR

A. To help the pupils understand that Jesus in the Blessed Sacrament is true God, and to guide them in the development of habits of respect, reverence, and personal love for Jesus in the Eucharist and in the Holy Sacrifice of the Mass.

B. To foster correct and reverent habits of behavior in church.

C. To develop a knowledge of God's nature and principal attributes so that the pupil is led to see God as his Creator and Heavenly Father, whom he should love and serve with his whole heart.

D. To know and appreciate God's great love for men, especially as shown in the Redemption of man through the Passion, Death, Resurrection, and Ascension of Jesus Christ.

E. To develop the knowledge of religious truths as a basis for a deeper love for vocal and mental prayer, and to understand and memorize the following prayers: "The Sign of the Cross," "Hail Mary," "Morning Offering," "The Lord's Prayer," "Angel of God," "Prayers Before and After Meals," "Morning and Night Prayers," "Glory Be to the Father," and the "Apostles' Creed."

F. To develop the knowledge that Mary is the Mother of God, and to instill in pupils a great love for her and a desire to honor her.

G. To celebrate some important feasts of the Church.

UNIT ONE

The Church — God's House
Time: 3 weeks

I. INTRODUCTION FOR THE TEACHER

Unit One is intended to give first graders some understanding of the following basic concepts: the presence of God in all Catholic churches, the role the priest plays, the purpose of the objects used in the worship of God, the reverence the child must have for the house of God and in the house of God. The teacher must take the children to church at least twice during the first week of school in order to acquaint them with the various objects in it. In the first visit she must impress upon them the fact that the church is God's house and the home of Jesus on earth, thereby arousing in the children reverence and respect for the Blessed Sacrament.

II. OBJECTIVES OF THE UNIT

A. To develop the knowledge that the church is God's house and the home of Jesus on earth.

B. To develop the knowledge that Jesus in the Blessed Sacrament is God.

C. To develop habits of respect, reverence, and personal love for Jesus in the Blessed Sacrament.

D. To become acquainted with the objects in the church as a means of fostering a feeling of respect for them.

E. To know the importance and dignity of the priesthood, and to develop habits of respect for priests.

F. To know how and when to make the "Sign of the Cross" and to develop the habit of making it devoutly.

III. SUBJECT MATTER

A. The home of Jesus on earth
B. The presence of God in all Catholic churches
C. Jesus lives with us in the Mass
D. Reverence in church
E. "Sign of the Cross"

1

F. The priest
G. Objects in church
H. Liturgical feasts:
1. Nativity of the Blessed Virgin Mary — September 8
2. Holy Name of Mary — September 12

LESSON 1

I. SUBJECT MATTER

The Home of Jesus on Earth

II. OBJECTIVES

A. To encourage a personal love for Jesus, the Friend of children.
B. To develop the knowledge that the church is the house of God and the home of Jesus on earth.

III. SUGGESTED PROCEDURE

A. Approach

Informal discussion: Who helped you get ready for school this morning? (Mother.) What does your mother do for you every day? Is there someone else who does many things for you every day? (Father.) What does he do for you? Why do our mothers and fathers do so many nice things for us every day? (They love us.) Perhaps they have already told you about Someone who loves you more than they do — Someone who is your very best Friend. Do you know who that is? (God.) Can you tell us some of the things you know about God? (Allow children to discuss freely.) Jesus is God. He is our Friend. Here is a picture of Jesus with some little children. Listen carefully and I will tell you about Him.

B. Presentation

1. Story: "Jesus Blesses the Little Children"

One day Jesus was very tired. He sat down to rest. Many little children who were playing nearby saw Jesus, so they quickly ran up to Him. Some mothers brought their children to Him, too. How happy these children were to be near Jesus. They knew very well that Jesus loved them, because He was always so kind to them. Each child tried to be as close to Jesus as possible.

Some men, who were Jesus' friends, tried to send the children away. "Go away," they said, "Jesus is very tired and cannot be bothered now." Jesus was tired, but not too tired for His little children. He needed rest, but He forgot about Himself and thought only of making the children happy. So He said, "Do not send the children away. They are My children and I love them." How happy the children were to hear this. They all began to tell Jesus many things, especially that they loved Him. Jesus blessed them and talked with them for a long time.

After a while it was time for Jesus to go away because He had work to do. The children did not want Jesus to go away. "Don't go away," they said over and over. "We love You. Please stay with us always." Jesus loved the children so much that He did want to stay with them.

2. The Home of Jesus on Earth

If you could have been there with those children, how happy you would have been. Jesus knew that we, too, would like to be near Him. So He thought of a wonderful plan. He thought of a place where He would stay so He could be near us all the time. Do you know where that place is? Yes, it is the church. Do you know where the house of Jesus is in church? (Show picture of altar.) Jesus is in this little house on the altar. This little house is called the "tabernacle." Jesus lives in the tabernacle all day and all night. He is waiting for His little children like you to come and talk to Him. How happy He is when He sees His little friends come to visit Him.

We will all go to visit Jesus soon. Then Jesus will bless us because He loves us. During the year we will learn many other nice things about Jesus. We will also learn what we can do to make Him happy.

Thank Jesus now for loving us so much. Thank Him for staying in the tabernacle for us. Couldn't we tell Jesus that we love Him, too? Let's do it now.

C. Organization

1. Why did Jesus want to rest?
2. What did the children do when they saw Jesus?
3. Who felt sorry for Jesus because He was disturbed?
4. Did Jesus feel bad because the children disturbed Him? Why not?
5. What did the children tell Jesus?

6. What would you tell Jesus if you were there?
7. Can we go to visit Jesus now?
8. Where is the home of Jesus on earth?

D. Virtues and Practices

1. Thank Jesus for loving you and staying here on earth for you.
2. Tell Jesus that you love Him and want to learn more about Him.
3. Try to be kind to others, because Jesus was very kind.

IV. SUGGESTED LEARNING ACTIVITIES

A. Dramatize the story; "Jesus Blesses Little Children."
B. Compose original prayers to Jesus, our best Friend.
C. Picture Study: Vogel's "Christ Blessing Little Children."
D. Poem: "Finding You" — *The Child on His Knees*, pp. 32–33.

V. TEACHER REFERENCES (cf. p. 303 ff.).

A. Sister Mary, *et al.*, *The Catholic Mother's Helper*, pp. 32–33.
B. Dennerle, *Leading the Little Ones to Christ*, pp. 3–7.
C. Fitzpatrick, *Religion in Life Curriculum, First Grade Manual*, pp. 12–14.
D. Holy Bible — Mk. 10:13–16.

LESSON 2

I. SUBJECT MATTER

The Presence of God in All Catholic Churches

II. OBJECTIVES

A. To develop the knowledge that Jesus in the Blessed Sacrament is God, and that He is present in every Catholic church.
B. To develop a personal love for Jesus in the Blessed Sacrament and to encourage the practice of visiting Him.

III. SUGGESTED PROCEDURE

A. Approach

Who remembers something we learned about a dear Friend of little children? (Show picture of Jesus and children again; allow children to discuss briefly.) Yesterday we learned that Jesus lives in church. Does anyone remember what we call His little house? Yes, it is the tabernacle. (Show the picture and discuss.)

B. Presentation

1. Jesus in the Blessed Sacrament Is God

Jesus is holy God. His home is in heaven, but it is also in the church. No matter when you go into the church, you will find Jesus there. He is waiting for you. He wants you to talk to Him. He wants you to say, "Jesus, I love You."

2. The Presence of God in All Catholic Churches

Jesus must surely love us. He stays in the tabernacle all the time waiting for us. Jesus is not only in our church but He is also in all Catholic churches. (Discuss some of the Catholic churches in the vicinity.) Every Catholic church has a tabernacle in which Jesus lives. Every Catholic church has a light burning somewhere near the tabernacle. That little light tells us that Jesus is in the tabernacle. The little light is called a sanctuary light. (Discuss the sanctuary lamp in our church: where located, what it looks like, why it is there.)

3. Why Jesus Lives in the Tabernacle

We cannot see Jesus when we go into the church because He is in the tabernacle, but Jesus sees us. Even though we cannot see Him, we know that He is there. Jesus promised to stay close to us and He keeps His promise. He loves us so much that He wants to stay near us and help us.

Whenever you go into the church to visit Jesus, look right up at the tabernacle. Tell Jesus that you know He is there and that you love Him. Jesus will look at you with a smile and will bless you for coming to visit Him. Go to Him every time you get a chance. He loves to see you and wants to talk to you. You wouldn't want to disappoint your Friend, would you? I have a surprise to tell you — we will go to visit Jesus today. (Plan a visit to church with the children. Discuss what to look for.) What will we say to Jesus when we go there? (Discuss briefly what children can say to Jesus.)

C. Organization

1. Where is the home of Jesus on earth?

2. What is the tabernacle?
3. How long does Jesus stay in the tabernacle?
4. Why is a little light burning beside the altar?
5. What do we call the little light?
6. Why does Jesus stay in the tabernacle?
7. When could you go to visit Jesus?

D. Virtues and Practices

1. Make extra visits to Jesus in the Blessed Sacrament.
2. Thank Jesus for staying in the tabernacle to be near you.

IV. SUGGESTED LEARNING ACTIVITIES

A. Compose original prayers to Jesus in the Blessed Sacrament.
B. Story: "Jesus in the Tabernacle," Sr. Mary, *et al., The Catholic Mother's Helper,* pp. 35–36.
C. Poem: "My Visits," Belger, *Sing a Song of Holy Things,* pp. 4–5.

V. TEACHER REFERENCES (cf. p. 303 ff.).

Sister Mary, *et al., The Catholic Mother's Helper,* pp. 33–36.

LESSON 3

I. SUBJECT MATTER

Jesus Continues to Live With Us Through the Mass

II. OBJECTIVES

A. To know that Jesus becomes present on the altar during the Consecration of the Mass.
B. To instill habits of reverence during Mass, especially at the Consecration.

III. SUGGESTED PROCEDURE

A. Approach

Yesterday we talked about Jesus living in the tabernacle. Does anyone know how Jesus comes to live there?

B. Presentation

1. When and How Jesus Comes to Live in Our Altar

Jesus died to save us. He died many years ago. Every day at Mass Jesus again offers His death on the cross to God the Father for us.

During Mass the priest takes the place of Jesus. Of course, you know who Jesus is. (God.) Did Mother or Daddy ever tell you what God can do? (Everything.)

Before Jesus died on the cross for us He did a very wonderful thing to show His great love for us. He wanted to stay with us on earth all the time, so He gave us the Mass and the Blessed Sacrament. Did you ever go to Mass? (Discuss.) Every time the priest says Mass, he brings Jesus down on the altar. The priest says Mass every day. So, our Lord comes down on our altars every day and lives with us all the time.

2. What the Priest Does and What We Should Do During the Consecration

Next time you go to Mass, listen very carefully. When you hear the bell ring, that means that Jesus is coming. Watch carefully! The priest, through the power of God, changes bread and wine into the Body and Blood of Jesus. The Body of Jesus is called the Sacred Host. After the priest changes the bread into the Body of Jesus he lifts up the Sacred Host for us to see. We should look at it and say, "My Lord and my God" and think about Jesus. This means that we believe the bread is now the Body of Jesus. After that, the priest, through the power of God, changes the wine into the Blood of Jesus. Then he lifts up the golden cup, called a chalice, for us to see. We should look at it, bow our heads and say, "My Jesus, Mercy." This means that we believe the wine is now the Blood of Jesus. (Show pictures of Consecration and Elevation. Discuss.)

3. By Good Conduct We Can Show Jesus How Grateful We Are for All He Does for Us

The part of the Mass in which the priest changes bread and wine into the Body and Blood of Jesus is called the Consecration. This part of the Mass is so holy that we must be especially quiet. All we can hear are the bells, which tell us Jesus is on our altar. We should tell God how much we love Him and thank Him for dying for us and for coming down from heaven to live with us. (Practice actions at Consecration and Elevation.)

C. Organization

1. Whose place does the priest take during Mass?
2. What does the priest do at Mass?
3. How do you know when it is time for the Consecration?
4. What should you do when you hear the bells ring?
5. What prayer should you say when you see the Sacred Host?
6. What does the prayer "My Lord and my God" mean?
7. Why should we be especially quiet at the Consecration of the Mass?

D. Virtues and Practices

1. Behave properly and devoutly during Mass.
2. Pay special attention and be very, very quiet during the Consecration of the Mass.
3. Love and thank Jesus for coming on our altar during Mass.

IV. SUGGESTED LEARNING ACTIVITIES

A. Dramatize conduct during the Consecration.
B. Show filmstrip, "The Mass for Young Children," by S.N.D. — Catechetical Guild.
C. Story: "Jesus' Workshop," Brennan, *For Heaven's Sake,* pp. 68–70.
D. Poem: 1. "The Bell," S. E., *Poems for God's Child,* p. 50.*

THE BELL

First, "God is holy," sings the bell
Then, "God is coming," can't you tell?
And then in song as glad and clear
As joyous angels: "God is here!"
The last time that it rings it's three
Is just before God visits me,
To say to him, "I welcome Thee."
I wish my voice might always say,
Just as the bell, "God comes this way."

V. TEACHER REFERENCES (cf. p. 303 ff.).

A. Dennerle, *Leading the Little Ones to Christ,* pp. 85–93, 246–247.

---

* Quotations from *Poems for God's Child* throughout this manual have been made possible through the courtesy of the owner of the copyright, The St. Anthony Guild Press.

B. Sister of N. D., *Religious Teaching of Young Children*, pp. 130–132.

LESSON 4

I. SUBJECT MATTER

Reverence in Church

II. OBJECTIVES

A. To develop a personal love for Jesus in the Blessed Sacrament.
B. To learn how to behave reverently in church.

III. SUGGESTED PROCEDURE

A. Approach

Tell the story of a little boy who went to visit a king or president. Discuss his behavior in the presence of such a great person.

B. Presentation

1. Boys Remove Hats; Girls Wear Head Coverings

Jesus is greater than any person in this world because He is God. When we go to visit His house, the Catholic church, there are certain things we should do in order to be very polite to so wonderful a Person. (Discuss what some of these things are.)

When boys go into the church the first thing they do is remove their caps or hats. For girls it is just the opposite. They must be sure to have their heads covered. It is good church manners for boys to remove their caps and for girls to have their heads covered.

2. Use of Holy Water

Inside the church near the door is a holy-water font. Dip the tips of the fingers of the right hand into the holy water and very carefully make the Sign of the Cross like this — (Demonstrate, children practice). When you do this God blesses you as you enter the church.

3. Genuflecting and Greeting

You should walk very quietly and slowly down the aisle of the church with hands folded. You should look toward the altar where

Jesus is. When you come to the pew into which you are going, kneel on your right knee. This is called genuflecting. (Demonstrate, children practice.) While you are genuflecting, keep your hands folded and say a little prayer to Jesus such as, "Jesus, I love You." Remember, Jesus is God, our King. That is why we genuflect or kneel on the right knee before Him. (Children practice genuflecting and saying prayer.)

4. Talking to Jesus

After you are in the pew, kneel up straight with your hands folded. Then talk to Jesus. What are some nice things you can say to Jesus?

5. Respectful Posture and Conduct

During Mass watch what the Sisters and others who know how to act do. Sometimes they kneel, sometimes they stand, and sometimes they are seated. Do what they do. When it is time to kneel, do not half-sit and half-kneel. That is not polite. If you are ill sit down or leave the church. Since you are in the presence of God, one way of showing how much you think of Him is to keep silence. Never laugh and talk in church. This shows you know that Jesus is on the altar. He is God Himself.

C. Organization

1. Why should we be polite in church?
2. What do boys do as soon as they go into church?
3. What do girls always wear in church?
4. Why do we use holy water as we go into church?
5. How should we walk into church?
6. What do we mean by genuflecting?
7. What should we do as soon as we are in the pews?
8. Why do we keep silence in church?

D. Virtues and Practices

1. Always use holy water reverently.
2. Genuflect properly.
3. Be polite to God by kneeling up straight.
4. Keep silence in church and pray.

IV. SUGGESTED LEARNING ACTIVITIES

A. Discuss pictures of children in church and note what they are doing.

B. Compose little prayers to say to Jesus while we are waiting for Mass to begin, or when we go to pay Jesus a little visit.

C. Go to church and practice proper behavior.

D. Story: "We Don't Talk in Church," Aurelia-Kirsch, *Practical Aids for Catholic Teachers*, p. 131.

E. Poem: "In Church," Thayer, *The Child on His Knees*, pp. 12–13.

V. TEACHER REFERENCES (cf. p. 303 ff.).

A. S.N.D., *Religious Teaching of Young Children*, pp. 132–134.

B. Sr. Mary, *et al.*, *The Catholic Mother's Helper*, pp. 33–34.

C. Dennerle, *Leading the Little Ones to Christ*, pp. 7–8, 28–29.

LESSON 5

I. SUBJECT MATTER

Prayer: The Sign of the Cross

II. OBJECTIVES

A. To teach the children how to make the Sign of the Cross.

B. To know when to make the Sign of the Cross.

C. To foster the habit of making the Sign of the Cross well.

III. SUGGESTED PROCEDURE

A. Approach

Have you ever noticed the sign at the corner of your street? Why is it there? That's right. It tells you the name of the street. The traffic guard holds up a sign to stop. Our building has a sign on it. It tells us the name of our school. It also tells that this is a Catholic school.

B. Presentation

1. How and Why We Make the Sign of the Cross

We have a sign that shows we are Catholic children. It shows that we belong to God. Do you know what this sign is? It is the Sign of the Cross. We make it like this. (Show how to make the Sign of the Cross by using the cross drawn on the board.) We make a cross to bless ourselves and to show that we believe that in God there are three Persons, God the Father, God the Son, and God the Holy Spirit. Can you make the Sign of the Cross well? (Teach words. Practice words and actions.)

2. When to Use the Sign of the Cross

There are many times when we can make the Sign of the Cross. Everyone knows that we make the Sign of the Cross when we enter church, before and after we say our prayers, when we begin school. But there are other times when we should make it too. Maybe some of you can tell when it would be good to make the Sign of the Cross. (Discuss.) We should make the Sign of the Cross when we wake up in the morning. By doing this we tell God that we are thinking about Him the first thing in the morning. Above all, make the Sign of the Cross whenever you are tempted to do something wrong. When you get angry and want to rage and break things, calmly make this prayer. It will help remind you that you are dear to God and that He wants you to be good.

C. Organization

1. What special sign do Catholics have?
2. What does our sign tell people?
3. What does it tell God?
4. Why do we make the Sign of the Cross?
5. How do we make the Sign of the Cross?

D. Virtues and Practices

Make the Sign of the Cross carefully and devoutly.

IV. SUGGESTED LEARNING ACTIVITIES

A. Children make the Sign of the Cross on a large crucifix.
B. Recording: The Sign of the Cross — Catholic Children's Record Club.
C. Teach and recite the salute to the crucifix. "O saving Cross of Jesus Christ, Glorious Flag of the Catholic Church, I salute Thee."

V. TEACHER REFERENCES (cf. p. 303 ff.).

A. Sr. Mary, *et al.*, *The Catholic Mother's Helper*, pp. 17–19.
B. S.N.D., *Religious Teaching of Young Children*, p. 121.
C. Dennerle, *Leading the Little Ones to Christ*, pp. 8–9.

D. Fitzpatrick, *Religion in Life Curriculum, First Grade Manual*, pp. 15–16.

E. C. C. Weiser, *Religious Customs in the Family*, pp. 25–26.

LESSON 6

I. SUBJECT MATTER

The Priest

II. OBJECTIVES

A. To know the importance and dignity of the priesthood.

B. To develop the habit of respect for priests.

III. SUGGESTED PROCEDURE

A. Approach

Show the picture: "Jesus Blessing Little Children." Who are the other men in the picture? (Jesus' helpers.) Does Jesus have any helpers today?

B. Presentation

1. The Power of the Priest

The priest is Jesus' special helper. He takes the place of Jesus here on earth. Jesus has given him many special powers. The priest has the power to say Mass. He has the power to bring Jesus down to our altars every day at Mass. The priest has the power to help us in many ways. Can you name some ways in which the priest can help us? (Discuss.)

2. Other Works of the Priest

The priest teaches us about God. We should be happy to listen to the priest when he talks to us in church and in school. When he baptizes babies, they become God's children and get the right to go to heaven. When little boys and girls, or big men and women, lose the right to go to heaven by committing big sins, the priest can take away these sins. The priest can give Jesus to many people in Holy Communion. He prays for us and helps us all the time.

3. Reverence Toward the Priest

We know that the priest takes the place of Jesus here on earth, so we must always be very polite toward him. When little boys meet a priest, they should tip their caps and say with a smile, "Good morning, Father!" or "Good afternoon, Father!" Little girls should smile and greet the priest also.

4. Gratitude to God for Priests

Remember that Jesus loved children so much that He sent priests to teach them, bless them, and make them good and happy. Little children must love the priests, obey them, and pray for them. We should thank Jesus each day for giving us good priests to help us.

C. Organization

1. Who takes the place of Jesus here on earth?
2. Why did Jesus give us priests?
3. What are some of the things priests do for us?
4. How should we act when we meet a priest?

D. Virtues and Practices

1. Pray for God's helpers, especially the parish priests.
2. Show respect and reverence for the priests by greeting them properly, etc. (Here stress naturalness in greeting rather than the sterile type of greeting.)

IV. SUGGESTED LEARNING ACTIVITIES

A. Dramatize ways of greeting priests.
B. Poem: "The Priest," S. E., *Poems for God's Child*, p. 53.

THE PRIEST

He is a man,
Yet God obeys when he commands;
He is a man,
And yet God rests within his hands;
He is a man,
Yet in his voice God's voice rings clear;
He is a man,
But at his whisper — God is here!

V. TEACHER REFERENCES (cf. p. 303 ff.).

A. Dennerle, *Leading the Little Ones to Christ*, pp. 14–19.
B. S.N.D., *Religious Teaching of Young Children*, pp. 131–132.

LESSON 7

(It may take more than one day.)

I. SUBJECT MATTER

The Objects in the Church

II. OBJECTIVES

A. To become acquainted with the objects in church.
B. To foster a feeling of respect for the sacredness of the objects in church.

III. SUGGESTED PROCEDURE

A. Approach

When we made our first visit to the church, we saw many, many things. This morning we are going to talk about some of these things. Then we will look at them again when we make our next visit to God's house.

B. Presentation

1. The Altar and the Objects on the Altar

(Show pictures of objects as they are mentioned in the lesson.) Where does Jesus live in the church? Yes, in the tabernacle. Where is the tabernacle? Yes, it is on the altar. The altar is the table upon which the Mass is offered. The altar is covered with white cloths. Above the altar is a large crucifix to remind us of Jesus' great suffering because He loved us so much. On the altar are candles which are burned during Mass. There are also three cards that look like framed pictures. During the Mass the priest reads the prayers that are printed on them. The priest reads other prayers from a large book called a missal.

2. *The Sanctuary and the objects Within the Sanctuary*

Do you know what the communion rail is? It is the place where people kneel to receive Holy Communion. The part of the church between the communion rail and the altar is called the sanctuary. It is the holiest part of the church. Inside the sanctuary we see the altar where Jesus is. Sometimes we also see two other altars there. One is the Blessed Virgin's altar, and the other is St. Joseph's altar. (Specify the one that is found in your church.) Sometimes priests say Mass at these altars. The sanctuary lamp is also in the sanctuary. Do you remember what it is and why it is there? (Discuss.)

3. *Shrine, Statues, and Pictures*

There are other small shrines in the church to honor some of Jesus' special friends in heaven. (Mention the statues and pictures or windows of various saints.) Our church is named in honor of one of these special friends. Who is that special friend? (Discuss parish's name.)

4. *Stations of the Cross*

Have you ever noticed the pictures or figures around the church? There are fourteen of them. These pictures are called the Stations of the Cross. They tell us the story of Jesus' suffering and death on the cross. Jesus suffered because He loves us and wants us to be in heaven with Him some day. Often thank Jesus for loving us so much.

When we make our next visit to church, we shall look for all of the things we have talked about in this lesson.

5. *Vestments Worn at Mass*

The next time you go to Mass, watch the priest to see what he wears at Mass. Does he wear the same things at Mass that he wears on the street? The things he wears at Mass are called vestments. Some of the things the priest wears are white, and some are of different colors. What colors of clothes or vestments have you seen Father wear? (Discuss.) What does the priest carry with him when he goes to the altar to say Mass? (Discuss.)

C. Organization

1. What is the tabernacle in the church?
2. What are some of the things that we see on the altar?

16

3. How many altars are there in our church?
4. What is the name of our church?
5. What statues are in our church?
6. Why does the sanctuary lamp burn all day and all night?

D. Virtues and Practices

1. Have a respect for holy things.
2. Be grateful to God for giving you the gift of faith.

IV. SUGGESTED LEARNING ACTIVITIES

A. Plan another visit to church and talk about what to look for there.
B. Discuss the visit to church.
C. Make an experience chart of what was seen in church.
D. Show and discuss pictures of church objects.
E. Poems: "The Altar," S. E., *Poems for God's Children*, p. 50; "The Candles," *ibid.*, p. 50.

THE ALTAR

The altar is God's table where
Our gifts to Him are made,
And Jesus is the greatest Gift
Upon the altar laid.
We give ourselves to God with Him,
And when His Father sees,
He says, "For love of my dear Son
I will love all of these."
The altar is God's table — see
How God our Father bends
To set a feast of Bread and Wine
For us He calls His friends.

THE CANDLES

The candles stand like sentinels
Straight and still and white.
They burn and burn themselves
     away
To please God with their light.
Your little candle, Lord, am I.
See how my love burns bright!

V. TEACHER REFERENCES (cf. p. 303 ff.).

A. Fitzpatrick, *Religion in Life Curriculum, First Grade Manual*, Vol. 1, pp. 138–142.
B. S.N.D., *Religious Teaching of Young Children*, pp. 134–135.

LESSON 8

I. SUBJECT MATTER

Nativity of the Blessed Virgin Mary — September 8

II. OBJECTIVES

A. To impart knowledge of the Blessed Virgin's childhood.
B. To instill an early love for the Blessed Virgin in the hearts of the little ones.

III. SUGGESTED PROCEDURE

A. Approach

Each one of you has a birthday. Did you know that the Blessed Virgin Mary has a birthday, too? Her birthday is on September 8. Let me tell you about her.

B. Presentation

1. Story of Joachim and Ann

A long time ago a very holy man and woman, named Joachim and Anne were lonely because they had no children. They prayed for many years for a little child. Finally, God sent them a beautiful baby girl. This baby was very dear and very special to God, because He had planned that she would some day be the mother of Jesus. Her name was Mary. (Show pictures of Mary as a child and as Mother of Jesus.) Joachim and Anne were very happy. They did not know that she was a special child.

2. Mary's Virtues

Mary did not know God's plan for her. She grew up into a very good and holy child. She loved God above all things. She loved her mother and father very dearly and did everything she could to please them. She obeyed them in every little way. You can be like the child Mary by trying to obey as well as she did. (Children tell ways in which they can be like Mary as a child.)

C. Organization

1. Why was Mary so special to God?
2. What kind of child was Mary?

18

3. How did Mary help her mother and father?

4. In what ways do you think she obeyed her parents?

D. Virtues and Practices

1. Be obedient at home.

2. Show love toward your family.

3. Show kindness toward classmates.

4. Do something to make Mary happy on her birthday.

IV. SUGGESTED LEARNING ACTIVITIES

A. Story: "The Story of Mary," Sister Marguerite, *Their Hearts Are His Garden*, pp. 102–104.

B. Poem: "Mary's Birthday," Belger, *Sing a Song of Holy Things*, p. 2.

V. TEACHER REFERENCES (cf. p. 303 ff.).

A. Sister Mary, *et al.*, *The Catholic Mother's Helper*, pp. 55–57.

B. Aurelia-Kirsch, *Practical Aids for Catholic Teachers*, pp. 191–192.

LESSON 9

I. SUBJECT MATTER

Feast of the Holy Name of Mary — September 12

II. OBJECTIVES

A. To inspire reverence for the holy name of Mary.

B. To foster a desire for imitating Mary's virtues.

III. SUGGESTED PROCEDURE

A. Approach

Many little girls receive the name of "Mary" at baptism. Why do parents give this beautiful name to their children?

B. Presentation

1. Mary's Name

When the Blessed Virgin was born, her parents gave her the name of Mary. This is a beautiful name. Many parents give this name to their little girls. The mothers and fathers of these children want their children to be like Mary — holy, good, obedient, and kind.

2. How to Honor Mary's Name

All those who have the name of Mary should pray to her in a special way every day. We, too, should pray to her every day. What can we say to her? Whenever we say the name of Mary we should form a picture of her in our minds. She was the most holy woman that ever lived. Her holiness made her beautiful. No artist could ever paint a real picture of Mary. God alone made her as lovely as she is. Let us love the name of Mary, and pray every day that she will help us be good children. Let us greet Mary very often by repeating her name many times during the day.

C. Organization

1. Why do parents give the name "Mary" to their children?
2. Why should we pray to Mary every day?
3. When can we use the name of Mary?

D. Virtues and Practices

1. Show love for Mary by imitating her virtues.
2. Pray to Mary every day.

IV. SUGGESTED LEARNING ACTIVITIES

A. Sing songs in honor of Mary.
B. Practice printing the name of Mary.
C. Story: "Roses for Mary," Sister Marguerite, *Their Hearts Are His Garden*, p. 28.

V. TEACHER REFERENCES (cf. p. 303 ff.).

A. Dorcy, *Mary, My Mother*, pp. 9–11.
B. Aurelia-Kirsch, *Practical Aids for the Catholic Teacher*, pp. 192–193.

UNIT TWO

God Our Heavenly Father

Time: 6 weeks

I. INTRODUCTION FOR THE TEACHER

Unit Two treats of the attributes of God as related to the child's awareness that God is His heavenly Father. The child can become conscious, probably for the first time, of God's tremendous love for him, manifested in the works of creation: the angels, the world, and man. He is also made conscious of the enormity of sin and God's punishment of it. God's goodness and mercy are shown in the promise of the Redeemer and in His many gifts to us. The child is taught to thank God for His many gifts, in consequence of which he should be taught to develop a great love for God, his heavenly Father.

II. OBJECTIVES OF THE UNIT

A. To develop the knowledge that God is our heavenly Father.
B. To develop the knowledge of the nature and attributes of God as revealed in His works.
C. To develop a knowledge of the creation of the angels, of the world, and of man.
D. To develop the knowledge of the fall of the angels and of man and God's promise of a Redeemer.
E. To develop a personal love for God.
F. To develop an attitude of thankfulness to God for His gifts.
G. To understand and learn the prayers "Angel of God" and the blessings before and after meals.
H. To teach the first part of the Creed: "I believe in God, the Father almighty, creator of heaven and earth."

III. SUBJECT MATTER

A. Love and care of an earthly father.
B. Love and care of our heavenly Father.
C. God made us.
D. God is a spirit.
E. God is everywhere — He sees all we do, hears all we say, knows

all we think.

F. God's presence in baptized persons.

G. The three Persons in God — the Blessed Trinity.

H. God the Creator:
  1. Creation and fall of the angels:
     a) Good and bad angels.
     b) Prayer: "Angel of God."
  2. Creation of the world.
  3. Creation and fall of man — effects of Adam's sin.

I. God promised a Redeemer.

J. Gratitude to God for His gifts.

K. Prayer: "Grace before Meals."

L. Prayer: "Grace after Meals."

M. Liturgical feasts: (1) Guardian Angel — October 2; (2) St. Therese, Little Flower of Jesus — October 3; (3) St. Francis — October 4; (4) Our Lady of the Rosary — October 7; (5)

LESSON 10

I. SUBJECT MATTER

Love and Care of an Earthly Father

II. OBJECTIVES

A. To remind the child of his earthly father's goodness to him.

B. To inspire a spirit of love and obedience toward parents.

III. SUGGESTED PROCEDURE

A. Approach

Show a picture of a family at some activity. Do you know who belongs to this family? Discuss briefly, leading children to relate the picture to members of their own family.

B. Presentation

1. Love and Care Given by Our Earthly Father

The father is a very important person of the family. He loves every-

22

one very much. You love your father, too, for you know how much he has done and how much he does for you every day. Your father shows in many ways that he loves you and cares for you. When you need help, where do you go? To father. He is ready to help you any time of the day and every day of the year. When you are sick, father is there, ready to take care of you as much as possible. When you are sad, father can console you and make you happy again. Think of the many ways father surprises you. (Discuss.) We now know that father proves his love for us by all the kind things he does.

2. Father Provides for the Family

Your father goes to work every day to earn some money to buy things for the family. He works very hard to give you a home to live in, food to eat, clothes to wear, and many other things you and the rest of the family need. What are some of the things mother buys with the money father earns? (Discuss briefly.) Your father is also the one who makes sure you get a good Catholic education. He sends you to a Catholic school and gets all the things you need there.

3. Father Willingly Makes Sacrifices to Help Us

How often it happens that someone in the family is in need. Father needs something, too. But father loves you so much that he thinks of you first and gets what you need. Many times father gives up a trip or a treat just to help you. His love is very great. You will never know how many times father makes a sacrifice for you.

4. Respect Due to Father

Father takes God's place on earth. We must always remember to be kind to him. We must speak to him politely and respectfully at all times. (Discuss polite ways of greeting, respectful title, tone of voice, etc.) Polite way of speaking shows that you are a polite child. But polite way of acting proves that you are really polite. Being polite to father shows that you respect him. (Discuss various polite actions that could be shown to father.)

5. The Gratitude Children Owe Their Earthly Father

When you do something for someone, you naturally expect him to thank you and be grateful toward you. Think of all the things your father did for you. Do you remember to thank him for everything? Do you show by your actions that you are grateful to him?

You can make father very happy by being kind to him and the rest of the family. You can make father's job easier by obeying him willingly with a smile and listening to his advice. You can also show father your love for him by being helpful whenever possible. Can you mention some other ways you can show your love for father?

If you do all this your home will be a happy home because everyone will do something to make others happy.

C. Organization

1. How does your father show you that he loves you?
2. Why does he do all these things for you?
3. How can you show your love and gratitude?
4. How do we show respect for our fathers?

D. Virtues and Practices

1. Show love for your father by being respectful, obedient, truthful, helpful, patient, considerate.
2. Show your father that you appreciate the home he gives you.
3. Be helpful and willing to give up little things you want.

IV. SUGGESTED LEARNING ACTIVITIES

A. Dramatize ways of helpful and courteous behavior at home.
B. Draw pictures to illustrate kindness at home.
C. Stories: "Alice's Shoes," Sister Marguerite, *Their Hearts Are His Garden*, pp. 41–42; "Father Helps," *ibid.*, pp. 43–44.
D. Poem: "Helping Others," Belger, *Sing a Song of Holy Things*, p. 82.

V. TEACHER REFERENCES (cf. p. 303 ff.).

A. S.N.D., *Religious Teaching of Young Children*, p. 81.
B. Schumacher, *I Teach Catechism, Vol. I*, pp. 1–5.

LESSON 11

I. SUBJECT MATTER

Love and Care of Our Heavenly Father

II. OBJECTIVES

A. To develop the knowledge that God is our heavenly Father.

B. To instill in the children a deep love for our heavenly Father.

III. SUGGESTED PROCEDURE

A. Approach

Work, sacrifices, surprises, and gifts are some ways through which your father shows his love for you. He cares for you and does many kind things to make you happy. However, there is Someone who loves you more than your earthly father.

B. Presentation

1. God Is Our Heavenly Father

God, our heavenly Father, is the best of fathers. From His heavenly home, He watches over us day and night, lovingly sending us all the good things we need. God, even more than our earthly fathers, thinks of us every minute of the day. He listens to us when we speak to Him. He sees us everywhere and knows all our needs. God, our kind heavenly Father, takes the best care of us because He knows all about us.

2. God Made Us to Show His Goodness

God shows us His goodness by making everything we see around us — flowers, trees, stars, sun, moon, etc. The most important creature that God made is a human person. God made you and God made me. He made your mother, father, brothers, sisters; in other words, God made everyone in the whole world. Do you know why? God wanted to show us His goodness; therefore, He made us all. Isn't it wonderful that God thought of us and loved us so much?

3. God Made Us to Be Happy With Him in Heaven

God made us to show His goodness. He also made us because He wants us to be happy with Him in heaven. Heaven is a beautiful place. That is our heavenly home. God is waiting for us all to come there and enjoy it with the angels and saints. We are happy with our family in our earthly home, but we will be happier with God in heaven.

4. We Belong to God

Our fathers and mothers always say we belong to them. But God has more right to us. We really belong to Him because He made us for

Himself. God wanted us, God made us, and now God takes care of us. No one can do more for us than God. We are His children. Therefore, we should always try to please Him in all we do and say, so that some day we can be happy with Him in heaven.

5. Ways We Can Show God Our Love

Just as we like to show our love and make our parents happy, we should try to show God our love, too. There are many chances during the day in which we can do it. Praying to God is loving Him. God loves to see you say your daily prayers in the nicest way. How pleased He is when He sees you are an obedient child. We can love Him by being kind to others. Each day we have many chances to prove our love for God. Can you mention other ways?

C. Organization

1. Why do we call God our heavenly Father?
2. Who made us?
3. Why did God make us?
4. What does God do to make us happy?
5. How can we show our love for God's goodness to us?

D. Virtues and Practices

1. Praise God for being so great and good.
2. Thank God for His goodness to you.
3. Obey His laws.
4. Show kindness and helpfulness to others.
5. Learn all you can about God.

IV. SUGGESTED LEARNING ACTIVITIES

A. Compose original prayers of love and gratitude.
B. Stories: "God's Love," Sister Marguerite, *Their Hearts Are His Garden*, p. 3; "God's Happiness," *ibid.*, pp. 6–10.

V. TEACHER REFERENCES (cf. p. 303 ff.).

A. Sister Mary, *et al.*, *The Catholic Mother's Helper*, pp. 20–21.
B. S.N.D., *Religious Teaching of Young Children*, pp. 81–84.
C. Schumacher, *I Teach Catechism*, Vol. I, pp. 1–8.

LESSON 12

I. SUBJECT MATTER

Why God Created Us

II. OBJECTIVES

A. To understand God's purpose in creating us.
B. To appreciate His great love for us.

III. SUGGESTED PROCEDURE

A. Approach

Do you remember why God made us? God made us to show His goodness and to make us happy with Him in heaven. To share the happiness of heaven we must do what God wants us to do.

B. Presentation

1. We Must Know God

It is nice to know your friends. It is much nicer to know God, our heavenly Father. We know that He is a good and kind Father. He loves us and cares for us every day. As the days go by we will learn more and more about God in our religion lessons. We will learn how wonderful and powerful He is. The priest in church and our parents at home will tell you many things about God, too. Just think — you will know Him more and more as your best Friend. Then you will try to be like Him in everything you do and say.

2. We Must Love God

We love our friends because we know them. If we know God we will love Him, too. The more you learn about God, the more you will love Him. Every time you think of God whisper to Him a secret that you love Him. Whisper it to God now. (Minute meditation.) Prayer is talking to God; it is also loving God. When you pray God listens, because He knows you love Him.

3. We Must Serve God

We must not only *tell* God we love Him, but, above all, we must *show* how much we love Him. Doing things for love of God proves our love. A child who really loves God will gladly serve Him. To

27

"serve" God means to do everything He wants us to do. Saying our daily prayers, helping at home, studying in school are some ways we serve God. Obeying right away, telling the truth, being kind to others also proves that we love and serve God. Can you mention other ways we serve God?

God loves us because He made us. God made us to show His goodness and to be happy with Him in heaven. To be happy with God in heaven, I must know Him, I must love Him and must serve Him. Heaven will be mine if I do all that for love of God.

C. Organization
1. Why did God make you?
2. What must we do to be happy with God in heaven?
3. How do we learn to know God?
4. How do we show our love for God?
5. How do we serve God?

D. Virtues and Practices
1. Do things that will please God.
2. Learn more about God, so you can love Him more and serve Him better.

IV. SUGGESTED LEARNING ACTIVITIES

A. Discuss and illustrate ways to please God.
B. Story: "A Queen Learns a Lesson," Brennan, *Going His Way,* pp. 32–35.
C. Poem: "God and I," Belger, *Sing a Song of Holy Things,* p. 1.

V. TEACHER REFERENCE

Fitzpatrick, *Religion in Life Curriculum, First Grade Manual,* pp. 34–36.

LESSON 13

I. SUBJECT MATTER

Presence of God

II. OBJECTIVES

A. To develop the knowledge that God is everywhere and that He is a spirit.
B. To encourage the practice of recalling the presence of God during the day.

III. SUGGESTED PROCEDURE

A. Approach

What makes the kite go high up in the air? Can you see the wind? How do we know there is such a thing as wind? We do not see it, but we know it is there by the things it does.

B. Presentation

1. God Is a Spirit

God is here, but we do not see Him. This very minute God is in this room looking at you and me. Why can't we see Him? God is a spirit; that means, He has no body. We cannot see Him with our eyes or touch Him with our hands. He is invisible — cannot be seen. However, He is real, more real than anything else.

2. We Will See God in Heaven

Since God is a Spirit, He cannot be seen with our eyes. But God promised that He will share heaven with us if we love Him. In heaven we will see God. Won't it be wonderful to see Him for ever and ever?

3. God Is Everywhere

God is our heavenly Father. He is not only in heaven. He wants to be near us all the time, because He loves us and cares for us. Therefore, God is everywhere. Right now God is in this room. He is very pleased seeing how you are listening about Him. At this same time, God is with your father at work and with your mother at home. He is also pleased with them because He knows that they work to help you. This very minute God is in every building in the world, He is everywhere. No matter where we go, it may be way up high or all the way down, God is there, too.

Is God in this place? (Show picture of children in church. Discuss.)

Is God on the playground? (Show picture of children at play. Discuss.) Show and discuss other pictures stressing the presence of God everywhere.

How good it makes us feel to know that God is everywhere with us. He wants to make sure that you are happy everywhere. Think of God everywhere you go. Thank Him for His loving care.

C. Organization

1. Why can't we see God?
2. Why do we say that God is a spirit?
3. When will we see Him?
4. Where is God?

D. Virtues and Practices

1. Try to be good at all times because God is near.
2. During the day think of God being near you.

IV. SUGGESTED LEARNING ACTIVITIES

A. Discuss ways of turning our thoughts upward and inward to God during the day in secret prayer.
B. Story: "The Voice at the Window," Brennan, *For Heaven's Sake,* pp. 7–9.
C. Poem: "God's Greatness," Belger, *Sing a Song of Holy Things,* p. 9.

V. TEACHER REFERENCES

A. Dennerle, *Leading the Little Ones to Christ,* p. 52.
B. Schumacher, *I Teach Catechism,* Vol. 1, pp. 9–12, 18–19.

LESSON 14

I. SUBJECT MATTER

God Sees All We Do, Hears All We Say, and Knows All We Think

II. OBJECTIVES

A. To develop the knowledge that God sees everything, hears everything, and knows everything.
B. To foster love of and the spirit of prayer to God, who knows everything about us.

III. SUGGESTED PROCEDURE

A. Approach

Did you ever play the game of "Hide and Seek"? When you played it, you made sure to hide where no one could see you. But, Someone saw you. Do you know Who?

B. Presentation

1. God Sees Everything

God saw you playing the game. God is everywhere and He sees everything. No one can hide from Him. No matter where you go, no matter what you do, God sees it. What can God see right now? (Discuss briefly.)

If God sees us now, why can't we see Him?

God loves us and wants to be near us. How pleased He must be when He sees that you are kind and obedient. How pleased He must be when He sees you say your daily prayers in the nicest way. Is God pleased with us now? Why? (Discuss briefly.)

When you go to church, God sees you there. When you are in school, God sees you there. When you are outdoors, God sees you there. When you are at home, God sees you there, too. God sees us everywhere. When it is dark. When it is light. Nothing is hidden from God. He made everything and He sees everything. He sees us when we work or play. When we eat or sleep. When we study or pray. Let us remember, everywhere we go, that "God sees us" and we surely will be good.

2. God Hears Everything

God sees us wherever we are and He hears whatever we say. He hears everything, even a tiny whisper. God hears us while we are at home and He hears us while we are in school. He hears us at prayer time and He hears us during play time. What does God hear now? (Discuss briefly.)

God wants to hear us say good things and to have a kind word on our lips for those we meet. He has given us the power to speak, and He wants us to use this power in such a way that it will draw us closer to Him. Can you tell some kind words that God is very pleased to hear? (Discuss, briefly, courteous words, i.e., thank you, please, I'm sorry, etc.)

3. God Knows Everything

God sees everything, God hears everything, and God knows everything. When we look up at the sky at night we can see stars, stars, and more stars. We haven't the slightest idea how many there are. But God knows. He knows how many stars are in the sky, how many leaves are on all the trees, and how many drops of water are in all the lakes, oceans, and rivers. He knows everything because He made everything. He is a powerful God.

He knows everything about us, too. He knows what we did last year, what we are doing now, and what we will do tomorrow. He knows all our thoughts and all our desires. How pleased He must be when He knows that our thoughts are good and kind.

God knows more about us than our own parents.

He knows what we need and wants to give us everything that will help us get to heaven.

God wants us to ask Him for the things we need. He is willing to help.

C. Organization

1. When does God see us?
2. Can we hide anything from God?
3. What can God hear?
4. Does God know what we're thinking about?
5. How much does God know?

D. Virtues and Practices

1. Form the habit of praying to God, who sees, knows, and hears everything.
2. Guard your thoughts, words, and actions because you do not want to displease God.
3. When you do not feel like being good, remember that God sees you.

IV. SUGGESTED LEARNING ACTIVITIES

A. Discuss and dramatize ways of speaking kindly to parents, friends, teachers, and others.
B. Poems: "Night and Day," Fitzpatrick, *Religious Poems for Little Folk,* p. 96; "God's Greatness," Belger, *Sing a Song of Holy Things,* p. 9.

V. TEACHER REFERENCES

A. S.N.D., *Religious Teaching of Young Children*, p. 91.
B. Sr. Mary, *et al.*, *The Catholic Mother's Helper*, pp. 23–24.
C. Schumacher, *I Teach Catechism*, Vol. I, pp. 16–17.

LESSON 15

I. SUBJECT MATTER

God Is Present in Us and in Others Through Baptism

II. OBJECTIVES

A. To develop the knowledge of the presence of God in us through Baptism.
B. To develop the habit of thinking of God's presence within us.

III. SUGGESTED PROCEDURE

A. Approach

God, our heavenly Father, made us that some day we will be happy with Him in heaven. We cannot be happy with God in heaven now. We must prepare ourselves upon earth for the heavenly home. However, God loved us so much that He wanted to be near us at all times. Therefore, He came to live in us.

B. Presentation

1. God Lives in Us Through Baptism

When you were baptized God chose you for something special. He came to live in you. God lives in me, in you, and in everyone who was baptized. You are like "little churches" or "little tabernacles" where God lives. How fortunate we are to have God close to us in the tabernacle of our heart. How happy God must be to find our hearts a pleasant place to live.

2. We Must Desire to Live for God

God lives in us because He loves us. We, too, love God; therefore, we will try to live for God. Everything we do and everything we say will be done for love of God. God is our Special Friend who likes to listen to us. Tell Him all about yourself, especially that you want to live for Him alone.

3. God Gives Us Grace

God helps us prepare for heaven. He gives us His help called "grace." The great gift God gave us at Baptism was sanctifying grace. Grace helps us to be good; it helps us do what God wants us to do. It helps us on our way to heaven. Grace makes us holy and pleasing to God.

4. God Lives in Others Who Are Baptized

Every man, woman, and child was made by God to live happily with Him in heaven. Every baptized person has God living within him. He may be colored, Eskimo, Indian, Japanese, or whatever you want, but God considers him as His special friend. Kindness shown to others is kindness shown to God, who lives within them. We should treat others as brothers and sisters and as living temples of God.

C. Organization

1. When did you become a child of God?
2. Who lives in you?
3. Does God live in other children too?
4. Why should we be kind to other children?
5. What can we do to make God feel happy in our hearts?

D. Virtues and Practices

1. Talk to God during the day, remembering that He is in your heart.
2. Try to be God's true child by being kind, unselfish, brave, etc.
3. Speak and act kindly to others, regardless of race and color.

IV. SUGGESTED LEARNING ACTIVITIES

A. Discuss pictures depicting good acts of children.
B. Dramatize acts of kindness to others.
C. Poem: "God's Homes," *Poems for God's Child,* p. 19.

GOD'S HOMES

I know that God is everywhere
And all about us — like the air.
God lives in Heaven, away up high
Above the earth and air and sky.

To share our little joys and tears
He lived on earth for thirty years.
In every Mass He comes again;
His joy is still to dwell with men.
And when I go to church, He's there —
He says it is "His House of Prayer."
God lives in every soul in grace,
And makes of it a holy place.
Within my heart, though none can see,
Lives God — He is at home with me!

V. TEACHER REFERENCE

S.N.D., *Religious Teaching of Young Children*, p. 85.

LESSON 16

I. SUBJECT MATTER

Three Persons in God — the Blessed Trinity

II. OBJECTIVES

A. To develop the knowledge that there is one God, but three Persons in that one God.
B. To stimulate love for the Blessed Trinity.

III. SUGGESTED PROCEDURE

A. Approach

We have learned wonderful things about God. Did we ever stop to think about God?

B. Presentation

1. God Always Was and Always Will Be

A long, long time ago there was no earth, nothing at all. There was only God. Everything upon earth and all the people in the world had a beginning. God made them all. But no one made God. God always was. He never had a beginning. God, the powerful Spirit, is eternal. He made everything. God is the same now. He will never change. He will never die. He always was and He will always be.

2. There Is Only One God

There cannot be another true God. No one can be more powerful than God. No one can equal Him. He is the One who made everything and takes care of everything. He is the only One who sees everything, hears everything, and knows everything. He lovingly watches over His creation and guides all things.

3. There Are Three Persons in God

God is a powerful Spirit. He is one God, but three Persons are present in Him at the same time. You are one person, I am one person, but God is greater. In God there are three divine Persons.

Each Person has a special name. The first Person is God the Father; the second Person is God the Son; the third Person is God the Holy Spirit. Each Person is the one same God. The three Persons love us equally. The three Persons in God take care of us and help us to get to heaven.

4. The Blessed Trinity

The three Persons in one God have a special name, the Blessed Trinity. Blessed means they are all holy. Trinity means three. (Present the symbol representing the Blessed Trinity. Explain briefly.)

Whenever you hear the name "Blessed Trinity" think of "three Persons in one God."

We can praise the Blessed Trinity by some prayers. You already know one — the Sign of the Cross. (Recite the prayer slowly, stressing the names of the three Persons.)

Another prayer we will soon learn is "Glory Be." (Recite this prayer slowly, stressing the names of the three Persons.)

We can also praise the Blessed Trinity by our kind acts, kind words, doing things cheerfully and in many other ways. Whatever I do for love of God, I really do for love of the Blessed Trinity.

C. Organization

1. Is there only one God?
2. How many persons are there in God?
3. What are the names of the three Persons in God?
4. What is the Blessed Trinity?

5. Is the Father God?
6. Is the Son God?
7. Is the Holy Spirit God?
8. Are the three Persons within me? Why?

D. Virtues and Practices

1. Pray often to the Blessed Trinity living in you.
2. Make the Sign of the Cross often, to tell God that you believe there are three Persons in one God.

IV. SUGGESTED LEARNING ACTIVITIES

A. Poem: "Blessed Trinity," Belger, *Sing a Song of Holy Things*, p. 6.
B. Draw symbols of the Trinity: triangle, clover, cross.

V. TEACHER REFERENCES

A. Sister Mary, *et al.*, *The Catholic Mother's Helper*, pp. 57–58.
B. S.N.D., *Religious Teaching of Young Children*, pp. 93–102.
C. Schumacher, *I Teach Catechism*, Vol. I, pp. 21–25.

LESSON 17

I. SUBJECT MATTER

God the Creator

II. OBJECTIVES

A. To develop the concept of the term "Gifts of God."
B. To develop a deeper sense of gratitude to God for the gifts of creation.
C. To teach the first part of the Creed: "I believe in God, the Father Almighty, Creator of heaven and earth."

III. SUGGESTED PROCEDURE

A. Approach

What do you usually receive on your birthday? Who gave them to you? People who love you give the presents. Today we will learn about some wonderful presents we received from God. He gave us more gifts than anyone in the world.

B. Presentation

1. Explanation of the Term "Gift"

A gift is a present. It is something nice we give to those we love and respect. We give gifts to our friends to tell them that we love them. Look at this gift. (Show a gift with tag "From Father to Mother." Discuss briefly.) Some gifts are small and some gifts are big.

2. God's Gifts to Us

God's gifts are the greatest of all. Everywhere you look you see gifts from God. Look up at the sky. You could almost hear the stars, the moon, and the sun saying, "We are a gift from God for you." Look around the earth. We can see trees, flowers, and other things that grow. As you look at them say to yourself, "They are gifts from God for me to make me happy." Think of your home, your parents, brothers, and sisters; they are gifts from God, too. A very great gift God gave you is a body and a soul. He gave you life. We could keep on mentioning more and more gifts from God. No one loves us more than God and no one gave us more gifts than God.

3. God, Creator of Heaven and Earth

We know that God lived before anything else was made. There was nothing at all — just God. To give gifts to others, God made us and He made all the gifts for us. God made everything out of nothing.

God wanted a place for His angels and saints, so God created the beautiful heaven. God has only to want a certain thing and there it is — it comes into existence. God wanted the earth for us, so He created it out of nothing.

4. Heaven and Earth Our Two Homes

God gave us an earthly home, but it will not last forever. It will come to an end when we die. Then God wants to take us to our heavenly home, where we will be happy with Him for ever and ever. No one can tell us how beautiful heaven is. It will be the happiest place to live because we will be with God.

5. Explanation of Terms: Create, Creator, Creatures

Only God can create, that means, He can make anything He wants out of nothing. He just wants it, by His power there it is. Since God is Almighty and can create anything we call Him the Creator.

No one other than God is a Creator. We always need something to make something. (Cite examples.) God alone is the Creator. All the things that God created belong to Him. They are called God's creatures. Can you name some of God's creatures?

6. God Is Almighty

Isn't God wonderful? Isn't He powerful to be able to do anything He wishes? We say God is Almighty. He can create anything He wishes. Nothing is too hard for Him to do.

7. Apostles' Creed

We believe in God and in all that He can do. He is very powerful and can do many things. He is the Almighty Creator of heaven and earth. In a special prayer, called "Apostles' Creed" or "I believe in God," we tell Him what we do believe. (Teach first part of Apostles' Creed: "I believe in God, the Father Almighty, Creator of heaven and earth.")

C. Organization

1. What is another name for presents?
2. From whom do we receive gifts?
3. What do people want to tell us when they give us gifts?
4. What great gifts did God give us?
5. What does "create" mean?
6. Why is God called "Creator"?
7. Why do we say "God is Almighty"?

D. Virtues and Practices

1. Thank God for His gifts of heaven and earth.
2. Be happy to give gifts to others.

IV. SUGGESTED LEARNING ACTIVITIES

A. Discuss personal experiences in giving and receiving gifts from others.
B. Discuss the phrase of the Apostles' Creed: "Creator of heaven and earth."
C. Discuss pictures illustrating God's gifts.

V. TEACHER REFERENCE

Sister Mary, *et al.*, *The Catholic Mother's Helper*, pp. 25–26.

LESSON 18

I. SUBJECT MATTER

Creation and Fall of the Angels

II. OBJECTIVES

A. To develop a knowledge of the creation and fall of the angels.
B. To develop an attitude of love for the angels in general.

III. SUGGESTED PROCEDURE

A. Approach

God was very happy in heaven, but He was so good and kind that He wanted others to share the happiness of heaven with Him.

B. Presentation

1. God Created Angels

God wanted some beautiful creatures to live with Him in heaven. By His almighty power, God created many wonderful angels to share His heavenly glory. The angels were God's first creatures. They were pure spirits like God. They did not have a body.

2. God's Gifts to the Angels

When God created the angels they were pure spirits, filled with grace. God gave each angel the power to understand things easily. God gave angels a free will to choose and do whatever they wanted. The angels were powerful. They could move about very swiftly; that is why we usually draw angels with wings. They were all very, very good. God loved them and He was pleased with them.

3. Test of the Angels

God made every angel to enjoy heaven with Him one day. But, before they could enter heaven, God gave them a test to prove if they really loved Him. God wanted them to obey Him. But something

40

sad happened. Lucifer, one of the greatest angels, and some other angels refused to obey. How sad to think that the angels did not pass the test. Michael, a powerful angel, and the rest of the good angels who obeyed God were very displeased with what had happened. "No one is like God," they said. "We must fight the disobedient angels. We will praise and obey God."

4. Punishment and Reward

The bad angels received their punishment. They were cast into a place called hell. They were not beautiful any more. They are very unhappy and will have to suffer for ever and ever in hell because they disobeyed God.

The good angels entered heaven where they have the happiness of seeing God. They praise and honor God. They know Him better than we do. They love Him more than we do; they never make Him sad.

The good angels will be in heaven forever because they proved to God that they loved Him.

C. Organization

1. Why did God create angels?
2. What test did God give the angels?
3. Did all the angels do what God asked them to do?
4. How did God punish the bad angels?
5. What reward did God give the good angels?
6. What reward will God give us if we are good?

D. Virtues and Practices

1. Obey God by obeying your parents and those in authority.
2. Be good so you can stay on God's side.
3. Be busy so the devil can't tempt you to sin.

IV. SUGGESTED LEARNING ACTIVITIES

A. Discuss the reward of obedience in the home.
B. Story: "Saint Michael and the Angels," Sister Marguerite, *Their Hearts Are His Garden*, pp. 91–93.

V. TEACHER REFERENCES

A. Sister Mary, *et al.*, *The Catholic Mother's Helper*, pp. 29–30.
B. Fitzpatrick, *Religion in Life Curriculum, First Grade Manual*, pp. 17–19.

C. Dennerle, *Leading the Little Ones to Christ*, pp. 38–45.

D. Schumacher, *I Teach Catechism*, Vol. I, pp. 26–30.

LESSON 19

I. SUBJECT MATTER

What the Good and Bad Angels Do

II. OBJECTIVES

A. To understand the work of angels.

B. To appreciate God's goodness in giving each of us a guardian angel.

III. SUGGESTED PROCEDURE

A. Approach

Who were the first creatures that God created? What happened to some angels? The good angels received their reward from God. They entered heaven joyfully.

B. Presentation

1. Good Angels Adore and Praise God

How happy the angels were when they entered heaven and saw God face to face. God made the angels to share His happiness and serve Him in providing for the needs of men. Each angel has something special to do. The angels are busy. Some angels are always near God's heavenly throne. There they adore God and sing His praises. They want us to praise God, too. They pray for us to God.

2. Good Angels Act as Messengers

Some angels are God's special messengers. God sends them down to earth to give a message to someone. Do you know of anyone who received a message through an angel? An angel came to Mary to tell her that she was chosen to be the Mother of Jesus. Angels came to the shepherds to announce that Jesus was born. (Show pictures.)

3. Good Angels Are Our Guardians

God gave each one of us an angel from heaven to be our guardian angel. Our guardian angel is near us all day and all night. Wherever we go, our guardian angel goes, too. God gave us this special angel because He knows we need someone to protect us and guide us along the way to heaven.

4. Bad Angels Try to Get Us to Do Wrong

How sad it is to know that the bad angels will never see God. They are not happy. They will never live in heaven. They do not love God any more, and they don't want you to love Him either. They are jealous that God loves you and wants you in heaven. They try very hard to keep you away from heaven. The bad angels tempt us to do something wrong, to disobey Mother or Father or to be unkind to someone. We must be brave as Angel Michael. Do not give in to the bad angels. Obey, do something kind instead. Ask your good angel to help. Let the bad angel be a loser.

C. Organization

1. What are some of the things good angels do?
2. Who are the guardian angels?
3. What do bad angels try to make us do?
4. What will you do if a bad angel tells you to be naughty?
5. What does "tempt" mean?

D. Virtues and Practices

1. Try to please God by being good.
2. Talk to your guardian angel during the day.
3. Send the bad angel away if he comes near by saying a prayer.
4. Thank your guardian angel for his love and care.

IV. SUGGESTED LEARNING ACTIVITIES

A. Stories: "Paul's Angel," Sister Marguerite, *Their Hearts Are His Garden,* pp. 38–39.
B. Poem: "The Angels," Belger, *Sing a Song of Holy Things,* p. 10.

V. TEACHER REFERENCES

A. Sister Mary, *et al., The Catholic Mother's Helper,* pp. 29–31.
B. Schumacher, *I Teach Catechism,* Vol. I, pp. 30–33.

LESSON 20

I. SUBJECT MATTER

Prayer: "Angel of God"

II. OBJECTIVES

A. To teach a prayer to the guardian angel.
B. To learn to say the prayer independently, and to love to say it often.

III. SUGGESTED PROCEDURE

A. Approach

God did not want to leave us alone upon earth. He gave each one of us a guardian angel to be with us all the time.

B. Presentation

1. Our Guardian Angel Is Always With Us

My guardian angel is beside me listening to what I'm saying. Your guardian angels are standing beside you watching how attentively you are listening. How happy they are when they see you good and kind and brave. We need help to remain good and kind and brave. Our guardian angel is willing to help us whenever we ask. We will learn a special prayer in honor of the guardian angel.

2. Words of the Prayer

When we begin the prayer we call upon our guardian angel, addressing him as "Angel of God." Since we know that he is our guardian angel, we say, "my guardian dear." When we say, "to whom God's love commits me here," we show that we believe that God has given us each a guardian angel. We ask our guardian angel to be near us during the day, "ever this day be at my side." We then tell our guardian angel in what way we need his help "to light and guard, to rule and guide. Amen." (Explain each briefly.)

Recite the entire prayer again in sequence, paying particular attention to correct pronunciation of words to prevent incorrect learning.

3. When to Say the Prayer

Say the special prayer to your guardian angel every morning and every night. Say it again during the day when you need his help. Sometimes we don't know what to do or we are in danger. Quickly think of your guardian angel who is near you and ask for the needed help. He is always listening and very willing to help.

Sometimes we are tempted to do something wrong. Call upon your guardian angel to protect you from hurting God.

Say the prayer asking your guardian angel to help you do good acts instead. It is also a good practice to say this prayer before going to sleep, using the words, "ever this night" for "ever this day." (Discuss briefly upon what other occasions children could invoke help of their guardian angels by reciting the prayer.)

C. Organization

1. To whom do you speak in this prayer?
2. What do you mean when you say: "To whom His love commits me here"?
3. What does "Ever this day be at my side" mean?
4. Why do you want your angel to stay with you?
5. What does "To light and guard, to rule and guide" mean?

D. Virtues and Practices

1. Form the habit of saying the prayer frequently and well.
2. Often speak to your angel in your own words.

IV. SUGGESTED LEARNING ACTIVITIES

A. Give the necessary practice and drill.
B. Discuss situations during which children should pray to their guardian angels.
C. Discuss why children should pray to their angels.
D. Class recites "Angel of God."

V. TEACHER REFERENCES

A. Schumacher, *I Teach Catechism*, Vol. I, pp. 32–33.
B. S.N.D., *Religious Teaching of Young Children*, p. 123.
C. Aurelia-Kirsch, *Practical Aids for Catholic Teachers*, p. 194.

LESSON 21

I. SUBJECT MATTER

Creation of the World

II. OBJECTIVES

A. To develop a knowledge of why God created the world.
B. To develop an attitude of thanksgiving to God for all His gifts to mankind.

III. SUGGESTED PROCEDURE

A. Approach

Have you ever thought of the many wonderful things we can see in the world? Do you know that God made them for you?

B. Presentation

1. God Created the World

God, our heavenly Father, thought of us a long, long time before we were born. He wanted us to be happy upon earth and some day to be happy with Him in heaven. Being good and kind, God decided to make many beautiful things. Everything that is in the world was created by God. He created it for us because He loved us.

2. God Created Everything

God is Almighty. He has the power to do all things. He wished that there would be light. "Let there be light," He said. By His power, light began to spread upon earth, God called the light day. The darkness was called night. Now we have day and night.

"Let there be a sky," God said. And so it happened. The beautiful sky was above while below was all water. God didn't want only water over the earth. In His powerful way God said, "Let all the waters below the heavens be gathered into one place and let dry land appear." And so it was. Now we have oceans, lakes, rivers, and other bodies of water. God saw that it was good, God wanted the land to look beautiful. "Let there be beautiful things that grow," He said. God created many beautiful flowers, many different kinds of trees and everything that grows in the gardens, fruits and vegetables, God saw that it was good. God wanted the sky to look beautiful, too. So He said, "Let there be lights for the day and for the night on the Heavens." He created the sun that lights up and warms the earth, and the moon and stars that shine during the night. God also created many fish to fill the waters. There were fish of all colors and all sizes. God also thought of the birds that could sing for us. He created many beautiful birds that filled the air with their happy songs praising God, their Creator. Then God created many animals that moved around the earth. God saw that it was all good. He was pleased with all His creatures. Heaven and earth, objects on the sky, in the water, upon land, and in the air are all creatures of God, created by His almighty power for us.

3. God Created Man

Finally God created the most important creature on earth, man. God created man to love and serve Him upon earth and some day to be happy with Him in heaven. God created man, body and soul, and gave him many marvelous gifts.

4. God Made the Seventh Day Holy

The Bible tells us that God created everything. Then it says that God rested. It says this because God wants us to set aside one day of the week for special prayers and praise for Him. God wants us to rest from daily hard work on Sundays. We must use the day to praise God and thank Him for His loving care. (Discuss ways to keep Sunday holy.)

C. Organization

1. Why did God create the world and all the things in it?
2. What was the first thing He made?
3. Name some other things that God made?
4. What was the greatest thing that God made?
5. What should we say to God every day for all His gifts?
6. What did God do on the seventh day?
7. How do we keep Sunday holy?

D. Virtues and Practices

1. Thank God for His gifts by using them in the right way.
2. Share your gifts with those who have little. Do not waste anything.
3. Keep the Lord's day holy.

IV. SUGGESTED LEARNING ACTIVITIES

A. Children collect pictures of things God has made, for a class scrapbook or a bulletin-board display.
B. Clay modeling of objects that God has made.
C. Draw a frieze showing the various stages of Creation.
D. Children retell the story of Creation to the class.
E. Story: "God's Secret," Brennan, *For Heaven's Sake*, pp. 3–6.
F. Poem: "The Creation," Fitzpatrick, *Religious Poems for Little Folks*, p. 14.
G. Hymn: "God the Creator" *Music Hour Kindergarten — First Grade*, p. 1

V. TEACHER REFERENCES

A. Fitzpatrick, *Religion in Life Curriculum, First Grade Manual*, pp. 19–28.
B. Schumacher, *I Teach Catechism*, Vol. I, pp. 33–36.
C. Sister Mary, *et al.*, *The Catholic Mother's Helper*, pp. 25–28.

LESSON 22

I. SUBJECT MATTER

Adam and Eve

II. OBJECTIVES

A. To develop a knowledge of God's gifts to man.
B. To develop an attitude of thanksgiving to God for His gifts.

III. SUGGESTED PROCEDURE

A. Approach

Look at this beautiful picture that shows God's wonderful world. (Show pictures illustrating various objects of creation.) Can you tell what God created? Now that the world was created, God wanted someone to use it and enjoy it.

B. Presentation

1. God Created Adam

All these wonderful creatures cannot know God and cannot love God. Why? God wanted some creatures to know Him, to love Him, and to share His happiness in heaven. That is why He created a very important creature, man. He created man's body from earthly matter and made man a living being by breathing into him a spiritual soul. Man was a very important living creature, made to the "image and likeness of God." He was called Adam, a Hebrew word for "man." Adam is our first parent.

Because He made man to His own "image and likeness," God wanted man to live forever with Him in heaven. The gifts of intellect and will enable man to know and love God.

2. God Created Eve

God didn't want Adam to live alone. He wanted Adam to have a companion in life. God, therefore, created the first woman, Eve.

The Bible tells us that God made Eve's body out of a part of Adam's body. God also breathed into her a soul. Eve, too, was a very important creature, with body and soul from God. Eve, like Adam, was created to the image and likeness of God. Adam and Eve are our first parents upon earth.

3. God's Gifts to Our First Parents

God gave our first parents many gifts. The gift of body and soul was one great gift given to them. A greater gift was sanctifying grace. It made them children of God. Sanctifying grace made them holy and pleasing to God. Adam and Eve received healthy bodies, too. They were never sick, they never suffered any sorrow or pain, they were never hungry. Adam and Eve understood everything easily. It was easy for them to be good, they never felt an urge to do something wrong.

4. Garden of Paradise

God placed Adam and Eve in a beautiful garden called the "Garden of Paradise." It was here that Adam and Eve enjoyed living under

God's loving care. Adam and Eve were busy and happy all day. They enjoyed everything that God created.

C. Organization

1. Who was the first man God created?
2. How did God create his soul?
3. Why did God create Eve?
4. What kind of place did God give Adam and Eve to live in?
5. Why are Adam and Eve called our first parents?
6. What did God give Adam and Eve that makes them greater than the animals?
7. How can we thank God for making us?

D. Virtues and Practices

1. Thank God for giving you life.
2. Show proper care and respect for your body: cleanliness, good health habits, wearing modest clothing, etc.
3. Respect the bodies of others.
4. Thank God for making you.

IV. SUGGESTED LEARNING ACTIVITIES

A. Illustrate the beautiful Garden of Paradise.
B. Illustrate the various animals for a booklet.
C. Draw a ladder illustrating different creatures God made, starting with the lowest and placing man at the very top.
D. Story: "Creation," Sister Mary, *et al., The Catholic Mother's Helper*, pp. 37–38.

V. TEACHER REFERENCES

A. Dennerle, *Leading the Little Ones to Christ*, pp. 30–35.
B. Fitzpatrick, *Religion in Life Curriculum, First Grade Manual*, pp. 28–30.
C. Sister Mary, *et al., The Catholic Mother's Helper*, pp. 26–28.
D. Schumacher, *I Teach Catechism*, Vol. I, pp. 36–38.

LESSON 23

I. SUBJECT MATTER
The Fall of Man

II. OBJECTIVES

A. To develop a knowledge of the fall of man.

B. To instill a hatred for sin and a sorrow for sin.

III. SUGGESTED PROCEDURE

A. Approach

God loved our first parents. He gave them many gifts to make them happy upon earth, and some day to make them happy with Him in heaven. Adam and Eve loved God, too. They tried to please God all the time.

B. Presentation

1. God's Command to Our First Parents

God wanted to see whether Adam and Eve really loved Him. He gave them a special command, which was very easy to keep. God told them to enjoy and eat anything in the Garden of Paradise, except the fruit from one tree. God showed Adam and Eve the tree from which they were not to eat. God promised them more happiness if they obeyed. If not, they would be unhappy, they would suffer, and some day they would die. It was an easy command.

2. Eve's Temptation by the Devil

Adam and Eve were happy in the Garden of Paradise. But one day something happened. Eve was tempted by the devil, whom the Bible pictures in the form of a serpent. The devil talked to Eve and asked her why she didn't eat the fruit from the tree. Eve, in surprise, answered that God had told her and Adam that they would be punished and would die if they should disobey His command. But the devil lied to Eve. He told her that they would never die. The devil tempted Eve to disobey God. Eve looked at the tree, it looked beautiful. The fruit looked delicious. Poor Eve listened to the serpent. She pulled off a fruit, ate some, and gave some to Adam, Adam ate it, too. Immediately something happened to them. They did not feel happy any more; they were frightened. Quickly, Adam and Eve hid themselves. But they could not hide from God.

3. Punishment of Adam and Eve

God knows everything. He knew what Adam and Eve did. God was very displeased with Adam and Eve. They made God angry because they disobeyed Him. They committed sin. It was the first sin committed upon earth. God asked Adam what happened, Adam blamed Eve and Eve blamed the serpent. That was no excuse. God had to punish Adam and Eve.

Adam and Eve were told they must leave the Garden of Paradise, never to return there again. They would suffer much. They would need to work hard now to be good. Their wills were weakened. Their minds were darkened. And saddest of all they lost sanctifying grace. Without this grace they could not enjoy heaven. Heaven was closed.

4. Effects of Original Sin Upon Us

God wanted Adam and Eve to pass on to us all the graces He gave them at their creation. But it did not happen as God wanted. Instead, their first sin, called original sin, is passed on to everyone who is born. But God, who is so good, has given us the wonderful sacrament of baptism. When you were baptized, God's grace freed you from original sin and flooded you with His own life.

C. Organization

1. What was the greatest gift God gave Adam and Eve?
2. What was the law God gave to Adam and Eve?
3. Why did God give them such a law?
4. Did Adam and Eve obey God's law? Why?
5. What was the punishment for this sin of disobedience?
6. What happened to Adam and Eve when they sinned?
7. What great gift did they lose?

D. Virtues and Practices

1. Obey your parents and teachers.
2. Be sorry for your sins.
3. Trust in God's love and mercy.
4. Thank God for your chance to win heaven.
5. Resolve to resist temptation and avoid occasions of sin.

IV. SUGGESTED LEARNING ACTIVITIES

A. Discuss how a child can show obedience to God by obeying His representatives.
B. Children retell the story of the fall of man.
C. Story: "Obedience," Sister Marguerite, *Their Hearts Are His Garden*, pp. 46–47.

V. TEACHER REFERENCES

A. Sister Mary, *et al.*, *The Catholic Mother's Helper*, pp. 39–41.
B. Dennerle, *Leading the Little Ones to Christ*, pp. 49–53, 57–60.
C. Fitzpatrick, *Religion in Life Curriculum, First Grade Manual*, pp. 30–33.
D. Schumacher, *I Teach Catechism*, Vol. 1, pp. 38–40.

LESSON 24

I. SUBJECT MATTER

A. God's Love and Mercy in Promising the Redeemer
B. Effects of the sin of Adam and Eve on Us

II. OBJECTIVES

A. To develop a knowledge of the love and mercy of God.
B. To instill in the children a hatred for sin.

III. SUGGESTED PROCEDURE

A. Approach

Adam and Eve disappointed God. They failed to return their love to God for the numerous gifts He gave them. For their sin of disobedience they were punished.

B. Presentation

1. God Promised a Redeemer

God still loved Adam and Eve. He knew they were sorry for what they did. He wanted to give them another chance. Once again God showed that He was kind and merciful. God promised Adam and Eve that He will send a wonderful Person, a Redeemer, to help them. The Redeemer or Saviour will come to lead them to heaven. Adam and Eve were glad that God still loved them and promised to send the Saviour.

2. What the Redeemer Would Do

God told Adam and Eve that the Redeemer would come upon earth to save them from their sins and from hell. The Saviour would suffer a great deal to make up for their sins and sins of all the people.

He would help them get back again the sanctifying grace which was lost through sin.

The Saviour would open heaven again. Someday they could be happy with God in heaven.

3. What We Must Suffer Because of Sin

Adam and Eve's sin is passed on to everyone. Because of original sin we find it hard to be good. Our will is weak, we must try again and again to choose and do what is right to please God.

Because of original sin we do not understand everything. We must study and learn more. Sometimes our bodies suffer and we become sick. And someday we will die.

C. Organization

1. What promise did God make to Adam and Eve?
2. What is original sin?
3. Did we commit that sin?
4. How is original sin taken from us?
5. What are some of the things we must suffer because of Adam and Eve's sin?

D. Virtues and Practices

1. Keep our promises made to God.
2. Try not to offend God by sin.
3. Obey God's laws at all times.
4. Thank God for His love and mercy.

IV. SUGGESTED LEARNING ACTIVITIES

A. Discuss the difference between the promise made by God and those which we have made and have not kept.
B. Stories: "God's Promise," Sister Mary, *et al., The Catholic Mother's Helper*, pp. 42–43; "Barbara's Heavenly Dress," Sister Marguerite, *Their Hearts Are His Garden*, pp. 33–35.

V. TEACHER REFERENCES

A. Dennerle, *Leading the Little Ones to Christ*, pp. 62–66.
B. Sister Mary, *et al., The Catholic Mother's Helper*, pp. 42–43.
C. Schumacher, *I Teach Catechism*, Vol. I, pp. 40–43.

LESSON 25 (This lesson may take more than one day.)

I. SUBJECT MATTER

Gratitude to God for His Gifts

II. OBJECTIVES

A. To develop an attitude of thankfulness to God for His gifts.
B. To compose original prayers of thankfulness.

III. SUGGESTED PROCEDURE

A. Approach

God, our heavenly Father, created everything for us to show His goodness and love. Do we remember to thank Him for all the marvelous gifts He gave us?

B. Presentation

1. Our Gratitude to God

A good child will thank God every day for the many gifts received. But on Thanksgiving Day we owe Him a special "thank you." Every day, from the day we were born, God has thought of us, cared for us, and showered gifts upon us to show His goodness and generosity. His loving care of us will never end.

2. Gift of Our Creation

Our life and all that we have we owe to God. He made us because of His love and His desire to share heaven with us. Your body with all its parts comes from God. Your eyes, which show you many beautiful things, are God's gift. Your ears, which tell you many wonderful things, come from God. All your powers, everything you can do comes from God. You are alive because God gave you an immortal soul. You are dear to God, because He wants to live in you. What great treasures God gave you to make you what you are. Have you ever thought of thanking Him for all that? Now could be a good time to do it. (Minute meditation.)

3. Gift of Food, Clothing, and Shelter

God is our loving Father. He makes sure that we have everything we need to live a happy way. He is the generous Giver. God takes care of our body and our soul. Think of the delicious food we have at our meals. That is a gift from God for our body. (Discuss original source of food as God's creation.)

Our soul needs food, too. God gives us Himself in Holy Communion. We do not receive Jesus in Holy Communion yet, but we can make a Spiritual Communion. (Explain briefly.)

Our clothing, too, is a gift from God. God created many things from which clothing is made. (Discuss source of clothing as God's creation.)

Our homes, where our family lives and prays together, are gifts from God. (Discuss source of our dwelling places as God's creation.)

4. Gifts of Creation

Looking around us we can see many, many gifts that God gives to make us happy and because He loves us. The sun, stars, and moon in the sky, flowers and trees, birds and animals, and many other things we can find are gifts from God. (Discuss purpose of each object and how it helps us to think of God.)

5. Gift of Good Parents

God, our heavenly Father, is a Spirit whom we cannot see. He knows that we need someone to take care of us upon earth, someone who will take His place. He gave you a good and kind father and mother. Think of the many ways they show you their loving care and kindness. (Discuss briefly.)

God wants us to be kind to our parents, too. Show them that you love them by obeying them and praying for them every day. How thankful we should be to God for giving us our parents.

6. Gift of Faith

God has chosen us for a special place, His heavenly home. He placed us in a Catholic family where we learn about God, where we learn how to pray, and where we learn how to get to heaven. He gave us the gift of faith which enables us to believe everything we learn about God. We believe in God.

7. Other Gifts

Besides these marvelous gifts, we have schools, churches, friends, animals. God has made all these and many, many more. Doesn't His goodness to you make you want to thank Him more and more?

Don't you think you should do all you can to show Him how much you love Him?

C. Organization

1. What are some of the gifts that God has given us?
2. How does God share His goodness with us?
3. How can we share God's gifts with others?
4. What do we owe God?
5. How can we show our thankfulness to God?

D. Virtues and Practices

1. Show God by your actions that you appreciate His gifts.
2. Share with those who have little food, clothing, etc.
3. Help the missions.

IV. SUGGESTED LEARNING ACTIVITIES

A. Make up an original litany of thanksgiving.
B. Make a Thanksgiving poster to show God's gifts to us.
C. Make a chart of original thank-you prayers.
D. Arrange a bulletin board of pictures of gifts from God.
E. Poems: "Prayer of Praise," *Hear Our Prayer,* Garden City Publishing Co.; "Little Joys," *Poems for God's Child*, p. 21; "Our Thank-You Day," Belger, *Sing a Song of Holy Things*, p. 21.

LITTLE JOYS

Thank You, dear God, for little joys;
For Ginger's baby kittens,
And for my Irish setter, Bob,
And for my furry mittens.
I thank You for my roller skates,
And for my new speedy sled,
And for my sandpile, and my swing,
And for my cozy bed.
I thank You for big things many times,
But, dear God, now and then,
I like to thank You for little joys
Of all day long.   Amen.

V. TEACHER REFERENCE

Aurelia-Kirsch, *Practical Aids for Catholic Teachers*, pp. 33–38.

LESSON 26

I. SUBJECT MATTER

Grace Before Meals

II. OBJECTIVES

A. To know and understand the prayer to be said before meals.
B. To develop the habit of always asking God's blessing before meals.

III. SUGGESTED PROCEDURE

A. Approach

God is the kind Giver of all the gifts we receive daily. He thinks of us and takes care of us. He provides the food we need for our bodies.

B. Presentation

1. We Pray Before Meals

Every time we sit down at the table for a meal, we see God's gifts. God gives the food we need to make us grow strong and healthy. He wants us to remember that all the food is given to us from His "bounty." (Explain term "bounty.")

Before the meal we should ask God to bless us and bless the food we are about to eat. (Show pictures and discuss.)

We say a special prayer called "Grace Before Meals."

2. Words of the Prayer

We first ask God to bless us and bless the food. We say, "Bless us, O Lord, and these Thy gifts." We know the food comes from God. So we say, "which we are about to receive from Thy bounty." We then end the prayer through Jesus. We say, "through Christ, our Lord. Amen."

Repeat the entire prayer slowly and distinctly, stressing difficult words to prevent incorrect learning.

C. Organization

1. Why do we pray before meals?
2. What do we ask God to do?
3. How should we say this prayer?

58

D. Virtues and Practices

1. Always say your "Grace Before Meals."
2. Give good example to others by saying this prayer well.

IV. SUGGESTED LEARNING ACTIVITIES

A. Recording: "Grace Before Meals," Catholic Children's Record Club
B. Illustrate how we say grace before meals.
C. Say the prayer before lunchtime each day in the classroom.

V. TEACHER REFERENCE

S.N.D., *Religious Teaching of Young Children*, p. 124.

LESSON 27

I. SUBJECT MATTER

Grace After Meals

II. OBJECTIVES

A. To teach prayer: "Grace After Meals."
B. To develop the habit of thanking God daily for His gifts.

III. SUGGESTED PROCEDURE

A. Approach

Before we ate our meals we asked God to bless us and bless the food. Do you know what we should do after the meal?

B. Presentation

1. We Pray After Meals

After each meal we should remember to thank God for the food He gave. We say a special prayer called "Grace After Meals." Saying prayers after meals will help us remember that food is a benefit from God. (Explain the term "benefits." Show picture and discuss.)

2. Words of the Prayer

The first thing we tell God is "Thank You." We say, "We give Thee thanks." We know God is all powerful. We call Him "O Almighty God." We continue: "for all Thy benefits." We end the prayer: "who liveth and reigneth world without end. Amen."

We also add another prayer for the poor souls in purgatory. We ask God to be merciful to them. We say: "May the souls of the faithful departed through the mercy of God rest in peace. Amen."

Recite the prayer again, slowly and distinctly, stressing in particular the difficult words to prevent incorrect learning.

C. Organization
1. What gifts does God give us every day?
2. What does God expect us to say? Why?
3. How can we thank God for His gifts?

D. Virtues and Practices
1. Start the practice of saying grace after meals at home.
2. Give good example by saying this prayer well.
3. Say grace after meals in school individually.

IV. SUGGESTED LEARNING ACTIVITIES

A. Recording: "Grace After Meals," Catholic Children's Record Club.
B. Individual recitation of the prayer.
C. Story: "The Chicken and the Sparrow," Brennan, *For Heaven's Sake,* pp. 82–84.

V. TEACHER REFERENCE

S.N.D., *Religious Teaching of Young Children,* pp. 124–125.

LESSON 28

I. SUBJECT MATTER

Feast of the Guardian Angels — October 2

II. OBJECTIVES

A. To know that God has provided each one of us with a heavenly protector.
B. To show appreciation to our guardian angels by thinking of them and praying to them.

III. SUGGESTED PROCEDURE

A. Approach

Our heavenly Father loves us so much that He gives us the best care He possibly can. God sends us helpers who tell us what to do. Can you name any?

B. Presentation

1. God Gave Us Each a Guardian Angel

When we were born God gave each one of us a special helper, a guardian angel, who would watch over us, protect us in danger, and lovingly guide us every day of our lives. Your guardian angel helps you along the road to heaven. He must bring you back to God when you die. Everyone has a guardian angel. Mother's angel is with her at home. Father's angel is with him at work. Your guardian angel is right beside you, very happy to see you a good child. My guardian angel is beside me, too.

2. Loving Care of Our Guardian Angel

You are never alone. Your guardian angel stays with you day and night. He loves you and helps you to be good. Your guardian angel protects you, body and soul. He wants you to be happy now and in heaven. Your guardian angel sees God. Wouldn't you want him to tell God nice things about you? He asks God to bless you and keep you always a kind and obedient child. (Discuss pictures — a child and his guardian angel from morning until night bringing out the constant presence of the heavenly spirit.)

3. We Show Our Love for Our Guardian Angel

Our guardian angel loves us. We should show him that we love him, too. Think of him often during the day, and ask for help whenever you need it. He loves to hear you talk to him. How pleased he is when he sees you being kind to others, and obeying mother and father. He knows you love him if you do everything to please God.

Every morning and every night and even during the day say the special prayer in honor of your guardian angel.

Teach or review the guardian angel prayer. See Lesson 20, p. 44 f.

C. Organization

1. When does God give each little child a guardian angel?
2. Why does God give everyone a guardian angel?
3. Why do we call our angels guardian angels?
4. Why don't the angels want us to commit sin?
5. What do we want our guardian angels to tell God about us?
6. How can I show my love for my guardian angel?

D. Virtues and Practices

1. Speak to your guardian angel often.
2. Think about him in time of danger.
3. Ask your guardian angel to help you love God more.

IV. SUGGESTED LEARNING ACTIVITIES

A. Discuss pictures of guardian angels.
B. Compose original prayers to your guardian angel.
C. Stories: "The Little Devil With the Long Tail," Brennan, *For Heaven's Sake,* pp. 18–21; "Dorothy's Angel," Sister Marguerite, *Their Hearts Are His Garden,* pp. 39–40; "An Angel Helps," *ibid.,* pp. 40–41.
D. Poems: "Angels," Thayer, *Child on His Knees,* p. 114; "The Angels," Belger, *Sing a Song of Holy Things,* p. 10.

V. TEACHER REFERENCE

A. Sister Mary, *et al., The Catholic Mother's Helper,* pp. 30–31.
B. S.N.D., *Religious Teaching of Young Children,* pp. 114–115.
C. Aurelia-Kirsch, *Practical Aids for the Catholic Teacher,* pp. 194–195.
D. Fitzpatrick, *Religion in Life Curriculum, First Grade Manual,* pp. 40–42.
E. Sister Marguerite, *Their Hearts Are His Garden,* pp. 89–91.

LESSON 29

I. SUBJECT MATTER

Feast of St. Therese — October 3

II. OBJECTIVES

A. To develop a knowledge of simple incidents in the life of St. Therese.
B. To know that we can get to heaven by doing ordinary things well for the love of God.
C. To try to imitate St. Therese in her "little way."

III. SUGGESTED PROCEDURE

A. Approach

Show pictures of St. Therese, Little Flower of Jesus. Who is this? What do you know about her? A saint is God's special friend. St. Therese, called the Little Flower of Jesus, is one of His friends.

B. Presentation

1. St. Therese as a Child

St. Therese belonged to a good Catholic family that loved God very much. Therese loved to pray together at home with her family. Everyone loved her, especially because she was the youngest. Therese was very devoted to her family and tried her best to be kind and helpful to them. She learned that to please God, she must learn to do things for herself and others, and not expect her sisters to do it for her.

Therese liked God's wonderful world. The flowers, stars, ocean, and others made her think of God and love God more.

Therese had great devotion to Blessed Mother. Mother Mary loved Therese, too. In fact, Mary cured her when she was very sick.

2. The Little Way of St. Therese

As a little girl, Therese loved God very much. She loved Him so much that everything she did was offered to God as a flower of love. Therese knew she was unable to do big things for Jesus, so she had her own little way of doing things. Whatever she did she tried to do well. In her little way she tried to do something she didn't like to do, obeyed quickly with a smile, told the truth if something happened, ate

63

something she didn't like. Can you tell some other ways in which we could follow St. Therese on her little way?

3. St. Therese as a Nun

It was very hard for St. Therese to become a nun. But she did not give up trying. As a nun, she tried more and more to do all little things for Jesus. She knew that it takes a hero to do small things well and to become a saint. Therese offered God all the unpleasant things she was asked to do, and all the pain she suffered. That was her little way of loving God.

4. St. Therese in Heaven

St. Therese wished to be in heaven with God for ever and ever. "I will spend my heaven doing good upon earth; I will ask God to send down a shower of roses," she would often say. St. Therese died as a young Sister. She's now a great saint in heaven. She is sharing in God's love and doing much good upon earth. She is praying for us and sending down the promised roses. Every time God gives us help through St. Therese's intercession, it is a rose from heaven.

C. Organization
1. How did St. Therese become a saint?
2. Why is she called the Little Flower of Jesus?
3. What can we do every day so that we, too, can become saints?

D. Virtues and Practices
1. Do the best you can just because you love God and want to please Him.
2. Ask St. Therese to teach you her "little way."

IV. SUGGESTED LEARNING ACTIVITIES

A. Dramatize incidents from the life of St. Therese.
B. Illustrate little acts we can do for the love of God.
C. Compose an original class prayer to St. Therese.
D. Story: "Stories of Saint Theresa," Sister Marguerite, *Their Hearts Are His Garden*, pp. 61–62.
E. Poem: "The Little Flower," Belger, *Sing a Song of Holy Things*, p. 12.

V. TEACHER REFERENCE

Practical Aids for Catholic Teachers, pp. 195–199.

LESSON 30

I. SUBJECT MATTER

Feast of St. Francis — October 4

II. OBJECTIVES

A. To learn about some events in the life of St. Francis of Assisi.
B. To imitate the virtues of St. Francis, especially his great love for God and His creatures.

III. SUGGESTED PROCEDURE

A. Approach

Today is the feast of someone who loved God very much, someone who loved God's creatures. It is the feast of St. Francis of Assisi.

B. Presentation

1. Early Life of St. Francis

St. Francis lived a long time ago in the town of Assisi in Italy. He was a rich boy, who had many pretty things and had everything he wanted. But that did not make him happy. He felt empty inside. His happiest moments were the times he could do good for others by his acts of kindness, cheerfulness, and helpfulness. Everyone called him "the cheerful kind boy."

2. Virtues of St. Francis

Francis loved everyone and everything that God created. He called them his brothers and sisters. (Explain "brother sun," "sister wind," etc.) No matter what he saw it taught him love of God. "Love God and praise God," he would often say. "Praise God that He made you out of love. Praise God that He made everything for love of us."

Francis realized that to show love for God, one must love to do good and help others, for in helping others we are doing something for God. He loved God so much and knew that God loved him that he was always friendly and cheerful. He did everything he could to make others happy.

3. St. Francis, a Franciscan

Francis tried to show others that God loved everyone. He found out that he could do this best by loving them and doing good things for them. So, he helped the poor, took care of the sick, begged for food for the hungry, and taught children about God. Some other men joined Francis. They, too, wanted to help others and do things for love of God. Francis and his helpers worked together, prayed together, and served God together. They soon were called the Franciscans. Today many boys and girls become Franciscans. They help others to live happily and some day be happy with God in heaven. There are many Franciscan priests, brothers, and sisters. They offer their lives to do good to others and help others to love God.

C. Organization

1. Why did St. Francis give up all his money and fine clothes?
2. Why was he especially kind to the poor?
3. Why was he kind to the birds and animals?
4. How can we show our love for God?

D. Virtues and Practices

1. Pray to St. Francis for the virtue of kindness.
2. Try to be kind to all of God's little creatures.
3. Be willing to give up little things to prove your love for God.

IV. SUGGESTED LEARNING ACTIVITIES

A. Discuss pictures of St. Francis.
B. Dramatize incidents from his life.
C. Discuss ways of helping the poor.
D. Discuss how to treat the animals.
E. Poems: "Saint Francis," Belger, *Sing a Song of Holy Things*, p. 13; "St. Francis Teaches the Children," *ibid.*, Sister Marguerite, pp. 31–33; "Saint Francis and His Little Brother."

V. TEACHER REFERENCES

A. Aurelia-Kirsch, *Practical Aids for Catholic Teachers*, pp. 199–200.
B. Dennerle, *Leading the Little Ones to Christ*, pp. 26–28.

LESSON 31

I. SUBJECT MATTER

Feast of Our Lady of the Rosary — October 7

II. OBJECTIVES

A. To give the children a simple but clear understanding of the rosary.

B. To develop love for the rosary and the frequent use of it.

III. SUGGESTED PROCEDURE

A. Approach

Can you guess what the child is doing in this picture. (Show picture of someone saying a rosary.) Everyone knows what this is. (Hold up a rosary.) Do you know the story of the rosary?

B. Presentation

1. Mary Gave Us the Rosary

A long time ago, a certain priest, Dominic, loved God very much and tried all he could to make others love Him, too. He wanted everyone to serve God.

Father Dominic loved Jesus and Mary. He asked them for help. He trusted in God and knew that God would help. He was not disappointed.

One day, Mother Mary appeared to Father Dominic holding a rosary in her hand. "Offer this prayer for sinners," she said. "It is a powerful prayer. The people will soon be good." And Mary was right. Many people returned to God. They came to love Him more and more and they loved Mary, too.

Father Dominic is in heaven now with Jesus and Mary. St. Dominic wants us to say the rosary every day.

2. How to Say the Rosary

Mother Mary taught St. Dominic how to say the rosary. It is made up of the Apostles' Creed, Our Fathers, Hail Marys, and Glory Bes. Some of these prayers we already know. The others we will soon learn. It is not necessary here to tell the children the names of the mysteries. Simply teach:

a) Parts of the rosary: crucifix, big beads, and small beads.

b) How to hold the rosary and use it properly,

c) Kind of prayers to say.

Recite one decade of the rosary each day in class. As different children recite the Hail Mary or Our Father, the rest of the class answers. This is a simple but effective way of teaching the children how to say the rosary properly.

3. Why We Say the Rosary

Mother Mary told St. Dominic to say the rosary every day. She also appeared several times to some good children (Fatima, Lourdes). Each time that Mary appeared, she asked the children to pray the rosary often and offer it especially for the conversion of sinners. Mary wants us to say the rosary every day. The rosary is Mother Mary's favorite prayer. We show Mary great love and honor when we say it devoutly. We can offer the rosary for ourselves, our parents, our friends, priests, and sisters or for anyone else. Mary is called Queen of the Holy Rosary. The entire month of October is dedicated to her. We show our love for Mary by saying our rosary every day during this month.

C. Organization

1. How can we show Mary our special love?
2. What is a rosary?
3. What prayers do we say on the rosary?
4. What prayer do we say most of the time on the rosary?

D. Virtues and Practices

1. Recite the "Hail Mary" devoutly to show Mary your love.
2. Carry the rosary respectfully and recite it daily.

IV. SUGGESTED LEARNING ACTIVITIES

A. Recite the rosary together in class, in church, or at home with the family.

B. Stories: "Roses for Mary," Sister Marguerite, *Their Hearts Are His Garden*, pp. 28–29; "Saint Dominic and the Rosary," *ibid.*, pp. 94–95; "Queen of the Rosary, Pray for Us," Dorcy, *Mary My Mother*, pp. 61–65.

V. TEACHER REFERENCE

Aurelia-Kirsch, *Practical Aids for Catholic Teachers*, pp. 200–203.

LESSON 32

I. SUBJECT MATTER

Feast of Christ the King — Last Sunday in October

II. OBJECTIVES

A. To acquaint the children with the fact that Jesus Christ is our King.
B. To infuse in the children love for and loyalty to their King.
C. To appreciate the work of the missionaries in spreading Christ's Kingdom today.

III. SUGGESTED PROCEDURE

A. Approach

Why does Jesus wear a crown on this picture? (Show picture of Christ the King.) Jesus is the greatest King that ever lived. He is the King of kings.

B. Presentation

1. Jesus Christ Is the King of Heaven and Earth

God is the great powerful King, who created heaven and earth. Everything belongs to God. Jesus is God. Therefore, we say Jesus Christ is the King of heaven and earth. He is the King of everything and everyone. We, too, are a part of God's creation. Therefore, God is our King, too.

2. Jesus' Kingdom Is in Heaven and Upon Earth

Jesus' kingdom is in heaven. All the angels and saints belong to His Kingdom. Jesus' kingdom is also upon earth. Everything and everyone that God created belongs to Jesus' kingdom.

3. Jesus' Kingdom Is in Our Hearts

Jesus' kingdom is in our hearts, too. We must let Jesus live in the kingdom of our hearts all the time. Keep your heart pure and holy for your King. Open your heart to this good and kind King. Let Him reign there and let your actions show that you believe that He is God and that He is your King. If we permit Jesus to stay in the kingdom of our hearts, He will take us to His heavenly kingdom when we die.

4. We Can Spread God's Kingdom Upon Earth

There are many boys and girls in the world that do not know about Jesus Christ our King. They have never learned to love Him. Many missionary priests and sisters want God's kingdom to be spread far and wide. They leave their homes and go far away to help others learn about Christ our King. (Give a short explanation about missionaries; their sacrifice and work.) We can spread Christ's kingdom, too. We can pray for the missionary priests and sisters that God will help them in their hard work. Our sacrifices will help them, too.

Discuss briefly other ways that we can spread God's kingdom upon earth, e.g., praying for pagan people.

C. Organization

1. Who is the greatest King?
2. Why is Jesus called the "King of kings"?
3. Where is God's kingdom?
4. Who belongs to God's kingdom?
5. What do missionary priests and sisters do?
6. What can we do to show God that we know He is our King?
7. How can we help spread God's kingdom?

D. Virtues and Practices

1. Pray for the spreading of Christ's kingdom on earth.
2. Pray for children in far-away countries, so they can have the chance to learn about God.
3. Offer little sacrifices for the missionary priests and sisters.

IV. SUGGESTED LEARNING ACTIVITIES

1. List some ways in which we can spread the kingdom of Christ by helping the missions.
2. Discuss pictures that show the work of missionary priests and sisters.
3. Stories: "Sharing Heaven," Sister Marguerite, *Their Hearts Are His Garden*, pp. 25–26; "Helping the Missions," *ibid.*, pp. 49–50.

V. TEACHER REFERENCES

A. Sister Mary, *et al.*, *The Catholic Mother's Helper*, pp. 96–98.
B. Fitzpatrick, *Religion in Life Curriculum, First Grade Manual*, p. 118.

UNIT THREE

The Lord's Prayer
Time: 3 weeks

I. INTRODUCTION FOR THE TEACHER

Unit Three develops the concept of prayer, but it is chiefly concerned with the teaching of the seven petitions of the "Lord's Prayer" as separate topics in order to facilitate the comprehension and memorization of this important prayer. Each petition is taken as a complete lesson and is elaborated upon in such a manner as to make it meaningful to the small child. The pronunciation and enunciation of the difficult words must be stressed, also. When the child understands the prayer, he will learn to love it and make it an important part of his daily life and prayers.

II. OBJECTIVES OF THE UNIT

A. To develop the knowledge that prayer is talking to God or thinking about Him.

B. To develop a great love for the "Lord's Prayer" as it is the prayer taught by Christ Himself.

C. To teach the children to say the "Lord's Prayer" meaningfully.

D. To foster the desire to pray for the extension of Christ's kingdom here on earth.

E. To foster an attitude of dependence upon God, who is the Provider of all our needs.

F. To grow in confidence in the love and mercy of God.

III. SUBJECT MATTER

A. What prayer is

B. Why we pray

C. How we should pray

D. Prayer: "Our Father"
   1. Father-child relationship expressed in the prayer
   2. The seven petitions of the "Our Father"

E. Liturgical feasts: (1) All Saints — November 1; (2) All Souls — November 2; (3) Presentation of Mary — November 21.

LESSON 33

I. SUBJECT MATTER

The Meaning of Prayer

II. OBJECTIVES

A. To develop the knowledge that prayer is conversation with God.
B. To instill habits of prayerfulness in daily living.

III. SUGGESTED PROCEDURE

A. Approach

Do you think that Jesus ever talked to His heavenly Father the way you do to yours? Did He ever think about Him? talk about Him?

B. Presentation

1. Prayer Is Talking to God

Yes, Jesus talked to His heavenly Father very many times. That is why we say that Jesus prayed, because talking to God is a prayer. Whenever we pray we are really talking to God, our heavenly Father, the way Jesus did.

2. Prayer Is Thinking About God

Jesus liked to think about His heavenly Father. He did that very many times, too. This also was a prayer. Whenever you are thinking about God you are really praying. Whenever you are listening to a story about Jesus in school, church, or home, and you are lovingly thinking about Him, that is a prayer. When you are looking at a picture of Jesus, you are thinking of God. God is very pleased with this, because thinking about God is a prayer.

3. Prayer Is Loving God

Jesus loved His heavenly Father. That too was a prayer, because loving God is a prayer. We do not always have to say words when we pray, because prayer is not only talking to God but also loving God and thinking about God.

4. What Are Some of the Things You Talk About When You Pray?

72

What are some of the things you can tell God when you talk to Him? (Here the teacher should obtain from the children some of their own ideas about prayer.) Children may compose their own prayer. When you pray you can tell God anything.

C. Organization

1. What is prayer?
2. When we are praying, whom should we think about?
3. Do we always have to use words when we pray?
4. Why does God want us to love Him?
5. What are some things we could talk about with God?

D. Virtues and Practices

1. Turn your work and play into prayer.
2. Make a little intention at the beginning of your important acts.
3. Tell Jesus about our little joys and sorrows.
4. Think of God when you pray, even though you do not understand all the words.

IV. SUGGESTED LEARNING ACTIVITIES

A. Show the children how to make a minute meditation about the good, kind God.
B. Poem: "How to Turn Fun into Prayers," *Child on His Knees*, p. 126.

V. TEACHER REFERENCES

A. S.N.D., *Religious Teaching of Young Children*, pp. 119–121.
B. Schumacher, *I Teach Catechism*, Vol. I, pp. 52–54.

LESSON 34

I. SUBJECT MATTER

Why We Pray

II. OBJECTIVES

A. To develop a knowledge of the various types of prayer.
B. To develop an attitude of prayerfulness in daily living.

III. SUGGESTED PROCEDURE

A. Approach

You already know what prayer is. Today we will talk about some of the reasons why we pray.

B. Presentation

1. We Pray to Praise God

We pray to praise God. When we praise God we are telling Him how great, wise, good, and almighty He is.

2. We Pray to Express Love of God

We should pray because we love God and not just because we need something. When we tell God we love Him, we do not have to think of hard words. We can just say, "I love You, dear God."

3. We Pray to Express Thanks to God

God has given us so many wonderful things. It is polite to say "Thank You" to God after we receive something from Him. God is very good to us. We should say "Thank You" to God very often.

4. We Pray to Express Sorrow for Sin

We ought often to tell Jesus we are sorry for our sins. Sin displeases God. When we tell God we are sorry, God forgives us our sins. Every time that we tell God that we are sorry for our sins we should also tell God we will try to be better. God loves us even though we are naughty. He only hates the sins we commit.

5. We Pray to Help Others

We cannot always help people when they are in trouble, but God can. We can pray to God, asking Him to help all those people who need help. That is the best thing we can do for others.

6. We Pray for Our Needs

We should also pray to God when we are sick. He will either help us get well or make us brave enough not to complain. There are so many things that we need. So isn't it best to ask our heavenly Father for them? He knows what is best for us. He will either give us what we want or else surprise us by giving us something better. But sometimes He asks us to suffer patiently with Jesus and like Jesus,

C. Organization

1. Why do we praise God?
2. Why should we tell God that we love Him?
3. Is it polite not to thank God for all His gifts?
4. What happens when we tell God we are sorry for our sins?
5. What is the best thing we can do for others?
6. Why should we pray for ourselves?

D. Virtues and Practices

1. Pray because you love God, and not just because you need something.
2. Remember to say "Thank You" after you receive something from God.
3. Often tell Jesus how sorry you are for your sins.

IV. SUGGESTED LEARNING ACTIVITIES

A. Compose original prayers of praise, love, thanksgiving, sorrow for sin, and petition.
B. Poem: "God's Help," Belger, *Sing a Song of Holy Things*, p. 50.

V. TEACHER REFERENCE

Schumacher, *I Teach Catechism*, Vol. I, pp. 54–56, 58–61.

LESSON 35

I. SUBJECT MATTER

How We Should Pray

II. OBJECTIVES

A. To develop the idea of right attitude toward prayer.
B. To develop the ability to pray with love and devotion.

III. SUGGESTED PROCEDURE

A. Approach

Yesterday we talked about some of the reasons why we pray. Can you name them? How do you think we ought to pray?

B. Presentation

1. We Should Pray With Love, Attention, and Devotion

What is prayer? Yes, prayer is talking to God, thinking about God, trusting God, and loving God. This will help us remember to pray in a holy way. Whom should we be thinking about when we are praying? Yes, we should be thinking about God. If we do so, we are praying with attention and devotion.

2. We Should Be Respectful When We Pray

When we are saying our morning or night prayers we ought to kneel and fold our hands. (Demonstrate.) This will show God that we honor Him. Whenever we are in church we must remember to be polite, too. It is not good manners to sit down as soon as we enter. We must remember at all times that we are in God's house. When you enter church, walk up the aisle, genuflect carefully, enter the pew, kneel down, fold your hands, and say some prayers. If you are really tired, you could sit down after a while.

3. We Can Pray at All Times

We do not always have to kneel or fold our hands when we pray. God will listen to us all the time. We can pray to Him while we dress, play, or work. We can change our whole day into a prayer by doing everything just the way Jesus did when He was a Child. (Cite example how this practice could be done.)

C. Organization
1. How should we pray?
2. How should we kneel?
3. How should we have our hands?
4. Why should we try to pray well?
5. When can we pray?

D. Virtues and Practices
1. Pay attention to what you are saying when you pray.
2. Try to pray devotedly.
3. Let your body help you pray well.

IV. SUGGESTED LEARNING ACTIVITIES

A. Discuss pictures of children at prayer.
B. Dramatize how we should pray at church, at school, at home.

C. Story: "When Mary Was a Little Girl," *Mary, My Mother,* pp. 13–17.

V. TEACHER REFERENCES

A. Schumacher, *I Teach Catechism*, Vol. 1, pp. 56–58.
B. S.N.D., *Religious Teaching of Young Children*, pp. 119–120.

LESSON 36

I. SUBJECT MATTER

A. The Lord's Prayer — the Best Prayer
B. The Father-Child Relationship — "Our Father, Who Art in Heaven"

II. OBJECTIVES

A. To develop a great love for the "Lord's Prayer" because Christ Himself taught us the prayer.
B. To learn and understand the meaning of the words: "Our Father, Who Art in Heaven."

III. SUGGESTED PROCEDURE

A. Approach

What prayers do you say at home? Today we are going to talk about a prayer that Jesus taught His friends. Do you know what that prayer is? Would you like to begin learning it today?

B. Presentation

1. The Apostles Ask Jesus to Teach Them to Pray

Very often the friends of Jesus saw Him go away from the crowd and pray. They wanted to pray the way Jesus prayed. One day they said, "Lord! teach us how to pray." Jesus answered, "When you pray say, 'Our Father who art in heaven . . . ,' " etc.

2. The First Words of the Lord's Prayer: "Our Father Who Art in Heaven"

We call God our Father because He loves us as a father loves his children. God made us. He watches over us. He gives us all we have. He punishes us so that we will be good. But He forgives us if we are sorry. And He loves us so much that He wants to take us to heaven when we die.

3. God's Home in Heaven

Where is God? That is true, God is everywhere, but it is in heaven especially that angels and saints honor and pray to God. Heaven is God's special home. That is why we say "Who art in heaven." Heaven is our home too. That is where God wants to take us after we die.

4. Universality of the Love of God

God is our Father. He is not only my Father or your Father, but the Father of all of us, that is, of all the people in the whole world. Because God is their Father, all people are God's children. Now let me see if you can think. If God is our Father and we are His children, then what are we all? Yes, we are all brothers and sisters. Brothers and sisters must love one another. If we would remember this, there will be no unkindness, hate, or fighting.

5. Special Honor and Love Should Be Given to God

If we want to be happy with God in heaven we must know, love, and serve God. We must love all as brothers and sisters. Can you tell of some ways in which we can really show God that we are His children?

C. Organization
1. What did the Apostles want Jesus to teach them?
2. What did our Lord say to the Apostles?
3. Does God love you more than your father loves you?
4. What have we received from God?
5. Are all people God's children?
6. Where is God especially honored?
7. Where is our true home?
8. What do you mean when you say "Our Father, who art in heaven"?

D. Virtues and Practices
1. Desire to go to heaven — your true home.
2. Often pray to your Father in heaven.

IV. SUGGESTED LEARNING ACTIVITIES

A. Discuss Picture 1 of the "Our Father" series ("The Lord's Prayer" — Gouppy) or "The Our Father for Children," Miki. (See Bibliography.)
B. Recall previously developed concept of God, our heavenly Father.
C. Recording: "The Lord's Prayer," Catholic Children's Record Club.
D. Begin memorization of the Lord's Prayer, adding to it as each petition is presented.
E. Poem: "Our Father, Who Art in Heaven," School Sisters of Notre Dame, *The Our Father for Little Ones.*

V. TEACHER REFERENCES

A. Dennerle, *Leading the Little Ones to Christ,* pp. 290–291.
B. Fitzpatrick, *Religion in Life Curriculum, First Grade Manual,* pp. 117–118.

LESSON 37

I. SUBJECT MATTER

Petition One: "Hallowed Be Thy Name"

II. OBJECTIVES

A. To guide the children to say the Lord's Prayer meaningfully.
B. To foster an attitude of respect and honor for God's name.

III. SUGGESTED PROCEDURE

A. Approach

God is our Father in heaven. God is holy. God's name is holy too. Today we shall talk about ways we can praise and honor His holy name.

B. Presentation

1. Explanation of the Phrase: "Hallowed Be Thy Name"

Another name for "hallowed" is holy. "Hallowed be Thy name"

means that God's name is holy and that we want to praise God's name. When we praise a person we are telling everyone how good and kind he is so that others can love and praise him. We want God to be praised by ourselves and others. We say "Hallowed be Thy name" to tell God this.

2. Use of God's Name

God's name is holy. We must use God's name only in a holy way. We use God's name in a holy way when we pray or when we say something nice about God. Everyone does not love and honor God's holy name. Some people use God's name when they are angry. Sometimes boys and girls use God's name when they make silly promises. It displeases God when we use His holy name carelessly.

3. Our Desire That Everyone Praise and Respect God's Name

When we say "Hallowed be Thy name" we are also asking God to help all people honor and praise God's holy name. We can also say this part of the prayer to make up for the people who do not love and praise God and keep His name holy. We can honor God's name in a special way when we bow our head every time we hear the name of Jesus.

C. Organization
1. How do you praise someone?
2. Why do we praise God?
3. What is another name for "hallowed"?
4. Does everyone love and respect God's name?
5. What do we want to tell God when we say, "Hallowed be Thy name"?

D. Virtues and Practices
1. Use God's name with respect.
2. Bow your head at the name of Jesus.
3. Make up to God for the misuse of God's name.

IV. SUGGESTED LEARNING ACTIVITIES
A. Discuss Picture 2 of the "Our Father" series (Gouppy or Miki).
B. Individual recitation of the phrase, "Hallowed be Thy name."
C. Poem: "Hallowed Be Thy Name," School Sisters of Notre Dame, *The Our Father for Little Ones.*

V. TEACHER REFERENCES

A. Dennerle, *Leading the Little Ones to Christ*, pp. 291–292.
B. Fitzpatrick, *Religion in Life Curriculum, First Grade Manual*, p. 118.

LESSON 38

I. SUBJECT MATTER

Petition Two: "Thy Kingdom Come"

II. OBJECTIVES

A. To guide the children to say the Lord's Prayer meaningfully.
B. To inspire the children with zeal for God's glory.

III. SUGGESTED PROCEDURE

A. Approach

Recall the first petition of the prayer. Children recite the first part and discuss the meaning.

B. Presentation

1. Explanation of the Phrase: "Thy Kingdom Come"

A kingdom is a country that belongs to a king. The king rules over the land and takes care of the people who live in his country. A king must be good to his people; the people should love and serve the king.

2. God the King of All Lands

Who is the greatest king in the whole world? What is His kingdom? (Heaven and earth.) God is a good King. He loves us and watches over us because we belong to Him and His kingdom. God wants us to love and serve Him. How can we serve God?

3. God the King of Our Hearts

Many people on this earth know nothing at all about God and His kingdom. They do not even know who God is. No one ever told them anything about God. That is why they do not pray to God or love or serve God. We want all people in the whole world to know about God, to love Him, and to serve Him; so we pray "Thy kingdom come."

4. Our Work as Apostles in Spreading the Kingdom of God

We can help in many ways those who do not know about God.

> We can pray for them.
> We can tell them about God.
> We can give them good example.
> We can help missionaries.

Missionaries are priests and Sisters who go to faraway countries where people do not know God. Today even some lay people go to mission lands to help priests and Sisters. They teach these people who God is and how they can love and serve Him. These missionaries need our prayers. They need money too to help build churches and to get the other things that will help the people to get to know God. God needs many missionaries. Perhaps God may some day call someone in this class to be His helper.

C. Organization

1. What do we call the country that belongs to a king?
2. Who is King of heaven and earth?
3. Do all the people in the world know about God?
4. Tell some ways in which you can help people know and love God.
5. What does "Thy kingdom come" mean?

D. Virtues and Practices

1. Pray for the spread of Christ's kingdom.
2. Be thankful for a Catholic home and education.

IV. SUGGESTED LEARNING ACTIVITIES

A. Discuss Picture 3 of the "Our Father" series (Gouppy or Miki).
B. Discuss the power of good example in the home, at school, in church, at play.
C. Poem: "Thy Kingdom Come," School Sisters of Notre Dame, *The Our Father for Little Ones.*

V. TEACHER REFERENCES

A. Dennerle, *Leading the Little Ones to Christ,* p. 292.
B. Fitzpatrick, *Religion in Life Curriculum, First Grade Manual,* p. 118.

LESSON 39

I. SUBJECT MATTER

Petition Three: "Thy Will Be Done on Earth as It Is in Heaven"

II. OBJECTIVES

A. To make the third petition of the Lord's Prayer meaningful.
B. To foster the habit of doing God's will at all times.

III. SUGGESTED PROCEDURE

A. Approach

Discuss how people obey a king if they love him.

B. Presentation

1. Obedience of Angels and Saints in Heaven

In heaven angels and saints love God so much that they always do only what God wants and as God wants. They do God's will. To do God's will means to do what God wants.

2. Doing God's Will on Earth

Just as angels and saints in heaven do the will of God, so all people on earth ought to do God's will. God our King is asking us to do His will. We are happy only when we are doing God's will. We show our love for God when we do what He wants us to do.

3. Doing What God Wants

Discuss things God wants us to do:

> Believe in Him.
> Love Him.
> Obey parents.
> Tell the truth.
> Be kind.
> Avoid sin bravely.
> Pray well.
> Do only what is right.

We should not complain when God sends us sorrow or disappointment. God knows what is best for us. We should be happy with whatever God sends us.

4. *The Third Petition of the Lord's Prayer*

In the third petition of the prayer Jesus taught us, we say, "Thy will be done, on earth as it is in heaven." When we say this, we promise God that we will do what He wants us to do. We know that He is a wise, loving Father who wants us to be happy. We know too that we are weak and that we sometimes want to do things that are displeasing to Him. God will, however, always give us help to do His will.

C. Organization

1. How do the angels and saints do God's will?
2. How can you do God's will on earth?
3. How should we act when God sends us joy?
4. How should we act when God sends us sorrow?
5. What does God want us to do?
6. What does "Thy will be done on earth as it is in heaven" mean?

D. Virtues and Practices

1. Do God's will by obeying your parents.
2. Accept whatever God sends you.
3. Try to do always what God wants.

IV. SUGGESTED LEARNING ACTIVITIES

A. Discuss how the will of God is done in heaven and how we can do it on earth.
B. Discuss Picture 4 of the "Our Father" series (Gouppy or Miki).
C. Poem: "Thy Will Be Done," School Sisters of Notre Dame, *The Our Father For Little Ones.*

V. TEACHER REFERENCES

A. Fitzpatrick, *Religion in Life Curriculum, First Grade Manual,* pp. 118–119.
B. Dennerle, *Leading the Little Ones to Christ,* p. 192.

LESSON 40

I. SUBJECT MATTER

Petition Four: "Give Us This Day Our Daily Bread"

II. OBJECTIVES

A. To make the fourth petition of the Lord's Prayer meaningful.
B. To foster the habit of thanking God for all His gifts.

III. SUGGESTED PROCEDURE

A. Approach

God has already given us so many gifts. The rest of this prayer is one of asking God for some very special gifts.

B. Presentation

1. Gifts We Need for Body and Soul

As long as we live on earth we need food, clothes, and a house to live in. Since God is our Father He gives us all these things and takes care of us just as our father at home does. There are things we need for our body and there are things we need for our soul, because as you already know we have a body and a soul. Our body needs food, sunshine, air, mother and father. Our soul needs Food too. Jesus gave us special Food for our soul, that is Holy Communion. You cannot receive Holy Communion yet but you can ask God to come to your heart and He will do so in a very special way. We call God's coming into our heart in this special way "Spiritual Communion."

2. Perseverance in Prayer for These Needs

God knows what we want and need for our body and our soul but He wants us to ask. That is what we do when we say "Give us this day our daily bread." We are asking God to give us and all the people today what we need to live for body and soul. Sometimes God doesn't give us what we want because it wouldn't be good for us or because we didn't ask God long enough. So, you see, God always answers prayers. Sometimes God says "no," but He gives us something else instead, and something better.

3. Gratitude to God for His Gifts

Since God is always giving us gifts, what does He expect in return? Yes, He expects us to say "Thank You" for His love and care. We can thank God for His gifts in many different ways: taking care of things He gives us, sharing things with others, and being satisfied with what we get.

C. Organization

1. What gifts do we need for our bodies?
2. What gift does God give for our soul?
3. How should we pray for these needs?
4. How can we thank God for these gifts?
5. What does "Give us this day our daily bread" mean?

D. Virtues and Practices

1. Thank God for His love and care.
2. Learn how to make a spiritual communion.

IV. SUGGESTED LEARNING ACTIVITIES

A. Discuss the things we need daily for our bodies.
B. Discuss briefly Holy Communion as Food for our souls.
C. Discuss Picture 5 of the "Our Father" series (Gouppy or Miki).
D. Make up original prayers of petition for our spiritual and bodily needs.
E. Poem: "Give Us This Day Our Daily Bread," School Sisters of Notre Dame, *The Our Father for Little Ones.*

V. TEACHER REFERENCES

A. Fitzpatrick, *Religion in Life Curriculum, First Grade Manual,* p. 119.
B. Dennerle, *Leading the Little Ones to Christ,* pp. 292–293.

LESSON 41

I. SUBJECT MATTER

Petition Five: "Forgive Us Our Trespasses, As We Forgive Those Who Trespass Against Us"

II. OBJECTIVES

A. To develop a knowledge of how God takes away our sins if we are kind and forgiving toward others.
B. To help the children grow in confidence in the love and mercy of God.

III. SUGGESTED PROCEDURE

A. Approach

Whenever we displease God, what do we want God to do? We want God to forgive us, don't we?

B. Presentation

1. Meaning of the Term "Trespasses"

Sometimes we do things that displease God. When we disobey, tell lies, miss Mass on Sunday, we commit sin and sin displeases God. "Trespasses" is another word for sin. You know that God rewards the good and punishes the bad things we do. How can you keep God from punishing you for the bad things you have done? A good child asks his father to forgive him if he has done wrong. That is the way we must ask God to forgive us our sins. "Forgive us our trespasses," means: "Forgive us our sins, dear God, forgive the bad things we have done against you."

2. Condition of Forgiveness — That We Forgive Others

Suppose a child begs his father to forgive him and then does not forgive his brother or sister when he or she does something against him. Will his father forgive such a child? Don't you think that the father will say, "You will not forgive your brother or sister, so I will not forgive you either." In the same way when we ask God to forgive us, He will not forgive unless we forgive all those who have hurt us.

3. How Should We Act When Someone Hurts Us?

When someone hurts us we should forgive right away. We should try to forgive others quickly; we should never pout or stay angry. When we have hurt someone we should apologize right away. God will not take our sins away if we do not forgive others. When I say, "Forgive us our trespasses . . ." I am asking God to forgive me and all people, and I am telling Him I will also forgive those who have hurt me.

C. Organization

1. What do we mean by "trespasses"?
2. What do we want God to do to us after we commit sin?
3. What must we do if we want God to take our sins away?
4. Will God take our sins away if we do not forgive others?

5. What does "Forgive us our trespasses, as we forgive those who trespass against us" mean?

D. Virtues and Practices

1. Be thankful to God for His priests, who have the power to take away sins.
2. Forgive others quickly and sweetly, never pout or stay angry.
3. Apologize right away when you hurt someone.

IV. SUGGESTED LEARNING ACTIVITIES

A. Tell the Gospel story of the unmerciful servant.
B. Discuss Picture 6 of the "Our Father" series (Gouppy or Miki).
C. Discuss how Catholic children should act toward one another at play.
D. Poem: "And Forgive Us Our Trespasses, As We Forgive Those Who Trespass Against Us," School Sisters of Notre Dame, *The Our Father for Little Ones*.

V. TEACHER REFERENCES

A. Fitzpatrick, *Religion in Life Curriculum, First Grade Manual*, p. 119.
B. Dennerle, *Leading the Little Ones to Christ*, pp. 293–294.

LESSON 42

I. SUBJECT MATTER

Petition Six: "And Lead Us Not Into Temptation"

II. OBJECTIVES

A. To guide the children to say the Lord's Prayer meaningfully.
B. To foster the attitude of trust in God and dependence upon His help for our needs.

III. SUGGESTED PROCEDURE

A. Approach

Children recite the Our Father as far as ". . . against us . . ."

(Give leads for the various parts of the prayer developed. Children respond with related part of the prayer.)

B. Presentation

1. Meaning of the Word: "Temptation"

When we say "Lead us not into temptation" we are asking God to help us keep away from persons, places, and things that will make us disobey Him. When I feel like doing something wrong then I have a temptation. This feeling or temptation is not a sin but it tries to make me commit sin. When I give in to temptation then I commit sin.

2. God's Grace Strengthens Us to Do What Is Right

God wants us to ask Him for help. He is ever ready to help us. Each day when we say this part of the Our Father, let us think, "Dear God, give me Your help to keep away from sin today." This help is grace. We need God's grace to fight the devil.

3. Avoiding Temptation

The devil is always busy trying to make someone commit sin. He bothers us most when we are not busy. Bad friends can make us commit sin by teaching to do the wrong things. There are places we should stay away from, because we may commit sin if we go to these places. This may happen when we go to see a bad movie. There are other things that make us commit sin such as bad TV programs, books, and magazines.

4. Prayer in Time of Temptation

When we are tempted to do something that is not right we should pray. God will help us if we ask Him for help. If we do not pray and give in to temptation then we commit sin. Pray to Mother Mary, too. She was pure, free from all sin. She is willing to help you keep away from sin too.

C. Organization

1. What is a temptation?
2. What does a temptation try to make us do?
3. Who can help us in time of temptation?
4. What will happen if we give in to temptations?
5. What should we do when we are tempted to do something that is not right?
6. What does "Lead us not into temptation" mean?

D. Virtues and Practices

1. Ask God to help you when you feel like doing something wrong.
2. Help others do good by giving good example.
3. Keep away from companions, TV programs, movies, magazines. etc., that are bad.

IV. SUGGESTED LEARNING ACTIVITIES

A. Discuss Picture 7 of the "Our Father" series (Gouppy or Miki).
B. Poem: "And Lead Us Not Into Temptation," School Sisters of Notre Dame, *The Our Father for Little Ones.*

V. TEACHER REFERENCES

A. Dennerle, *Leading the Little Ones to Christ,* p. 294.
B. Fitzpatrick, *Religion in Life Curriculum, First Grade Manual,* p. 119.

LESSON 43

I. SUBJECT MATTER

Petition Seven: "But Deliver Us From Evil"

II. OBJECTIVES

A. To guide the children to say the Lord's Prayer meaningfully.
B. To develop the habit of praying to God for help and protection.

III. SUGGESTED PROCEDURE

A. Approach

Today we will talk about the last part of the Our Father: "But deliver us from evil."

B. Presentation

1. Discuss the Meaning of the Word: "Evil"

The things which we call evil are sickness, death, hunger, war, and sufferings. But the greatest evil of all is sin; it keeps us from God.

2. Deliver Us From Evil

When we say the last part of the Our Father we are asking God to protect us from all these evils. God will keep these away from us if we ask Him and if it is really best for us to be kept away from them. Sometimes God permits some evil to happen to us. God has a very good reason for doing this. We should not complain or pout when suffering comes along but ask God to make us brave and strong enough to carry our little cross.

3. Prayerful Recitation of the Lord's Prayer

Recite the Our Father using leads appropriate for each phrase of the prayer.

Leads	*Prayer*
I call on my heavenly Father.	Our Father, who art in heaven
I tell God we want His name praised.	Hallowed be Thy name
I tell God we want Him to be the King of the whole world.	Thy kingdom come
I tell God I want to do what He wants me to do the way the angels do in heaven.	Thy will be done on earth as it is in heaven
I ask God to grant me what I need for body and soul.	Give us this day our daily bread
I ask God to forgive me for offending Him the way I forgive those who hurt me.	And forgive us our trespasses, as we forgive those who trespass against us
I ask God to help me to keep away from temptation.	And lead us not into temptation
I ask God to keep me away from all harm and misfortune.	But deliver us from evil
I tell God that I mean everything I said.	Amen.

C. Organization

1. What do we mean when we say "deliver us from evil"?

2. What evils can happen to us?
3. What is the greatest evil?

D. Virtues and Practices

1. Ask God to protect you from danger.
2. Pray to your guardian angel to help you.
3. Recite the Lord's Prayer devoutly.

IV. SUGGESTED LEARNING ACTIVITIES

A. Discuss Picture 8 of the "Our Father" series (Gouppy or Miki).
B. Individual recitation of the Lord's Prayer.
C. Poem: "But Deliver Us From Evil," School Sisters of Notre Dame, *The Our Father for Little Ones.*

V. TEACHER REFERENCES

A. Fitzpatrick, *Religion in Life Curriculum, First Grade Manual,* pp. 119–120.
B. Dennerle, *Leading the Little Ones to Christ,* p. 294.

LESSON 44

I. SUBJECT MATTER

Feast of All Saints — November 1

II. OBJECTIVES

A. To develop the knowledge of the purpose of this feast.
B. To awaken in the child the desire to share the happiness of the saints in heaven.

III. SUGGESTED PROCEDURE

A. Approach

In heaven all the people know that Jesus is God. Can you tell who these people are? (Show picture of saints in heaven.)

B. Presentation

1. Who the Saints Are

The saints were at one time boys and girls like you. Now they have reached their home, just as you hope to do. They are in heaven with God and His angels. They are God's close and special friends. When the saints lived upon earth they loved God more than they loved themselves. They loved no one more than God. They showed their love for God by doing everything for Him. They were willing to suffer for Him, even to die, as long as it pleased Him. Now they are always happy, seeing God face to face and enjoying the heavenly home.

2. Our Patron Saints

Among the saints in heaven are your patron saints. These are the saints in whose honor you were named. When you were baptized, those patron saints took you under their care and now they watch over you. pray for you to God, and do all possible to help you join them in heaven. Pray to your patron saint to help you become a saint, too.

Who is your patron saint? (Have several children name their patron saint.)

3. All Saints' Day

There are many saints in heaven. There are more than just those whose names we see on the calendar. Heaven is full of God's friends. The feast of All Saints, a holyday of obligation, is the day on which the Church honors all those men, women, and children who are sharing God's heavenly home. It is a day we should use to make up our minds to lead good lives and assure ourselves of becoming saints also. What joy is in heaven on All Saints' Day, when the Church honors them by special prayers. (Explain term "holyday of obligation," and how holydays must be observed.)

C. Organization
1. Who are the saints?
2. Why are the saints in heaven with God?
3. Who is your patron saint?
4. Does every saint in heaven have a special day on which we honor him?
5. Whom do we honor on All Saints' Day?
6. What must every Catholic do on that day? Why?

D. Virtues and Practices
1. Make little sacrifices for the love of God.

2. Show kindness to others.

3. Be obedient at all times.

IV. SUGGESTED LEARNING ACTIVITIES

A. Find out what patron saint each child has and tell some interesting events about those saints.

B. Begin a pictorial booklet of the saints.

C. Story: "Your Patron Saint," Sister Marguerite, *Their Hearts Are His Garden*, pp. 17–19.

D. Poem: "The Feast of All Saints," Belger, *Sing a Song of Holy Things*, p. 16.

V. TEACHER REFERENCES

A. Sister Marguerite, *Their Hearts Are His Garden*, pp. 95–97.

B. Aurelia-Kirsch, *Practical Aids for Catholic Teachers*, p. 205.

C. C. Weiser, *Religious Customs in the Family*, pp. 86–87.

LESSON 45

I. SUBJECT MATTER

Feast of All Souls — November 2

II. OBJECTIVES

A. To develop the knowledge of the purpose of this feast.

B. To develop a love for the holy souls and a desire to help them.

III. SUGGESTED PROCEDURE

A. Approach

On All Saints' Day we honor all the saints who live with God and the angels in heaven. On All Souls' Day we must remember the suffering souls who died for God.

B. Presentation

1. Certainty of Death

All people must die because of original sin. We are made up of body and soul. Because we have a body, we suffer, get sick, and some day will die. Our soul, however, will never die. It is immortal. If we love God perfectly upon earth and serve Him faithfully, we will go to heaven for an eternal reward. If we love God but do not make up for our sins, we must go to purgatory to suffer for a time.

2. Purpose of Purgatory

Many good people die before they had a chance to make up for all the little sins they committed. They cannot go to heaven until they are cleansed of all stain of sin. God loves these people and wants them with Himself. Therefore, in His mercy, He created a place called purgatory. The poor souls must remain there and suffer until they atone for all their sins. (Explain atone.) The poor souls in purgatory know that some day, when they will have been cleansed from the stain of sin, they will go to heaven forever.

3. We Can Help the Poor Souls

The poor souls in purgatory cannot help themselves any more. They look down to us, begging for help. We can do a great deal to help them. Our prayers, our little sacrifices, our Masses are some helps we can give. Each prayer, each sacrifice, each Mass offered for a person who has died and gone to purgatory will help bring him closer to heaven and sometimes help him enter into heaven. If any person enters heaven through our kind help we may be sure that he will never forget us. He will pray for us to God and some day come to our help if we must suffer in purgatory.

The Catholic Church remembers the poor souls in purgatory in a special way on All Souls' Day. During the whole month of November we remember to help the poor souls more than in any other month. They want to go to heaven as soon as possible, and they need our prayers and sacrifices to shorten their stay in purgatory. (Discuss what sacrifices could be made to help the poor souls.)

4. What We Can Do for Ourselves

We can help ourselves shorten our own stay in purgatory. In God's justice we must do penance to make up for our sins. Now is the time to do it while we are on earth. Our daily prayers well said, going to Mass often, obeying God's laws, making sacrifices for love of God, suffering willingly whatever suffering God sends, are some of the ways which will help us avoid purgatory or help us leave there quickly if we should have to go there. (Can you name other helpful ways?)

C. Organization

1. Why must we die?
2. What happens when we die?
3. Can the holy souls help themselves?
4. Can we help the holy souls get to heaven? How?
5. What can the poor souls do for us?

D. Virtues and Practices

1. Pray for the holy souls in purgatory.
2. Make sacrifices for the poor souls.

IV. SUGGESTED LEARNING ACTIVITIES

Stories: "Helping the Holy Souls," Sister Marguerite, *Their Hearts Are His Garden*, pp. 99–100; "A Party at School," *ibid.*, p. 97; "All Souls' Day," *ibid.*, pp. 97–99.

V. TEACHER REFERENCES

A. Aurelia-Kirsch, *Practical Aids for Catholic Teachers*, pp. 205–206.
B. S.N.D., *Religious Teaching of Young Children*, pp. 143–144.
C. C. Weiser, *Religious Customs in the Family*, pp. 87–88.

LESSON 46

I. SUBJECT MATTER

Feast of the Presentation of Mary — November 21

II. OBJECTIVES

A. To become familiar with the childhood of Mary and her consecration to God.
B. To foster a desire to imitate Mary in her generosity to God.

III. SUGGESTED PROCEDURE

A. Approach

Mary is the loveliest creature that God made. (Show picture.)

Today we shall hear a story of something that happened to Mary when she was a little girl.

B. Presentation

1. Mary's Great Love for God

You have heard about Mary. Anne was her mother and Joachim was her father. Mary was good. Because Mary obeyed God she had kept God's goodness. She loved God very much. God loved Mary more than anyone else He ever made. When Mary grew up God let her know that He had chosen her to be the mother of Jesus.

2. Mary Goes to the Temple to Give Herself to God

When Mary was a little child, Anne and Joachim took her to the temple of Jerusalem. There she went to learn all a Jewish girl needed to know. She learned how to cook, how to sew, how to spin the sheep's wool into yarn, and how to weave the woolen cloth. She learned how to help in the house. Mary learned to love God more and more each day of her life. Mary was a very special little girl. We should try to be like Mary who showed her love for God by always doing what God wanted her to do.

C. Organization

1. What did Mary do when she was three years old?
2. How did Mary show her great love for God?
3. How do you think Mary acted in the temple?

D. Virtues and Practices

1. Imitate the virtues of the child Mary.
2. Ask Mary to keep you like her.

IV. SUGGESTED LEARNING ACTIVITIES

A. Dramatize the story, "Mary Goes to the Temple."
B. Draw a picture about this story.

V. TEACHER REFERENCES

A. Sister Marguerite, *Their Hearts Are His Garden*, p. 103.
B. Dorcy, *Mary, My Mother*, pp. 13–17.

UNIT FOUR

God's Goodness in Sending His Son to Us

Time: 2 weeks

I. INTRODUCTION FOR THE TEACHER

Unit Four, the Christmas unit, prepares the child for the coming of the Christ Child by acquainting him with circumstances leading up to and centering around the birth of Christ. He hears the beautiful stories of Mary's Immaculate Conception, the angel's message to Mary, her acceptance of God's will, her visit to Elizabeth, and, finally, the nativity of the Baby Jesus. Christmas will now have a greater meaning for the first grader, because he has been made to realize God's goodness in sending His divine Son to open heaven for us.

II. OBJECTIVES OF THE UNIT

A. To acquaint the children with the events prior to and centering around the coming of the Christ Child.

B. To develop an understanding and an appreciation of the real meaning of Christmas.

C. To develop the knowledge that Jesus is God, the Promised Redeemer.

D. To foster the practice of pleasing the Christ Child by prayers and sacrifices in preparation for His coming.

E. To help the child live with Christ in His Church by means of the celebration of the liturgical seasons.

F. Teach the article of the Apostles' Creed: "And in Jesus Christ, His only Son, our Lord, who was conceived by the Holy Spirit, born of the Virgin Mary."

III. SUBJECT MATTER

A. Preparation for the coming of the Christ Child
   1. Man's preparation for the Redeemer
   2. Our preparation for the Christ Child
B. Mary is chosen to be the Mother of Jesus
   1. Mary is free from all sin
   2. Immaculate Conception, December 8

C. The Annunciation
D. The Visitation
E. Prayer: "Hail Mary"
F. The Nativity of our Lord
G. The meaning of Christmas
H. Liturgical feast
   St. Nicholas — December 6

LESSON 47

I. SUBJECT MATTER

Preparation for the Coming of the Christ Child

II. OBJECTIVES

A. To acquaint the children with the events of the coming of the Christ Child.
B. To foster practices of pleasing the Christ Child by prayers and sacrifices in preparation for His coming.
C. Teach phrase of the Creed: "And in Jesus Christ, His only Son, our Lord."

III. SUGGESTED PROCEDURE

A. Approach

How many of you remember the story of Adam and Eve? Adam and Eve disobeyed God's law and had to leave the Garden of Paradise. They lost many wonderful gifts, especially sanctifying grace. Without this gift neither Adam and Eve nor any of their children nor any people could enter heaven. But God in His mercy promised to send a Redeemer, that is, a Saviour.

B. Presentation

1. Waiting for the Redeemer — Advent

Adam and Eve did not live to see the Redeemer, nor did their children see Him. Many people lived and died upon earth, and still the Saviour did not come. We call this long time of waiting, Advent. Advent means coming of Someone, namely the Saviour.

2. People Prepared for the Saviour

During the long time of waiting for the Saviour some of Adam's children did some very special things.

a) They prayed each day so that God would send them the Saviour.

b) They made many sacrifices so that God would send them the Saviour.

c) They tried to be very good and do as God wanted them to do so that God would send the Saviour.

3. Church Prepares for Christ's Coming

We are waiting for Someone also. Do you know Who? Do you know the day which commemorates His coming? It is Christmas, the birthday of Jesus, our Saviour. We call the time of waiting and getting ready for Jesus, Advent. During the four weeks of Advent we get ready for Jesus just as the people did long ago:

a) By saying our prayers more carefully,

b) By making sacrifices for Jesus,

c) By trying hard to be good boys and good girls.

By doing these things for Jesus we will be getting ready for Jesus on Christmas Day. The prayers, sacrifices, and good works will be presents for Jesus on His birthday.

4. We Get Ready for Coming of Jesus

We will prepare our hearts for the coming of the Saviour on Christmas Day. During the four weeks of Advent we will do something special for Him. These special gifts will make Jesus feel welcome in our hearts.

We pray every day, but during Advent we can pray more often and more carefully. We can do all our work at home and in school we can work especially hard for love of Jesus. We can be more helpful at home and in school without being told.

Can you tell other special things we can do? Discuss the possible practices that could be done during Advent. Lead the children to the choice of one special practice during the entire season. Suggest and discuss the possibility of making a spiritual crib in their hearts.

C. Organization

1. What does the word "Advent" mean?
2. Why did God close the gates of heaven?
3. What did God promise to do some day?

4. How did the people get ready for Jesus' coming?
5. How can we get ready for Jesus' birthday?

D. Virtues and Practices

1. Trust God to keep His promises.
2. Don't give up when you pray for something.
3. Make little sacrifices to be ready for Christ's coming.
4. Be more happy to give gifts than to receive them.

IV. SUGGESTED LEARNING ACTIVITIES

A. Discuss how to prepare a crib in our hearts, e.g., post a layette for the Infant Jesus on the bulletin board and mark it *sold* after the *price* has been paid.
B. Make a calendar to show how many days until Jesus comes to us.
C. Teach the phrase of the Apostles' Creed, "And in Jesus Christ, His only Son our Lord."
D. Poem: "Why I Am Happy at Christmas," Belger, *Sing a Song of Holy Things,* p. 27.

V. TEACHER REFERENCES

A. Fitzpatrick, *Religion in Life Curriculum, First Grade Manual,* p. 55.
B. Schumacher, *I Teach Catechism,* Vol. I, pp. 44–47.
C. Sister Mary, *et al., The Catholic Mother's Helper,* pp. 73–74, 80–81.
D. Sister Marguerite, *Their Hearts Are His Garden,* pp. 77–78.
E. Weiser, *Religious Customs in the Family,* pp. 36–40.

LESSON 48

I. SUBJECT MATTER

Mary Is Chosen to Be God's Mother

II. OBJECTIVES

A. To acquaint the children with the feast of the Immaculate Conception.
B. To foster a love for purity.

III. SUGGESTED PROCEDURE

A. Approach

Advent is the time of waiting for Christmas, Jesus' birthday. Jesus will come to us from heaven as a little Baby. He needs someone to take care of Him. Whom did Jesus need? (Show picture of Mother Mary.)

B. Presentation

1. God's Plan for Mary

Jesus certainly needed a Mother to care for Him. Since God knows all things, He knew that Mary was going to be His Mother long before Mary was born. God had a special gift for Mary since she was to be His Mother. God's special gift for Mary was freedom from all sin. This is a special gift since all men are born with original sin. From the time Mary began to live she was free of original sin. She was the only person to have this special privilege from God. We call this special gift Mary's Immaculate Conception. Sinless at birth, Mary never committed a sin during her whole life, not even the smallest one. This means the devil never had any power over Mary.

2. Mary's Great Love for Purity

When Mary was a little girl, she was very, very good. Her mother and father loved her much because she always obeyed them and was good to them. All the little boys and girls who played with Mary loved her because she was kind. Everyone who met and worked with Mary noticed how very good Mary was. This was because Mary was free from all sin and was so brave. All through her life she tried to please God and never do anything to displease Him. Mary wants us to do the same thing, never to displease God by sin.

3. Feast of Immaculate Conception — December 8

The Church has a special day on which we celebrate the special gift of Mary's Immaculate Conception. This day comes in Advent, on December 8. On this feast the Church tells us that we must all go to Holy Mass to praise God for the special gifts He gave to His Mother Mary. It is the day that we should ask Mary to keep us free from sin, to help us when the devil tempts us to do evil things, to help us please her Son even if it is hard for us to be good. We need God's help, and Mary will ask her Son to help us be good boys and girls.

C. Organization

1. In what particular way was Mary different from all other creatures?
2. Why was Mary born free from original sin?
3. What virtue did she practice in a special way?
4. When do we celebrate the feast of the Immaculate Conception?
5. What could we ask of Mary?
6. What can we do to keep our souls pure?

D. Virtues and Practices

1. Watch over our thoughts, words, and actions.
2. Pray to Mary for the virtue of purity.
3. Assist at Mass in honor of Mary.

IV. SUGGESTED LEARNING ACTIVITIES

A. Discuss reason for Mary's preservation from original sin.
B. Story: "The Immaculate Conception," Dorcy, *Mary My Mother*, pp. 1–6.
C. Poem: "My Mother Mary," Belger, *Sing a Song of Holy Things*, p. 25.

V. TEACHER REFERENCES

A. Sister Marguerite, *Their Hearts Are His Garden*, pp. 7–8.
B. Schumacher, *I Teach Catechism*, Vol. I, pp. 41–42.

LESSON 49

I. SUBJECT MATTER

The Annunciation

II. OBJECTIVES

A. To acquaint the children with the Story of the Annunciation.
B. To foster the virtue of humility.
C. To teach the article of the Apostles' Creed: "Who was conceived by the Holy Spirit."

III. SUGGESTED PROCEDURE

A. Approach

When we want to let someone know about a plan we are making for them we either tell them, call them on a telephone, or perhaps send a friend. We call the person who tells our message a messenger. God wanted to tell Mary a special message. He chose Angel Gabriel as one of His special messengers.

B. Presentation

1. Angel Gabriel, a Messenger Angel

Angel Gabriel was privileged by God. He was sent down from heaven to Mary to announce that God wanted her to be the Mother of the Saviour. While Mary was at prayer, a bright light filled the room. Mary saw a beautiful angel from heaven within the midst of the light. Mary was very surprised to see the angel and a little afraid. She wondered what the angel had to tell her.

2. Angel Gabriel's Message

The angel said, "Hail, full of grace, the Lord is with thee." This meant that Mary was very holy and pleasing to God. The angel was telling her that she never had original sin or any other sin. He also told her that God was very pleased with her. Mary appeared afraid. The angel then said, "Do not be afraid Mary. I am Angel Gabriel. I came from God with a message. God wants you to become the Mother of the Saviour."

Mary wondered how this could happen. But the angel told her that the Saviour would be born through the power of the Holy Spirit. Mary answered in a humble way, "I am the handmaid of the Lord, I will do whatever He wants me to do." Then the angel told Mary some good news about her cousin, Elizabeth, that she would be blessed with a baby soon. Then Angel Gabriel went back to heaven to God and all the other angels.

3. Mary's Willingness to Please God

God made Mary especially to be His Mother. However, He still asked Mary whether she would be the Mother of the Saviour. Mary did not have to say yes, but she loved God so much that she was always willing to do His will. Mary was very humble when she called herself "a handmaid of the Lord." She didn't consider herself great, neither did she tell others about her fortune. Her humility, her purity, and her great desire to do God's will made her very pleasing to God.

C. Organization

1. Whom did God send to earth with a message?
2. How did the Angel Gabriel greet Mary?
3. What did his words "full of grace" mean?
4. What message did the angel tell Mary?
5. What was Mary's answer?
6. How do you think the angels in heaven felt when Mary gave her answer?

D. Virtues and Practices

1. Honor Mary because she is the Mother of God.
2. Imitate the humility of Mary.
3. Be ready to accept and do the will of God.

IV. SUGGESTED LEARNING ACTIVITIES

A. Dramatize the story of the Annunciation.
B. Discuss Picture 1 of the "Hail Mary" series ("The Hail Mary" — Gouppy; "The Hail Mary" — Miki). See Bibliography.
C. Teach the phrase of the Apostles' Creed: "Who was conceived by the Holy Spirit."
D. Poem: "Hail Full of Grace," Belger, *Sing a Song of Holy Things*, p. 55.

V. TEACHER REFERENCES

A. Dennerle, *Leading the Little Ones to Christ*, pp. 73–76.
B. Sister Mary, *et al.*, *Catholic Mother's Helper*, pp. 61–63.
C. Fitzpatrick, *Religion in Life Curriculum, First Grade Manual*, pp. 46–50.
D. S.N.D., *Religious Teaching of Young Children*, pp. 19–21.
E. Sister Marguerite, *Their Hearts Are His Garden*, pp. 111–113.
F. Holy Bible, Lk. 1:26–38.

LESSON 50

I. SUBJECT MATTER

The Visitation

II. OBJECTIVES

A. To acquaint the children with the feast of the Visitation.
B. To instill a deeper love and reverence for Mary, and the desire of imitating her virtues of kindness and charity.

III. SUGGESTED PROCEDURE

A. Approach

The Angel Gabriel, you will recall, told Mary a secret about her cousin Elizabeth. Do you know what that secret was? Yes, Elizabeth was going to become a mother of a baby.

B. Presentation

1. Mary's Visit to Elizabeth

Mary was very happy when she heard the secret about her cousin Elizabeth. Mary knew that Elizabeth was not young and that she would have many things to do before God sent the baby to her. Since Mary was always kind she decided to go to Elizabeth's house and help her.

We do not know how Mary went to Elizabeth's house — but we think she went along with some other people traveling along the same road. Her cousin Elizabeth lived quite a distance away from Nazareth. It probably took Mary three or four days before she reached Elizabeth. Mary did not mind the long tiresome journey. She was happy to do something good and kind for someone.

2. Elizabeth's Greeting to Mary

Mary finally reached Elizabeth's house. Elizabeth noticed Mary coming up the walk, and she went out to meet her. How happy Elizabeth was because Mary was coming to her! God let Elizabeth know about Mary's little secret. Elizabeth cried out with joy: "How good God is to me that He sends His Mother to see me." Then Elizabeth said something very wonderful about Mary: "Blessed art thou among women and blessed is the fruit of thy womb," she said. She meant that Mary was the holiest and blessed of all women who ever lived and will live upon earth. She also knew that Mary's Son, Jesus, is blessed, too.

Mary was very glad that Elizabeth knew her secret about the Saviour. She was so happy that she began to sing a beautiful song. In this song Mary praised God for all the kindness and goodness He showed. Mary praised God because she owed all her greatness to Him. Mary sang: "My soul doth magnify the Lord and my spirit has rejoiced in God my Saviour." (Explain briefly.)

3. Mary Helps Elizabeth

Everyone in Elizabeth's house was made happy by Mary. Mary was full of grace. God made her good and beautiful. Everyone noticed how kind and helpful Mary was.

Mary stayed at Elizabeth's house for a long time. All this while Mary and Elizabeth worked together and praised God together.

C. Organization

1. Who was Elizabeth?
2. Who told Mary a message about Elizabeth?
3. Why did Mary go to visit her cousin?
4. What did Elizabeth say when she saw Mary?
5. What did Mary answer her cousin?

D. Virtues and Practices

1. Show kindness toward the sick and the aged.
2. Think and say only kind things about others.
3. Make someone happy today by doing something kind for him.

IV. SUGGESTED LEARNING ACTIVITIES

A. Dramatize the story of the Visitation.
B. Discuss the picture of the Visitation (Gouppy or Miki).
C. Compose original prayers to Mary.
D. Discuss the charity and kindness of Mary toward others.

V. TEACHER REFERENCES

A. Fitzpatrick, *Religion in Life Curriculum, First Grade Manual,* pp. 50–52.
B. S.N.D., *Religious Teaching of Young Children,* pp. 22–23.
C. Holy Bible, Lk. 1:39–47.

LESSON 51

I. SUBJECT MATTER

Prayer: "Hail Mary" (This lesson will take more than one day.)

II. OBJECTIVES

A. To guide the children to say the Hail Mary intelligently.
B. To instill in the children great devotion and love for Mary.

III. SUGGESTED PROCEDURE

A. Approach

Today we are going to talk about a special prayer that we know very well. As we say this prayer together, let us listen to the words and try to remember if we heard them before. (Recite the Hail Mary.)

B. Presentation

1. Part One — We Praise and Honor Mary

When we said this prayer the first words were "Hail Mary." That is the way Angel Gabriel greeted Mary. Angel Gabriel also told Mary that she was pure and free from all sin. We, too, say this to Mary when we say "full of grace." We then say "the Lord is with thee." This means that God loves Mary and lives in her.

When Elizabeth met Mary she said something beautiful about her, too. "Blessed art thou among women and blessed is the fruit of thy womb, Jesus." Elizabeth's words mean that Mary is the holiest of all women and that Jesus is holy, too.

Angel Gabriel's words and Elizabeth's words were so beautiful that the Church wants us to tell them to Mary every time we pray.

2. Part Two — We Ask Mary to Bless Us

In the second part of the Hail Mary we ask Mary for some special favors. We tell her again that she is holy and that she is the Mother of God when we say, "Holy Mary, Mother of God." Since Mary never was under the power of the devil we ask her to pray for us sinners. We say: "Pray for us sinners." We call ourselves sinners because sometimes we do things that do not please God.

We want Mary to pray for us while we are still living so that we will be good. But we ask her to pray for us in a special way when we are dying. We say "now and at the hour of our death." We want the Blessed Mother to pray for us at that time so that we will be sorry for all our sins and say no to the devil when he tempts us to be bad.

Mary will ask her Son to forgive us for our many sins because she loves us very much and wants us to come to heaven with her and Jesus. The last word that we say is "Amen." This means "I mean every word I said in this prayer. I'm glad I said it."

3. Meaningful Recitation of Hail Mary Prayer

Teacher gives meaningful leads for each phase of the prayer; children respond with the proper phrase of the prayer.

Lead	*Response*
I greet Mary the way Angel Gabriel did.	Hail Mary
I tell Mary she is pleasing to God and free from sin.	Full of grace
I tell Mary that God is within her all the time.	The Lord is with thee
I tell Mary that she is the holiest among all the women.	Blessed art thou among women
I tell her that her Son, Jesus, is holy and blessed, too.	And blessed is the fruit of thy womb, Jesus
I tell Mary that she is God's Mother.	Holy Mary, Mother of God
I tell Mary what I want from her.	Pray for us sinners
I tell Mary when I want her prayers.	Now and at the hour of our death.
I tell Mary I mean what I have said.	Amen.

C. Organization

1. Who is the Blessed Virgin Mary?
2. How did the Angel Gabriel greet Mary?
3. What do the words "full of grace" mean?

4. What words of the "Hail Mary" do we say when we ask Mary to help us?
5. When do we want Mary to help us?
6. Why should we say the Hail Mary often?

D. Virtues and Practices

1. Recite the Hail Mary with devotion at all times.
2. Remember to say a Hail Mary in time of temptation.
3. Like Mary try to pray well.

IV. SUGGESTED LEARNING ACTIVITIES

A. Discuss pictures of the "Hail Mary" series as each phrase of the Hail Mary is presented ("The Hail Mary" — Gouppy; "The Hail Mary" — Miki). See Bibliography.
B. Individual recitation of the Hail Mary.

V. TEACHER REFERENCES

A. S.N.D., *Religious Teaching of Young Children*, pp. 121–122.
B. Dennerle, *Leading the Little Ones to Christ*, pp. 77–78, 295–296.

LESSON 52

I. SUBJECT MATTER

The Nativity of Our Lord

II. OBJECTIVES

A. To develop a knowledge of the circumstances of the birth of Jesus
B. To develop an appreciation of God's goodness in sending us Saviour.
C. To teach the article of the Apostles' Creed: "born of the Virgin Mary."

III. SUGGESTED PROCEDURE

A. Approach

Joseph and Mary began to get things ready for Jesus to come. Jesus would be God and Man at the same time. How happy Mary and Joseph felt because they would have the privilege to take care of Him.

B. Presentation

1. Mary and Joseph Go to Bethlehem

One day while Joseph was working a Roman soldier came with a message. He told all the people that they must go and sign their names into a book called a register. The Roman emperor wanted the exact number of people living in the Roman empire.

Joseph and Mary were always obedient, they tried to obey all the laws. Even now they prepared for their trip to Bethlehem, the home of Joseph and Mary's ancestors, to do as the emperor ordered. All St. Joseph and Mary had in order to make the trip was a donkey. (Why? Discuss briefly.) Mary rode on the donkey while Joseph walked alongside her. They traveled a long time on their tiresome journey, but at last they reached Bethlehem, cold, tired, and hungry.

Joseph felt sorry for Mary. He wanted by all means to find an inn (explain — motel) where at least Mary could rest. But it was too late. Many other people came to Bethlehem. All the rooms were taken. Joseph and Mary had to go to a stable for the night.

2. The Birth of Jesus

When Joseph and Mary came to the stable, Joseph soon made a pile of hay for Mary, so that she could have a soft place to rest.

During the night Baby Jesus, the Saviour, was born. Mary loved her Son, Jesus. She adored Him because He was God. How happy Mary was when she held her dear Son, who was God and Man, close to her bosom. Mary wrapped her Baby in infants' clothes and placed Him in a crib. Angels from heaven sang, "Glory to God in the highest." Mary and Joseph knelt down and adored Jesus.

3. Shepherds Visit Jesus

On a hillside near Bethlehem there were many shepherds watching their sheep. Suddenly a bright light appeared with angels around. The shepherds were frightened at first. Jesus had sent His angels to them with an announcement. "Fear not," the angels said to the shepherds, "I bring you glad tidings of great joy. For unto you is born this day a Saviour, who is Christ, you shall find the Child wrapped in swaddling clothes and laid in a manger." The sound of the angels' voice was the sweetest sound the shepherds had ever heard. They listened to the angels singing, "Glory to God in the highest; and on earth peace to men of good will."

The shepherds were very happy and excited. They hurried to the stable and found what they were told, the Saviour with His Mother and Joseph. The shepherds knelt down to adore Jesus.

C. Organization

1. Why did Mary and Joseph have to go to Bethlehem?
2. How did they get there?
3. Why didn't they find a place in the Inn?
4. Why was Jesus born in a stable?
5. Who came from heaven with Jesus?
6. Why did God let the shepherds know first about the birth of Jesus?
7. What should we say to Jesus on His birthday?
8. What day is His birthday?

D. Virtues and Practices

1. Offer your gifts at the crib.
2. Tell others the story of the birth of Christ.
3. Thank Jesus for coming to the earth for us.
4. Bring a non-Catholic to visit the crib.

IV. SUGGESTED LEARNING ACTIVITIES

A. Discuss pictures that depict the story of the first Christmas.
B. Dramatize the story of the Nativity.
C. Listen to recordings of the Christmas story.
D. Compose original prayers to the Infant Jesus.
E. Teach the phrase of the Apostles' Creed: "Born of the Virgin Mary."
F. Stories: "Waiting for Jesus," Sister Mary, *et al.*, *The Catholic Mother's Helper*, pp. 71–72; "A Journey to Bethlehem," *ibid.*, pp. 75–77; "The Shepherds," *ibid.*, pp. 78–81.
G. Poem: "A Christmas Wish," Belger, *Sing a Song of Holy Things*, p. 32.

V. TEACHER REFERENCES

A. Dennerle, *Leading the Little Ones to Christ*, pp. 79–85.
B. Fitzpatrick, *Religion in Life Curriculum, First Grade Manual*, pp. 53–56.
C. S.N.D., *Religious Teaching of Young Children*, pp. 24–29.
D. Sister Mary, *et al.*, *The Catholic Mother's Helper*, pp. 71–72, 75–81.

E. Sister Marguerite, *Their Hearts Are His Garden*, pp. 113–119.

F. Holy Bible, Lk. 2:1–20.

LESSON 53

I. SUBJECT MATTER

The Meaning of Christmas

II. OBJECTIVES

A. To appreciate the real meaning of Christmas.

B. To learn to enjoy giving rather than receiving.

III. SUGGESTED PROCEDURE

A. Approach

Pretend you are at a birthday party. At birthday parties all those who come usually bring a present for the person whose birthday it is. Suppose all the children are having a fine time, playing games, eating ice cream and candy. But there is one strange thing that happens. No one pays any attention to the one whose birthday it is, no one gives him presents, they give them to each other. And it is his birthday. How would you feel if you were that child?

B. Presentation

1. Christmas — the Birthday of Jesus

This very thing happens to Jesus every Christmas. Whose birthday is it? It is Jesus' birthday. That means that Jesus should be the one who receives the presents. But we are the ones who receive them. God does not mind that we have these presents, God wants us to have them. God is so good to us that He wants to share His birthday happiness with others. On Christmas Day He gives us His only Son, Jesus.

2. Our Gifts to the Christ Child

Do you know that you can give Christmas presents to Jesus, too? All your little sacrifices, your prayers said better, your effort in trying to be good boys and girls, are your presents to Jesus. You did many kind things during Advent. On Christmas Day you can tell Jesus that these presents were made out of love for Him.

3. The Gift of Our Hearts

There is a special gift Jesus wants from us. It costs nothing at all. This gift is the gift of our hearts. We can give Jesus our hearts by doing everything He wants us to all the time. We can prepare a spiritual crib (explain) in our hearts for the Christ Child on Christmas morning. Little acts of charity, little extra prayers, saving pennies for the missions, study in school, gentleness to others, helpfulness at home and school will help build a beautiful crib. (Cite examples of each — discuss other acts that could be done in building a spiritual crib in our hearts.)

4. Why We Give Gifts

You all like to receive gifts on Christmas, and you like to give them, too. God gave us many gifts because He loves us. On Christmas day He gave us His only Son, Jesus. Isn't Jesus the best gift of all? That is why we share with one another at Christmas time. We want to return our love and want to do something good to Jesus.

Is there anything you can give Jesus in return for His gift of Himself to you?

What do you think He would like best?

C. Organization

1. Who was God's gift to us?
2. What gift did the shepherds give Baby Jesus?
3. Why do we give gifts on Christ's birthday?
4. What gift can we give?

D. Virtues and Practices

1. Be satisfied with whatever is received at Christmas.
2. Share your toys with others.
3. Make your parents happy by being grateful for the gifts they give you.

IV. SUGGESTED LEARNING ACTIVITIES

A. Plan a gift for parents.
B. Make up a Christmas Litany.
C. Culminating activity: dramatize the entire Christmas story and sing Christmas hymns.
D. Story: "The Gifts We Bring," Sister Mary, *et al.*, *The Catholic Mother's Helper*, pp. 79–81.

E. Poem: "Happy Birthday Baby Jesus," Belger, *Sing a Song of Holy Things*, p. 30.

V. TEACHER REFERENCE

Sister Mary, *et al.*, *The Catholic Mother's Helper*, pp. 76–77, 79–81.

LESSON 54

I. SUBJECT MATTER

Feast of St. Nicholas — December 6

II. OBJECTIVES

A. To become acquainted with the story of St. Nicholas.
B. To strive to imitate the virtues of St. Nicholas.

III. SUGGESTED PROCEDURE

A. Approach

Today is the feast of a saint we love very much. He always had a friendly smile and a big kind heart. Now he is enjoying heaven with God. Many people imitate him today. Can you guess who he is? (Show picture of St. Nicholas.)

B. Presentation

1. Love of the Poor

St. Nicholas from his earliest years loved the poor people. When he was a little boy, he was good and kind to the poor children. As he grew older he loved God more and more. He loved God so much that he became God's special helper, a priest. Later he became a bishop. This means that he took care of very many people and tried to help them love God and go to heaven.

One wonderful thing about St. Nicholas was that he never let anyone know what he was doing for the poor. Secretly he would fix presents for the poor and take them to their houses. St. Nicholas did most of his kind deeds at night; he wanted God to know but no one else. As time went on the people soon learned from whom these presents came, but they never saw him give these presents.

When the bishop died the people missed him very much, but they celebrated his feast and tried to do what he did. His name, St. Nicholas was shortened. People called him St. Nick and children knew him as Santa Claus.

2. Others Imitate St. Nicholas

Many people did what St. Nicholas did, made others happy in some way. They especially showed their kindness to the poor. They were more happy when they gave to others than when others gave to them.

We, too, can make people happy by giving something to them. We do this especially at Christmas time to remind us about St. Nicholas but, most of all, to remind us of the Christ Child who gives us more than any other person.

Kindness to others will always be remembered. It makes them feel very happy. Someday, someone will do the same to us.

C. Organization
1. Who is the Christmas saint?
2. Tell some of the kind things he did.
3. How can we imitate him?

D. Virtues and Practices
1. Quietly do kind acts for others for the love of Jesus.
2. Be good to God's poor, especially on Christmas.

IV. SUGGESTED LEARNING ACTIVITIES

A. Dramatize ways of imitating St. Nicholas.
B. Legend: "St. Nicholas," Sister Marguerite, *Their Hearts Are His Garden*, pp. 62–65.

V. TEACHER REFERENCE

Aurelia-Kirsch, *Practical Aids for Catholic Teachers*, pp. 207–208.

UNIT FIVE

The Childhood of Jesus
Time: 4 weeks

I. INTRODUCTION FOR THE TEACHER

Unit Five acquaints the child with important events in the Hidden Life of Jesus, beginning with the Adoration of the Magi. The Flight into Egypt, its hardships, and the subsequent adjustment of the Holy Family to life in a strange country are presented to the first grader in a manner both simple and understandable. The child learns to know each member of the Holy Family in a very specific way as he learns about their life at Nazareth. The love that follows this knowledge makes the child want to imitate the virtues of the Holy Family, but, more especially, those of the Child Jesus, as exemplified in His life at home, at play, and at prayer.

II. OBJECTIVES OF THE UNIT

A. To develop a knowledge of the principal events pertaining to the Childhood of Jesus.
B. To develop an understanding that the Boy Jesus was a living reality, and that He is a model for all.
C. To foster a growing ability to pray as the Child Jesus did.
D. To appreciate and practice the virtues of courage, humility, and obedience as exemplified in the lives of Jesus, Mary, and Joseph.

III. SUBJECT MATTER

A. Adoration of the Magi
B. The Flight into Egypt
C. The Holy Family at Nazareth
    1. Joseph, the Head of the Holy Family
    2. Mary, the Mother of the Holy Family
    3. Jesus, the Child at home, at play, and at prayer
D. Liturgical feast
    1. Holy Name of Jesus — Sunday between the octave of Christmas and Epiphany

LESSON 55

I. SUBJECT MATTER

Adoration of the Magi

II. OBJECTIVES

A. To learn about the visit of the Magi.
B. To appreciate the zeal of the Magi and to imitate their zeal by doing immediately whatever God wants us to do.

III. SUGGESTED PROCEDURE

A. Approach

Who were the first ones to know of Jesus' birth? How did they find out?

B. Presentation

1. An Explanation of the Magi

The shepherds were the first to be told of Jesus' birth, but they were not the only ones to receive a sign. There were three wise men in a distant Eastern land who knew that God was going to send a Redeemer to the human race. They also knew that a very special star would appear in the East when the Redeemer would be born. The three wise men, also called the Magi, searched the skies every night, hoping that they would see the star. Then, one night, they *did* see it! They knew the Redeemer had come, and they were anxious to start out on their journey to find Him.

2. The Journey of the Magi

a) Explain the difficulties of travel in those days, even though the Magi had camels.
b) Tell how the star disappeared when they arrived at Jerusalem and, consequently, they had to seek refuge in Herod's palace.
c) Describe colorfully the palace of Herod.
d) Contrast the wicked King Herod with the Magi.
e) Explain Herod's false statement about wanting to adore the newborn King and the Magi's promise to return to him with the necessary information.

118

f) Tell how the star reappeared and the Magi were able to continue their journey.

3. Adoration of the Magi

The star came to rest over the stable and the Magi were filled with joy at finding the Christ Child. They knelt down and adored Him reverently. Then they offered Him their beautiful gifts of gold, frankincense, and myrrh. That night, as they were sleeping, an angel appeared to them and warned them not to go back to Herod because he really wanted to harm the child. The Magi obeyed and returned to their own country by a different route.

C. Organization

1. What sign did the Magi see?
2. How did the Magi travel?
3. What happened when they reached Jerusalem?
4. When did the star reappear?
5. Where did the star lead them?
6. How did the Magi adore the Infant Jesus?

D. Virtues and Practices

1. Sometimes do hard things for the love of Jesus.
2. Be reverent when you are in church.
3. Make a visit to Jesus.

IV. SUGGESTED LEARNING ACTIVITIES

A. Dramatize the story of the Magi.
B. Illustrate the story of the Magi.
C. Retell the story of the Magi using pictures.
D. Visit the crib in church.
E. Bring non-Catholic friends to visit the crib.
F. Stories: "The Visit of the Wise Men," Sr. Mary, *et al., The Catholic Mother's Helper,* pp. 82–84; "The King's Return Home," *ibid.,* pp. 85–86.
   Poem: "The Wise Men," Belger, *Sing a Song of Holy Things,* pp. 38–39.

V. TEACHER REFERENCES

A. S.N.D., *Religious Teaching of Young Children,* pp. 32–34.
B. Fitzpatrick, *Religion in Life Curriculum, First Grade Manual,*

pp. 71–75.

C. Dennerle, *Leading the Little Ones to Christ*, pp. 97–103.
D. Sr. Mary, *et al.*, *The Catholic Mother's Helper*, pp. 82–84.
E. Sr. Marguerite, *Their Hearts Are His Garden*, pp. 119–121.

LESSON 56

I. SUBJECT MATTER

The Gifts of the Magi

II. OBJECTIVES

A. To know what gifts the Magi offered.
B. To appreciate the significance of the gifts of the Magi.

III. SUGGESTED PROCEDURE

A. Approach

Why did the wise men come to see Jesus? They traveled a long distance to visit and adore the new King. Do you remember the names of the special gifts the Magi offered to Jesus?

B. Presentation

1. The Gifts of the Magi

The gifts the Magi offered were gold, frankincense, and myrrh. These are very special gifts and each one meant something. The gold showed that the Magi knew Jesus was a King, in fact, the King of kings and the Lord of all men. The incense showed that they knew Jesus was God, for incense is used in divine services. (Explain.) The myrrh showed that they knew that Jesus, as man, would die for our sins, as myrrh was a substance used in preparing bodies for burial. (Explain.)

2. Our Gifts to Jesus

Don't you want to be like the Magi? Don't you want to give Jesus some gifts in return for all He has given you? You can, you know.

You can give Jesus the gold of your love. Doing things for the love of Jesus, loving Him at prayer time, offering Him your heart filled with love is gold offered to Jesus.

You can give Jesus incense of prayers. Prayers, said with love and devotion, praise God and ascend into heaven.

You can give Jesus the myrrh of your sacrifices. Give Jesus yourselves. Give Him all you are and have.

3. Comparisons

Compare and discuss briefly the symbolic phases.

The star stopped above the stable to show Jesus is here.	The sanctuary light tells us Jesus is here in the tabernacle.
Jesus was born in a stable. Good people came to visit Him.	Jesus stays with us in the tabernacle. We can all visit Him.
The Magi knelt and adored Jesus when they came to visit Him.	We kneel and adore Jesus when we visit Him in church.
The Magi traveled a long distance to visit Jesus amid many hardships.	We live close to the church with no hardships at all.

C. Organization

1. What gifts did the Magi give the Christ Child?
2. What does the gold of the Magi mean?
3. What does the gift of incense show?
4. What does the myrrh show?
5. How can we give gifts of gold, incense, and myrrh to Jesus?

D. Virtues and Practices

1. Give your best to God.
2. Give help to your parish church.

IV. SUGGESTED LEARNING ACTIVITIES

A. Discuss the meaning of the gifts of the Magi.
B. Draw pictures of the gifts of the Magi.
C. Poems: "My Gift," Fitzpatrick, *Religious Poems for Little Folks*, p. 95; "Gifts," *ibid.*, p. 100.

V. TEACHER REFERENCES

A. Dennerle, *Leading the Little Ones to Christ*, pp. 98–99.
B. S.N.D., *Religious Teaching of Young Children*, pp. 32–33.
C. Holy Bible, Mt. 2:1–12.

LESSON 57

I. SUBJECT MATTER

The Flight Into Egypt

II. OBJECTIVES

A. To develop a knowledge of the hardships endured by the Holy Family in the Flight into Egypt.

B. To foster an attitude of obedience to the will of God in imitation of the Holy Family.

III. SUGGESTED PROCEDURE

A. Approach

Do you remember what King Herod asked the Magi to do on their way back from Bethlehem?

B. Presentation

1. The Magi Return Home

King Herod did not want to adore the Baby Jesus. He wanted to kill Him because he was afraid Jesus would take his place as king. While Herod was waiting for the Magi to return to Jerusalem, something else was happening in Bethlehem. An angel came to the Magi and told them not to go back to Herod because he intended to harm Jesus. The Magi obeyed the angel's message and returned home a different way. When Herod discovered that the Magi had taken a different route, he became very angry and ordered his soldiers to hurry to Bethlehem and kill all the boy babies, two years old and under. That was a very sad day in Bethlehem. Those little babies who were killed are called the Holy Innocents and we celebrate their feast day on December 28.

2. The Flight Into Egypt

An angel also appeared to Joseph in his sleep and told him that Herod intended to harm Jesus. (Stress the fact that the angel appeared to *Joseph* — head of the Holy Family.) The angel told Joseph to take Mary and Child and to flee at once to Egypt, which was a faraway country, and to stay there until told to return. Joseph obeyed immediately, and the Holy Family started on their long journey in

122

the middle of the night. They were well on their way by the time Herod's soldiers arrived in Bethlehem. (At this point, present a picture of the Flight into Egypt and discuss the hardships of the journey.)

C. Organization

1. Why didn't the Magi return to King Herod?
2. What did Herod do when the Wise Men did not return to Him?
3. How did God protect the Christ Child?
4. What did the angel tell Joseph to do?
5. What did Joseph do after he received the message?
6. What did Mary do after she heard about the heavenly messenger?
7. Why was it hard for Mary and Joseph to go to Egypt?

D. Virtues and Practices

1. Obey cheerfully when you are told to do something.
2. Make little acts of sacrifice willingly.

IV. SUGGESTED LEARNING ACTIVITIES

A. Discuss the virtues of Mary and Joseph and tell how we can imitate them.
B. Discuss little acts of self-denial that we can practice when obedience demands.
C. Dramatize the story of the Flight into Egypt.
D. Story: "Obedience — Truth," Sister Marguerite, *Their Hearts Are His Garden,* pp. 46–47.

V. TEACHER REFERENCES

A. S.N.D., *Religious Teaching of Young Children,* pp. 35–36.
B. Fitzpatrick, *Religion in Life Curriculum, First Grade Manual,* pp. 76–77.
C. Sister Mary, *et al., The Catholic Mother's Helper,* pp. 85–88.

LESSON 58

I. SUBJECT MATTER

Life of the Holy Family in Egypt

II. OBJECTIVES

A. To develop a knowledge of how God rewards the good and punishes the wicked.

B. To develop a desire to imitate the obedience of Mary and Joseph.

III. SUGGESTED PROCEDURE

A. Approach

Did you ever go on a long trip? How did *you* travel? How did the Holy Family travel to Egypt? It was a hard journey but Joseph and Mary were happy to protect Jesus.

B. Presentation

1. The Hardships of the Holy Family in Egypt

While Jesus, Mary, and Joseph were in Egypt, they must have suffered greatly. You see, they were strangers there and they missed their friends and relatives in their native land. They also had to learn the ways of the Egyptians. As you know, Joseph was the head of the Holy Family and he had to take care of Jesus and Mary. It must have taken him a long time to find enough work to keep his family safe and give them enough food and clothes. Jesus loved us so much that He even willed to suffer hardships as a little child.

2. The Return to Nazareth

Herod finally died, and an angel came to tell Joseph that he could take the Holy Family back to their home in Nazareth. How happy Joseph must have been! Can't you imagine how thrilled he and Mary were when they finally returned home and once again saw their friends and relatives? How do you think Jesus felt?

3. The Obedience of Joseph and Mary

Notice how obedient Joseph was to the angel, God's messenger. All the angel had to do was tell Joseph that God wanted him to do this or that, and Joseph did it immediately and cheerfully. When Joseph told Mary the angel's message she obeyed in the same way that Joseph did. Shouldn't we all try to be like Joseph and Mary?

C. Organization
1. Why was it hard for the Holy Family to live in Egypt?
2. Were Mary and Joseph happy there? Why?

3. What happened to King Herod while the Holy Family was in Egypt?
4. What did the angel tell St. Joseph to do after the death of King Herod?
5. Did Mary and Joseph obey the angel?

D. Virtues and Practices
1. Be ready to do God's will when someone in charge of you asks you to obey.
2. Think of Mary and Joseph when you are asked to do something hard.
3. Be good and God will reward your goodness.

IV. SUGGESTED LEARNING ACTIVITIES

A. Dramatize the angel's visit to Joseph and the return of the Holy Family to Nazareth.
B. Compose original prayers to Mary and Joseph, asking them to help us become more obedient.
C. Story: "Flight Into Egypt," Sr. Mary, *et al., Catholic Mother's Helper*, pp. 87–88.

V. TEACHER REFERENCES

A. Fitzpatrick, *Religion in Life Curriculum, First Grade Manual*, pp. 77–81.
B. Sister Marguerite, *Their Hearts Are His Garden*, pp. 122–124.

LESSON 59

I. SUBJECT MATTER

The Holy Family at Nazareth

II. OBJECTIVES

A. To become acquainted with the life of the Holy Family.
B. To appreciate and encourage the practice of the virtues exemplified in the life of the Holy Family.

III. SUGGESTED PROCEDURE

A. Approach

Discuss informally the members of our families. Do you know who belongs to the Holy Family? (Show picture.)

B. Presentation

1. The Holy Family

Look at Jesus, Mary, and Joseph. They are all holy. Jesus was God made Man. What a wonderful Son He must have been to His mother and foster father. Mary was sinless, and Joseph was a just, hardworking, patient, and obedient man. Is it any wonder, then, that we call them the Holy Family?

2. Joy and Happiness in the Holy Family

How happy the family of Nazareth must have been! Jesus, Mary, and Joseph loved each other. They especially showed their love by their kindness and helpfulness. They prayed together to show God their love. How Joseph and Mary must have thanked God for sending them so wonderful a Son. Each one did their best to make one another happy. What a happy home it was.

3. Joy and Happiness in Our Families

All of you love your mothers and fathers, your brothers and sisters. You like to help them out and be good to them. You know how happy everyone in your family is when you are all together and when you all work together in peace.

What ways can you think of to make your family a "holy" family? Do you think you could make your family happier if you were more obedient to your parents? Do you ever try to do little jobs around the house to help your mother even though you were not asked?

Discuss what the children could do to make their family a happy place to live.

C. Organization

1. Who belongs to the Holy Family?
2. Who was the holiest one in the Holy Family?
3. What did Jesus do to make Mary and Joseph happy?
4. What did Joseph do to make Jesus and Mary happy?
5. What did Mary do to make her home a happy one?
6. What can you do to make your home a happy home?

126

D. Virtues and Practices

1. Be quiet when another member of the family is speaking.
2. Give to others in the family the choice of the radio or TV program.
3. Be unselfish when you have fun with the members of your family.

IV. SUGGESTED LEARNING ACTIVITIES

A. Compose and chart a story about the Holy Family.
B. Learn and recite frequently the ejaculation: "Jesus, Mary, and Joseph, I give you my heart and soul" (Raccolta, 636).
C. Plan an imaginary visit to Nazareth; discuss what we shall see and do.
D. Story: "A Happy Family," Sister Marguerite, *Their Hearts Are His Garden*, pp. 133–135.

V. TEACHER REFERENCE

Fitzpatrick, *Religion in Life Curriculum, First Grade Manual*, pp. 39, 82–84.

LESSON 60

I. SUBJECT MATTER

The Home of the Holy Family

II. OBJECTIVES

A. To acquaint the children with the type of home in which Jesus lived.
B. To encourage the practice of helpfulness in the home by being satisfied with what parents can afford.

III. SUGGESTED PROCEDURE

A. Approach

Do you think that Jesus lived in the same kind of house you do? Would you have liked to visit the Holy Family? Today we will take an imaginary airplane trip to Nazareth. Close your eyes and think. Here we go, up in the air, across our country, across the ocean into the town of Nazareth. What do you expect to see? (Discuss briefly.)

B. Presentation

1. The Home of the Holy Family

Show pictures of the Holy Family. Try to have pictures which accurately illustrate:

Homes in Nazareth	Mary's loom
Village well	Pieces of furniture
Joseph's carpenter shop	Water jars
Tools Joseph used	Clothing

These pictures can give you some idea of what Jesus' home town was like. By means of leads, discuss whatever is depicted in the pictures, stressing particularly whatever information you wish the class to acquire.

2. The Holy Family Is Grateful

Jesus, Mary, and Joseph were the happiest people upon earth. Their house was a poor little house in Nazareth. But it was rich at the same time because Jesus lived there. They never complained about anything they didn't have. They were pleased with everything and thanked God daily for what they had to make their home a happy home.

3. Gratitude for Our Homes

God is good to us. He gave us a home. But it is up to us and the rest of the family to make our home a good and happy home. We cannot always have everything we want. But we can make the best use of whatever we have, be happy and satisfied with it. Above all, thank God daily for giving you so many things in your home.

C. Organization

1. Where did the Holy Family live?
2. What kind of home did Jesus live in?
3. Where did St. Joseph go to work?
4. Where did Jesus go to get water for His Mother?

D. Virtues and Practices

1. Be thankful for the conveniences of your home.
2. Be orderly for the sake of others at home and in school.
3. Take care of the things you use at home and in school.

IV. SUGGESTED LEARNING ACTIVITIES

A. Illustrate the home of the Holy Family.
B. Have a picture study of homes in Nazareth.
C. Compose original prayers to the Holy Family asking for blessings on our homes.

V. TEACHER REFERENCE

Fitzpatrick, *Religion in Life Curriculum, First Grade Manual,* pp. 85–88.

LESSON 61

I. SUBJECT MATTER

Joseph, the Head of the Holy Family

II. OBJECTIVES

A. To develop the knowledge that St. Joseph was the foster father of Jesus and the head of the Holy Family.
B. To appreciate the virtues shown by St. Joseph, and to develop the desire to imitate him.

III. SUGGESTED PROCEDURE

A. Approach

Recall the members of the Holy Family. Who is the head of the Holy Family? Why did the angels appear to Joseph instead of Mary when they brought their messages?

B. Presentation

1. Joseph, Head of the Holy Family

Joseph was the head of the Holy Family just as your father is the head of your family. The Gospels do not tell us much about Joseph. All we know about him from the Bible is that he was a very just man who obeyed God in all things and that he must have loved Jesus and Mary dearly. He had a big job to do, for he had to watch over the young Jesus and His Mother. He worked very hard in his trade as carpenter.

Have you ever seen real carpenters at work? They are very clever and skilled workers who take pride in their work. Don't you think that Joseph made some special things for Jesus and Mary? (Discuss briefly.)

Joseph was the provider for the family. With the money he earned in his carpentry, the family was able to get whatever it needed. How happy Joseph was to take care of Jesus, the Son of God, and Mary His Mother.

2. The Virtues of Joseph

God, the heavenly Father, was Jesus' real Father. Joseph was Jesus' foster father. Joseph, being a pure and virtuous man, was privileged by God to become the husband of Mary and the foster father of Jesus. He is especially known for his obedience to God. He quickly did everything God told him to do through his messengers. He was a good and kind father to his family.

Joseph loved Jesus and Mary. He worked hard to please them and make them happy. Joseph protected them from all danger.

3. Our Fathers Imitate Joseph

Like Joseph, your father, the head of the family, takes care of you and works hard to provide food, clothing, and shelter. Joseph thought of Jesus and Mary. Your father thinks of you all the time. He tries his best to make your home a happy home.

4. We Can Show Love for Our Fathers

How Jesus must have loved His hard-working foster father! He did many kind helpful things to make him happy. Can you tell some things you can do to make your father happy?

C. Organization

1. Who was St. Joseph?
2. Why was St. Joseph chosen to be the foster father of Jesus?
3. How is our father like St. Joseph?
4. How must we treat our father?

D. Virtues and Practices

1. Show appreciation of your father's work for the family.
2. Be patient with others.
3. Show kindness toward others at home and in school.
4. Be gentle in your words and actions.

IV. SUGGESTED LEARNING ACTIVITIES

A. Learn and recite the ejaculation: "Joseph, Head of the Holy Family, pray for us."
B. Poem: "Joy of St. Joseph," Belger, *Sing a Song of Holy Things*, ⁴p. 53.

V. TEACHER REFERENCES

A. Sister Mary, *et al.*, *The Catholic Mother's Helper*, pp. 69–70.
B. Fitzpatrick, *Religion in Life Curriculum, First Grade Manual*, pp. 38–39.

LESSON 62

I. SUBJECT MATTER

Mary, the Mother of the Holy Family

II. OBJECTIVES

A. To develop the knowledge of Mary's part in the life of the Holy Family at Nazareth.
B. To appreciate the work done by our mothers in imitation of Mary.
C. To love and obey our mothers as the Boy Jesus loved and obeyed His Mother.

III. SUGGESTED PROCEDURE

A. Approach

Who takes care of your home and does the cooking, washing, cleaning, and sewing?

B. Presentation

1. Mary, the Mother of the Holy Family

Mary took care of all these things for the Holy Family. You know how good your own mothers are to you and how hard they work to keep your home clean, to feed and dress you, and to take care of your fathers, too. Just think! Mary was God's mother. In earlier lessons we learned that she was completely sinless. How richly God must have

131

blessed her. She loved to take care of Jesus and Joseph, and worked hard to keep their home at Nazareth clean and beautiful. In those days you couldn't buy bread at the grocery store, nor could you buy your clothes ready to wear. Mary spent a lot of time baking bread, sewing clothes, and doing the necessary work around the house. She loved her work, for her labors helped make Jesus and Joseph happy.

2. Our Mothers Are Like Mary

Like Mary, our own mothers have a big job to do. They work very hard for us, but they are happy because they love us. They know that their hard work means that we will be well-fed and healthy.

3. How We Can Show Love for Our Mothers

You can imagine how much Jesus loved Mary, His mother, and how many little things He did to help her. Jesus wants you to be as good to your mothers as He was to His. Can you think of anything you can do to show your mothers that you are grateful to them for what they do for you?

C. Organization

1. Who took care of Jesus and Joseph at home?
2. What kind of work did Mary do?
3. What did she do for Jesus to show Him her love?
4. What did Mary do for Joseph to show him her love?
5. Why is your mother like Mary?
6. What could you do to show your mother you love her?

D. Virtues and Practices

1. Love and honor Mary as your heavenly mother.
2. Show your mother that you love her by helping her.
3. Be orderly for your mother's sake.

IV. SUGGESTED LEARNING ACTIVITIES

A. Dramatize some of Mary's activities in the home.
B. Compose prayers to Mary asking her to help us be kind and helpful to our mothers.
C. Discuss various pictures of Mary with the Christ Child.
D. Story: "When Jesus was a Little Boy," Dorcy, *Mary, My Mother,* pp. 31–36.
E. Poem: "To Our Lady," Thayer, *The Child on His Knees,* pp. 24–25.

V. TEACHER REFERENCE

Fitzpatrick, *Religion in Life Curriculum, First Grade Manual,* pp. 69–70.

LESSON 63

I. SUBJECT MATTER

Jesus at Home

II. OBJECTIVES

A. To develop a knowledge of the Christ Child in His earthly home.
B. To foster love and obedience in the home.

III. SUGGESTED PROCEDURE

A. Approach

What do you do to make your home a happy home? (Discuss briefly.) Jesus, too, made His home a very happy and pleasant place to live.

B. Presentation

1. Jesus' Love for His Parents

(Show pictures in which Jesus is helping His mother and foster father.) Look at these pictures. Can you tell that Jesus loves His mother and foster father? Think of how much you love your parents. Jesus was perfect, He was the God-Man, and you can imagine how dearly He loved His mother and foster father. He had even chosen Mary to be His mother before He was born and He had chosen Joseph to be His foster father and protector. To prepare them for their work, He had showered graces and blessings upon them. Jesus loved His parents because it was God's will. He loved them because they were holy and took care of Him.

2. Jesus' Conduct at His Home in Nazareth

Jesus appreciated everything that Mary and Joseph did for Him. He knew that they both worked very hard for Him, and that they made many little sacrifices just to make Him happy. Jesus was greater than Mary and Joseph. But He obeyed and respected them because God the Father wanted Him to.

Jesus repaid their love and devotion by obeying them immediately, by doing kind and helpful acts and by cheering them if something went wrong.

3. We Can Imitate Jesus in Our Home

Jesus is our Leader. He wants us to follow Him and be like Him in everything. Jesus wants us to obey and respect our parents because God wants us to. (Discuss briefly — Honor thy father and thy mother. Stress problems of obedience and respect toward parents.)

We can be like Jesus if we try to be good and kind boys and girls at home. You must know many little things you can do that will make your parents happy and proud of you. What are some of the things you can do?

C. Organization

1. How did the Child Jesus act in His home?
2. Was His home as nice as yours?
3. How did He behave toward His parents?
4. How can we imitate the Child Jesus?

D. Virtues and Practices

1. Pray for our parents every day.
2. Be helpful, tidy, and clean at home.
3. Obey your parents promptly and cheerfully.
4. Anticipate the wishes of your parents.

IV. SUGGESTED LEARNING ACTIVITIES

A. Talk about the home duties that Jesus performed and how He did them.
B. Discuss the obedience of Jesus to His own creatures, Joseph and Mary.
C. Make a picture booklet to show some ways in which we can imitate Jesus, the obedient Child.
D. Stories: "Kathleen Learns How to Be Happy," Sister Marguerite, *Their Hearts Are His Garden*, pp. 52–54.
E. Poem: "Just Think," Thayer, *The Child on His Knees*, pp. 49–50.

TEACHER REFERENCES

A. S.N.D., *Religious Teaching of Young Children*, pp. 40–41.
B. Fitzpatrick, *Religion in Life Curriculum, First Grade Manual*, pp. 82–90.
C. Sr. Mary, *et al.*, *The Catholic Mother's Helper*, pp. 89–91.
D. *Practical Aids for Catholic Teachers*, pp. 106–110.

LESSON 64

I. SUBJECT MATTER

Jesus at Play

II. OBJECTIVES

A. To acquaint the children with the fact that the Child Jesus was always kind and fair.
B. To foster a spirit of kindness and fair play.

III. SUGGESTED PROCEDURE

A. Approach

Every child likes to play games. Do you suppose Jesus ever played games? What games could He have played?

B. Presentation

1. Games Jesus Might Have Played

Sometimes it is hard for us to remember that Jesus was a real boy and that He liked to play with children of His own age. Of course, the boys in Nazareth did not play baseball or football, but they did have games of their own.

Like children everywhere, they probably had races and contests. They probably played ball and tag. They did have some toys to play with too.

2. Jesus' Conduct at Play

Everyone liked to play with Jesus. Do you wonder why? He was a friend who was always gentle and courteous at play. He was kind and considerate of other children. Jesus played with all children, especially the poor. Everyone likes to play with children who do not become angry when they lose the game. Jesus played fair and was a good sport. He was pleasant when He lost and when He won.

Jesus is our little Leader. He wants us to play the way He did and always be happy.

3. We Can Be Like Jesus at Play

Can you measure up to Jesus? You can surely think of many, many things you can do at play which will make you more like Him. Sometimes when you're tempted to get angry at your playmates, think of Jesus at play. Ask yourself, then, what Jesus would do if He were you. (Discuss with the children the traits they must strive to acquire while at play with their companions, i.e., fair play, good sportsmanship, kindness, courtesy, gentleness, etc.)

C. Organization
1. What games might Jesus have played?
2. Do we know how Jesus acted at play?
3. How can we imitate Jesus?

D. Virtues and Practices
1. Be fair and polite when you play.
2. Share your toys with other children.
3. Give a good example when you play.
4. Play with all children — poor, friendless, etc.
5. Show respect for all children, regardless of color, because they are all children of God.

IV. SUGGESTED LEARNING ACTIVITIES
A. Make up original prayers asking Jesus to help us play fairly.
B. Make an imaginary trip to Nazareth.
C. Discuss the virtues practiced by Jesus when He was a boy.
D. Poem: "Thoughts," Thayer, *The Child on His Knees*, p. 85.
E. Picture study: Murello, "Children of the Shell."

V. TEACHER REFERENCES
A. Fitzpatrick, *Religion in Life Curriculum, First Grade Manual*, pp. 91–95.
B. Sister Mary, *et al.*, *The Catholic Mother's Helper*, pp. 89–91.

LESSON 65

I. SUBJECT MATTER

Jesus at Prayer

II. OBJECTIVES

A. To develop an understanding of the way in which the Child Jesus prayed.

B. To foster a desire to pray as Jesus prayed.

III. SUGGESTED PROCEDURE

A. Approach

What are some of the things Jesus did every day? There was one thing Jesus did often because He liked to do it most of all. (Show pictures of Jesus at prayer.)

B. Presentation

1. Jesus Prayed as a Boy

Jesus always gave honor to His heavenly Father. When He prayed, He prayed perfectly: with love, with attention, with devotion. He knew that every minute of the day could be used to serve His heavenly Father, and He made every minute count.

2. Jesus Prayed That His Father's Will Might Be Done

Jesus prayed for many things, but in His prayers He always asked that His heavenly Father's will be done. God's will is good. His will is that there be peace and love on earth and that we shall all go to heaven to be happy with Him. Jesus wants us to do His heavenly Father's will at all times. We know God's will for us through our parents, priests, Sisters, and all those placed over us.

3. Jesus Prayed for Mary, Joseph, and All Men

Jesus wanted His mother and His foster father to have all good things. He wanted His heavenly Father to comfort them in sorrow and to lead them to Paradise. He prayed for His Apostles, that they might be strong and brave. He prayed for everyone, even those who hurt Him, because He wanted all men to be happy with Him in heaven.

4. Jesus Prayed for Himself as Man

Because Jesus was really man, He did not like suffering. He knew that some day He had to die an agonizing death on the cross. Like everyone else He feared death. But He prayed that His Father's will be done, even if it meant that He had to suffer as man.

5. How We Can Imitate Jesus at Prayer

We can make our whole day a prayer just as Jesus did by offering our day to God the first thing in the morning. What will help you keep your mind on your prayers? What can we pray for?

C. Organization

1. How did Jesus pray?
2. Why did Jesus pray?
3. When did He pray?
4. For whom did He pray?
5. How should we pray?

D. Virtues and Practices

1. Pray with your family and for your family.
2. Get the good habit of turning your work into prayer.
3. Accept God's will when we pray.

IV. SUGGESTED LEARNING ACTIVITIES

A. Picture study of the Boy Jesus at prayer.
B. Dramatize a fervent child at prayer.
C. Hymn: "Jesus Teach Me How to Pray," *Music Hour*, II, p. 1.
D. Poem: "Presents," Thayer, *The Child on His Knees*, p. 92.

V. TEACHER REFERENCE

Fitzpatrick, *Religion in Life Curriculum, First Grade Manual*, pp. 97–99.

LESSON 66

I. SUBJECT MATTER

A. Jesus Prayed Every Morning
B. Instruction on Morning Prayer

II. OBJECTIVES

A. To develop a knowledge of what a morning prayer should include.
B. To encourage the habit of saying our morning prayers regularly and devoutly.

III. SUGGESTED PROCEDURE

A. Approach

When you awaken in the morning from a good night's sleep do you say, "Good morning" to God? What do you think Jesus did every morning when He awakened?

B. Presentation

1. Jesus Prayed Every Morning

As soon as Jesus opened His eyes in the morning from His night's sleep, He turned His first thoughts to His heavenly Father. Reverently, with His hands folded He prayed and talked to God the Father. What do you think He might have told Him each morning when He prayed? (Discuss briefly.)

2. Jesus Wants Us to Pray Every Morning

Jesus is our little Leader. He wants us to think of God as soon as we awaken, just as He did. God wants to hear our prayer every morning. What could we say to God when we say our morning prayers?

We should remember to:

a) Thank God for His protection during the night.
b) Tell God how much we love Him in return for His love.
c) Ask God to help us with His grace.
d) Promise to try our best to do His will.
e) Make a morning offering of all our thoughts, words, and acts of the day.

3. Instruction on Morning Prayer

Help the children to develop the habit of making a good intention in the morning by saying their morning prayers. Teach a definite form of "Morning Offering." Suggest to them what other prayers they may choose to say. (Our Father or Hail Mary or Angel of God.)

This is an opportune time to encourage the children to say their morning prayers daily. Encourage the children to ask themselves:

Did I say my morning prayers today? If so, thank Jesus for helping you remember to say them.

If not — why? Ask Jesus to help you remember to say them to-morrow morning.

C. Organization

1. What did the Boy Jesus do as soon as He woke up every morning?
2. Why did Jesus pray to do His Father's will?
3. What should we thank God for every morning?
4. What does God like to have us tell Him?
5. What should we ask God to do for us every morning?

D. Virtues and Practices

1. Say your morning prayers every day.
2. Make a morning offering of all your thoughts, words, and actions of the day.
3. Be happy to greet God every morning.

IV. SUGGESTED LEARNING ACTIVITIES

A. Learn a "Morning Offering":
   "O my God, I offer Thee every thought, word, and act of today.
   Please, bless me, my God, and make me good today."

   Primer — *Living My Religion Series*

B. Compose original morning prayers.
C. Poems: "Different Ways," Thayer, *The Child on His Knees*, p. 123; "Early Prayer," *ibid.*, p. 21.

V. TEACHER REFERENCES

A. S.N.D., *Religious Teaching of Young Children*, p. 122.
B. Fitzpatrick, *Religion in Life Curriculum, First Grade Manual*, pp. 99–105.
C. Schumacher, *I Teach Catechism*, Vol. I, pp. 210–212.

LESSON 67

I. SUBJECT MATTER

A. Jesus Prayed Every Evening
B. Instruction on Evening Prayer

II. OBJECTIVES

A. To develop a knowledge of what an evening prayer should include.
B. To encourage the habit of saying our evening prayers every night.

III. SUGGESTED PROCEDURE

A. Approach

We know that the first thing Jesus did in the morning was to raise His thoughts to His heavenly Father and say His morning prayer. What was the last thing Jesus did at night?

B. Presentation

1. Jesus Prayed Every Evening

At night, before going to bed, Jesus prayed to His Father to thank Him for all the blessings He had received that day. He wanted His Father to be honored and loved and He showed us how to do this through prayer and adoration.

In all likelihood, the Holy Family said their night prayers together. What a beautiful heavenly sight to look at!

2. Jesus Wants Us to Pray Every Evening

A good child will remember to talk with God at bedtime. There are so many things we can tell Him. Shouldn't we:

    a) Thank God for all the favors we have received during the day?
    b) Ask Him for protection during the night?
    c) Tell Him we are sorry if we hurt Him during the day by doing something wrong?
    d) Pray for our parents, brothers, sisters, and others?

3. Instruction on Night Prayers

Discuss with the children what prayers may be said at bedtime. A definite practice in saying them will establish the habit more readily. Let a few children recite their night prayers to enable others to hear and see what could be done.

Teach the children how to think about themselves, about all the good things they did that pleased God that day and about all the naughty things they did that offended (hurt) God that day.

Teach them how to tell God they are sorry and promise to do better tomorrow. It is not too early to begin teaching a definite "Act of Contrition" which is a very important prayer in their lifetime.

Each day in class encourage the children to have a "secret checkup" with themselves and Jesus.

Did I say my night prayers last night?

If so, thank Jesus for helping you remember to say them.

If not — why?

Ask Jesus to help you remember to say them tonight.

C. Organization

1. Why did Jesus pray every evening?
2. What should we thank God for every evening?
3. What should we ask God to do for us during the night?
4. How can we get rid of our sins before we go to sleep?
5. For whom should we pray especially at night?

D. Virtues and Practices

1. Say our prayers every night.
2. Encourage members of our family to say evening prayers together.

IV. SUGGESTED LEARNING ACTIVITIES

A. Compose original prayers that could be included in our evening prayers.
B. Compose an original "Act of Contrition."
C. Story: "Aberdeen Angus," *For Heaven's Sake*, pp. 79–81.
D. Poem: "Afterwards," Thayer, *The Child on His Knees*, p. 26.

V. TEACHER REFERENCES

A. *Religion in Life Curriculum, First Grade Manual*, pp. 105–108.
B. Schumacher, *I Teach Catechism*, Vol. I, pp. 210–212.

LESSON 68

I. SUBJECT MATTER

Jesus Prayed Before and After Meals

II. OBJECTIVES

A. To develop the knowledge that meal prayers are necessary.

B. To develop the habit of saying meal prayers every day.

III. SUGGESTED PROCEDURE

A. Approach

What do you suppose Jesus did before He sat down to eat? What did He do after His meal?

B. Presentation

1. *Jesus Prayed Before and After His Meals*

Jesus also prayed before and after meals. Why? He wanted to ask His Father's blessing on the food He was about to eat and to thank Him after He ate for His goodness. Jesus did this to show us what to do. (Discuss picture.)

2. *We Must Pray Before and After Meals*

Just think of all the gifts of food God gives you every day. We must always remember to ask God to bless the food we are about to eat and to thank Him after we have eaten. (Discuss picture — stress respect, posture, and devotion at prayer.)

3. *Prayer Before and After Meals*

Review or reteach the prayers "Grace Before Meals" and "Grace After Meals." See Lessons 26 and 27, pp. 58–60.

C. Organization

1. Why did Jesus pray at mealtime?
2. Why should we pray before we eat?
3. Why should we pray after we eat?
4. How should we say meal prayers?

D. Virtues and Practices

1. Remember to say our meal prayers every day.
2. Pray before we eat, even though we are very hungry.

IV. SUGGESTED LEARNING ACTIVITIES

A. Review the prayers: "Grace Before Meals" and "Grace After Meals."

B. Children dramatize the saying of meal prayers.

V. TEACHER REFERENCE

S.N.D., *Religious Teaching of Young Children*, pp. 124–125.

LESSON 69

I. SUBJECT MATTER

Jesus in the Temple

II. OBJECTIVES

A. To show how Jesus observed feast days.
B. To foster the habit of observing Sundays and holydays in the proper manner.

III. SUGGESTED PROCEDURE

A. Approach

Jesus was God. He wanted to be like us and show us how to live to please God, especially by being obedient.

B. Presentation

1. Jesus Goes to the Temple

When Jesus was twelve years of age, He went with Mary and Joseph to Jerusalem to celebrate a special feast which lasted a few days. Jerusalem was many miles away from Nazareth, but Jesus was very pleased to walk all the way. While in Jerusalem, Jesus, Mary, and Joseph prayed in the temple, the house of God. (Explain term — "temple.") How happy Jesus was to be there. What a good example He showed the people. (Discuss briefly — what we could see Jesus doing in the temple — His polite manners in God's house.)

2. Jesus Is Lost

When the feast was over the families were returning home. Many people were traveling along the roads together. At the end of the first day's journey Mary and Joseph noticed that Jesus was not with the group. They looked everywhere, they asked everyone, but Jesus was not there. How Joseph and Mary worried that Jesus was lost.

3. Jesus Is Found

Since no one could tell them anything about Jesus, Mary and Joseph returned to Jerusalem, looking and inquiring as they went along. On the third day, as they entered the temple, Joseph and Mary noticed Jesus in the midst of some doctors, listening and telling them many wonderful things about God. (Explain terms — doctors, teachers.)

How surprised the men were to see that Jesus, a young Child, knew everything and even more and better than they did. The teachers did not know that Jesus was God.

4. Jesus Is Obedient

Joseph and Mary told Jesus how worried they were about Him. But Jesus very kindly said, "Did you not know I must be about My Father's work?"

Jesus returned to Nazareth with Mary and Joseph. Jesus was God, but He obeyed His parents in everything because He wants us to obey our parents, too.

C. Organization

1. Where did Jesus go when He was twelve years old?
2. What did Jesus do in the temple?
3. What happened when Mary and Joseph were returning home?
4. Where did they find Jesus?
5. What was He doing there?
6. What am I supposed to do on Sundays and holydays?
7. Am I ever allowed to miss from Mass on Sundays and holydays?

D. Virtues and Practices

1. Act properly when you go to Mass.
2. Be as happy to go to church as Jesus was.

IV. SUGGESTED LEARNING ACTIVITIES

A. Discuss our obligation to assist at Mass every Sunday.
B. Discuss the conduct of Jesus in the temple.
C. Dramatize the story of Jesus' becoming lost in the temple.
D. Poem: "Hide and Seek," Fitzpatrick, *Religious Poems for Little Folks*, p. 53.

V. TEACHER REFERENCES

A. Dennerle, *Leading the Little Ones to Christ*, pp. 110–117.

B. Sr. Mary, *et al.*, *The Catholic Mother's Helper*, pp. 92–95.
C. S.N.D., *Religious Teaching of Young Children*, pp. 37–39.
D. Sr. Marguerite, *Their Hearts Are His Garden*, pp. 129–133.

LESSON 70

I. SUBJECT MATTER

Feast of the Holy Name of Jesus — Sunday Between the Octave of Christmas and Epiphany, or January 2

II. OBJECTIVES

A. To acquaint the children with this special feast.
B. To foster devotion to the holy name of Jesus.

III. SUGGESTED PROCEDURE

A. Approach

When you pray, what titles or names do you give our Lord?

B. Presentation

1. When Jesus Received His Name

One of the names you call our Lord is "Jesus." We have a very special feast to honor the holy name of Jesus. It is celebrated on the Sunday between the octave of Christmas (January 1) and Epiphany (January 6). You remember the story of the Angel Gabriel's message to Mary — that she was to be the mother of God. In that message he also told her what the Child's name was to be. What was that holy name?

There was a law in those days that eight days after a Jewish boy was born he was to be brought to the temple to be circumcised and to receive his name. Mary and Joseph obeyed this law and brought the Baby Jesus to the temple where His name was given to Him for all to know. "Jesus" means "Saviour." Jesus would save us from our sins.

2. How We Should Honor Jesus' Name

The name of "Jesus" is so holy that God gave us a commandment about it. (Acquaint the children with the words of the Second Com-

146

mandment.) We should always bow our heads reverently when we say Jesus' name. His name should never be used in anger or in a careless way. We should use Jesus' holy name only to praise Him.

C. Organization

1. When did Jesus receive His name?
2. When should we use our Lord's name?
3. When is it wrong to use our Lord's name?

D. Virtues and Practices

1. Use the name of Jesus in the right way.
2. Say the holy name of Jesus often.
3. Bow your head when you say or hear the name of Jesus.

IV. SUGGESTED LEARNING ACTIVITIES

A. Make up original prayers or ejaculations in honor of the holy name of Jesus.
B. Poem: "The Holy Name of Jesus," Belger, *Sing a Song of Holy Things,* p. 37.

V. TEACHER REFERENCE

Fitzpatrick, *Religion in Life Curriculum — Grade One Manual,* p. 118.

UNIT SIX

The Public Life of Our Lord   *Time: 4 weeks*

I. INTRODUCTION FOR THE TEACHER

The public life of our Lord is introduced in this unit by means of stories describing our Lord's departure from His home in Nazareth, His particular way of choosing His Apostles, and the manifestation of His divine power in several of His miracles. A deep and growing appreciation of and reverence for the almighty power of God the Son should be instilled in the child as the miracles of Jesus are developed.

II. OBJECTIVES OF THE UNIT

A. To develop a knowledge of some outstanding miracles performed by Christ during His public life.
B. To develop an appreciation of the power of Jesus as shown by His miracles.
C. To instill the desire to imitate Jesus in the practice of His virtues and to find opportunities for their practice.
D. To foster a growing realization that Jesus is God.
E. To nurture the possible seed of religious vocation in the hearts of the children.
F. To encourage the children to pray for God's representatives.

III. SUBJECT MATTER

A. Jesus leaves His home at Nazareth
B. Jesus chooses His Apostles
C. Jesus Christ manifests His power and mercy by His miracles
    1. Wedding feast at Cana
    2. Miracle of the loaves and the fishes
    3. Calming of the storm
    4. Miraculous draught of fishes
    5. Jesus walks upon the water
    6. Raising of Jairus' daughter to life
    7. Raising to life of the widow's son
    8. Raising of Lazarus

9. Cure of the man born blind
10. The ten lepers
11. Man at the pool of Bethsaida
D. Liturgical Feasts
    1. Purification — February 2
    2. St. Blaise — February 3
    3. St. Valentine — February 14

LESSON 71

I. SUBJECT MATTER

Jesus Leaves His Home at Nazareth to Do His Father's Work

II. OBJECTIVES

A. To know why Jesus left His home in Nazareth.
B. To create in the children a desire to learn all they can about the Public Life of Christ.
C. To instill in the children a greater love for Jesus.

III. SUGGESTED PROCEDURE

A. Approach

Show the picture of the Child Jesus in the temple. Discuss the reasons why Jesus stayed in the temple, and why He went back to Nazareth to live.

B. Presentation

1. Happiness of Jesus at Nazareth

From earlier lessons we know why the family at Nazareth was the "Holy" Family. Jesus was very happy in the small village with His Mother and Joseph, and He loved to spend His days with them. Do you remember some of the many things Mary and Joseph did to make Jesus happy?

2. When Jesus Left His Home

As you know, Jesus was only twelve years old when He left His home the first time. We just talked about that story when we saw the picture. (Show picture once more.) Do you think Mary and Joseph knew what Jesus meant when He said, "Did you not know that I must be about My Father's business?" Nevertheless, He very obediently went back to Nazareth with them. Some time after this, Joseph died. What a happy death he had, with Jesus and Mary at his side!

When Jesus was about thirty years old, He left His Mother and began His public life.

3. Why Jesus Left His Home

Jesus left His home to do His Father's will. He had come into the world to redeem us from sin, to found His Church, and to teach us how to get to heaven. He had to teach the people right ideas about God and He also had to organize a group of Apostles who would carry on His work after He had returned to heaven.

C. Organization

1. How old was Jesus when He left His home at Nazareth?
2. Why did Jesus leave His home at Nazareth?
3. What would have happened to us if Jesus had not come to earth to live?

D. Virtues and Practices

1. Try to obey God as Jesus did.
2. Ask Jesus to help you to get to heaven.
3. Be happy to belong to the Church that Jesus started.

IV. SUGGESTED LEARNING ACTIVITIES

A. The children collect pictures of the miracles of Jesus.
B. Dramatize the scene in which Jesus said good-by to His Mother

V. TEACHER REFERENCE

Dennerle, *Leading the Little Ones to Christ*, pp. 121–123.

LESSON 72

I. SUBJECT MATTER

Jesus Chooses His Apostles

II. OBJECTIVES

A. To develop a knowledge of Jesus' choice of helpers.

B. To develop an appreciation for the work of the Apostles and a desire to imitate the Apostles.

C. To encourage the children to pray for God's representatives and for vocations.

III. SUGGESTED PROCEDURE

A. Approach

When Jesus lived on earth He wanted helpers to work with Him. Today we will see how He chose His helpers.

B. Presentation

1. Jesus Chooses His Apostles

When Jesus began His public life, He gathered around Him a group of men whom He would train to be leaders of His Church. These were the twelve Apostles. Many of them were simple fishermen like Peter, James, and John. One of them, Matthew, was a tax collector. They were all simple men, but Jesus would teach them the truth about God and Himself and He would give them wonderful powers so that they could carry on His work and bring the word of salvation to all men.

2. What Jesus Taught the Apostles

Jesus taught His Apostles that He was true God and true man. He taught them the mystery of the Blessed Trinity, and He showed them that the thing God chiefly wants is our love — love for Him and love for all men because of Him. He taught them that heaven was a gift from God, but that we could all gain it if we would only do what God wants us to do. He gave them all truth, so that they could rule the Church He would found and bring His message to all men.

3. How the Work of the Apostles Is Done Today

We know that the Catholic Church is the true Church of Christ. The Pope takes the place of Peter, the chief Apostle and first pope. The bishops of the entire world take the place of the other Apostles and, in union with the pope, teach us the same truths which Jesus taught His Apostles. We can help them in their work by being good Catholics, by learning more about our faith, and by giving good example.

C. Organization

1. What do we call Jesus' first helpers?
2. Why did Jesus choose His Apostles?
3. What are the names of some of the Apostles?
4. Does Jesus have any helpers today? Who are they?
5. How can we share in the work of the Apostles?

D. Virtues and Practices

1. Do something hard today to show Jesus that you love Him.
2. Help do God's work today by praying for the missionaries and by giving good example.
3. Ask Jesus to help you become one of His helpers some day.
4. Be polite and respectful to priests and Sisters.

IV. SUGGESTED LEARNING ACTIVITIES

A. Dramatize the scene of Jesus teaching the Apostles to pray.
B. Make up original prayers for the missionaries.
C. Carry on a mission activity in the classroom.
D. Poem: "Tell Me What," *The Child on His Knees*, p. 119.

V. TEACHER REFERENCES

A. S.N.D., *Religious Teaching of Young Children*, pp. 42–46.
B. Sr. Mary, *et al.*, *The Catholic Mother's Helper*, pp. 103–104.
C. Dennerle, *Leading the Little Ones to Christ*, pp. 166–172.
D. Holy Bible, Jn. 1:35–51.

LESSON 73

I. SUBJECT MATTER

The First Miracle — the Wedding Feast at Cana

II. OBJECTIVES

A. To increase knowledge of the power and kindness of Jesus Christ through the story of the wedding feast at Cana.
B. To know that Jesus proved He is God by changing water into wine.

C. To increase our love for the Blessed Mother.

III. SUGGESTED PROCEDURE

A. Approach

Did you ever go to a wedding reception? Once Jesus and His Mother were invited to a wedding feast and Jesus did something wonderful while He was there.

B. Presentation

1. The Story of the First Miracle

Jesus and Mary were at a wedding feast at Cana. During the feast, Mary noticed that the wine was coming to an end. She knew that the bridegroom would be embarrassed if there was no more wine for his guests. She quietly went up to Jesus and said, "Son, they have no wine." She then went to the chief waiter and his helpers and told them to do whatever Jesus told them to. Jesus told them to fill the large waterpots with water — up to the brim. He then told them to take the wine to the bridegroom and his guests. When the bridegroom tasted the wine he asked the chief waiter why he had kept the best wine until last. What had happened to the water? Jesus did something no one else could do. He worked a miracle, and this was His first miracle. How kind Jesus was to do this. He worked many more miracles during His public life. (Present a picture of this miracle.)

2. Jesus' Love for His Mother and for Men

This miracle not only shows us how powerful Jesus was, it also shows us how much He loves His Mother and all men. All Mary had to do was ask Him to do a favor, and He gladly performed a miracle. Jesus wants to do good things for you, too. Just ask Him, and ask Mary to beg Jesus for you.

C. Organization

1. What do we call the wonderful things that Jesus did to show that He is God?
2. What was His first miracle?
3. Who asked Jesus to help the poor people?
4. What did Jesus tell the waiters to do?
5. Why did Jesus do this wonderful thing?
6. Will the Blessed Mother take care of us too?

7. Because Jesus loves us so much, what will He do for us?

D. Virtues and Practices

1. Love the poor and the sick.
2. Believe that Jesus is God.
3. Ask Mary, your Mother, to help you in time of need.

IV. SUGGESTED LEARNING ACTIVITIES

A. Begin a bulletin-board display of Christ's miracles.
B. Picture study of the miracle: Wedding Feast at Cana.
C. Dramatize the story.
D. Discuss Mary's intercessory power.
E. Story: "The First Miracle," Sr. Mary, *et al.*, *The Catholic Mother's Helper*, pp. 104–105.
F. Poem: "The Wedding at Cana," Moran, *Verses for Tiny Tots*, p. 55.

V. TEACHER REFERENCES

A. Dennerle, *Leading the Little Ones to Christ*, pp. 245–246.
B. Holy Bible, Jn. 2:1–11.

LESSON 74

I. SUBJECT MATTER

Miracle of the Loaves and Fishes

II. OBJECTIVES

A. To increase knowledge of the power and kindness of Jesus.
B. To appreciate God's goodness in taking care of us physically as well as spiritually.

III. SUGGESTED PROCEDURE

A. Approach

Jesus proved that He was God by His miracle. What wonderful miracle did our Lord work at Cana?

B. Presentation

1. Happiness of Jesus in Teaching People

The people flocked to Jesus because He was so good and because He taught them such wonderful truths. One day, a great crowd of people — over 5000 — followed Him to a beautiful grassy hillside to hear Him tell them about God. Jesus was very happy that so many people wanted to learn about God and about heaven, and He gladly spoke to them.

2. Story of the Multiplication of the Loaves and Fishes

As the day wore on, the people got hungry. They were far from their homes and there was very little food. Nearby was a small boy with a few loaves and some fishes, but how could a crowd of so many people get enough from this? The Apostles wanted our Lord to send the people home. Instead, Jesus took the loaves and fishes and blessed them. Then He told the Apostles to give the people as much as they wanted. After all had been fed, the Apostles gathered up twelve baskets of food that had been left over. Do you think this was a great miracle? (Show a picture of the miracle.)

3. Purpose of the Miracle

By working such a great miracle, Jesus showed the people that He was truly what He claimed to be — the Son of God. In addition, He had told His disciples that He was going to leave them His own flesh to eat and His blood to drink. It was hard for the disciples to understand this, but this miracle prepared the way for them.

C. Organization

1. Did Jesus send the people home for food?
2. What happened when Jesus blessed the five loaves and two fishes?
3. Was there enough for everyone?
4. What did the people want Jesus to be?
5. What must we do to belong to Jesus' kingdom?
6. What lesson did Jesus teach us when He blessed the bread?

D. Virtues and Practices

1. Be kind to the poor, especially to the hungry.
2. Remember to say grace at meals.

IV

SUGGESTED LEARNING ACTIVITIES

A. Make an analogy between this miracle and the distribution of Holy Communion to the faithful.
B. Dramatize the story.

V. TEACHER REFERENCES

A. S.N.D., *Religious Teaching of Young Children*, pp. 49–51.
B. Dennerle, *Leading the Little Ones to Christ*, pp. 245–247.
C. Sister Mary, *et al.*, *The Catholic Mother's Helper*, pp. 115–118.
D. Holy Bible, Jn. 6:1–15.

LESSON 75

I. SUBJECT MATTER

Calming of the Storm

II. OBJECTIVES

A. To develop the knowledge that Jesus has power over nature.
B. To instill in the children great confidence in the power and goodness of Jesus.

III. SUGGESTED PROCEDURE

A. Approach

Did you ever see a storm on the lake? What happened to the water?

B. Presentation

1. Jesus and the Apostles on the Lake

One of Jesus' miracles took place on a stormy lake. He had gone out in a fishing boat with Peter and some of the other Apostles. They sailed far out onto the lake. Jesus was tired and fell asleep. A terrible storm suddenly rose up, causing waves to fall into the boat. The wind and the waves were getting worse but Jesus still didn't awaken. The Apostles thought the waves would drown them and they wanted Jesus to help them.

2. Jesus Shows His Power Over Nature

Peter was very frightened. He finally woke Jesus and said, "Save us,

Lord, we perish." Jesus then stood up in the boat and commanded the wind and waves to stop. Immediately, all was calm. Only God could do something like this. Why? (Show picture of the miracle.)

C. Organization

1. Where were Jesus and the Apostles?
2. How did the Apostles feel in the presence of Jesus?
3. What happened to Jesus?
4. What was happening while Jesus was sleeping?
5. Did Jesus know about the approaching storm?
6. How did the Apostles feel?
7. What did they do?
8. What did they ask for?
9. Did Jesus help them?
10. What did Jesus say to the wind and water?

D. Virtues and Practices

1. Pray whenever you are in danger.
2. Trust in God's loving care and goodness at all times.
3. Use blessed palm or candles during a bad storm.

IV. SUGGESTED LEARNING ACTIVITIES

A. Learn and recite the ejaculation "Heart of Jesus, I put my trust in Thee" (*Raccolta*, 226).
B. Discuss what we should do in time of physical danger.
C. Recording: "Jesus Calms the Storm."
D. Picture study and discussion of this miracle.

V. TEACHER REFERENCES

A. Sister Mary, *et al.*, *The Catholic Mother's Helper*, pp. 114–115.
B. Sister Marguerite, *Their Hearts Are His Garden*, pp. 140–141.

LESSON 76

I. SUBJECT MATTER

Miraculous Draught of Fishes

II. OBJECTIVES

A. To further develop the knowledge that Jesus is God, as is evident in His power of performing miracles.

B. To instill great love for Christ, who looks after our daily needs.

III. SUGGESTED PROCEDURE

A. Approach

Did you or your father ever go fishing? Did you ever catch any fish? Today's story is about a fishing trip the Apostles were on, but they didn't catch any fish.

B. Presentation

1. *The Apostles Fishing*

One day Peter and a group of the Apostles were in their boats on the Sea of Galilee. They had been fishing a long time, but as yet they hadn't caught any fish. That was very serious for them, as they depended on their fishing for a living. If they didn't catch some fish soon they would not be able to take care of their families. They finally decided to give up and turned their boats toward shore. As they neared shore, Peter saw Jesus coming toward them. The Apostles had already started hauling in their nets to clean them. Peter told Jesus how they had caught nothing after their many hours of fishing.

2. *Jesus Works a Miracle*

Jesus listened to Peter's story and then told him and the others to drop their nets into the water. The Apostles obeyed and were amazed at the great haul which filled their nets. So many fish were trapped in the nets that they began to break. The Apostles had to call others from shore to come and help them. (Show a picture of the miracle.)

C. Organization

1. What were the Apostles doing out on the lake?
2. Were they able to catch any fish?
3. What did they decide to do?
4. Who happened to come and see how they felt?
5. Did Jesus help the Apostles?
6. What did He tell them to do?
7. Did the Apostles obey Jesus?
8. What happened because the Apostles were obedient?

D. Virtues and Practices

1. Think of Jesus while you work.
2. Trust God to help you.
3. Obey as the Apostles did.

IV. SUGGESTED LEARNING ACTIVITIES

A. Discuss our dependence on God in order to do our work successfully.
B. Children retell the story in their own words.
C. Picture study and discussion of this miracle.
D. Poem: "The Draught of Fishes," Moran, *Verses for Tiny Tots*, p. 58.

V. TEACHER REFERENCE

Sr. Mary, *et al.*, *The Catholic Mother's Helper*, pp. 105–107.

LESSON 77

I. SUBJECT MATTER

Jesus Walks Upon the Water

II. OBJECTIVES

A. To develop the knowledge of the divinity of Christ as shown by His miracles.
B. To instill love for and trust in God at all times.

III. SUGGESTED PROCEDURE

A. Approach

Did you ever run through a puddle on a summer day? Do you think you could stand on *top* of the water? Why not?

B. Presentation

1. The Apostles Again Are Fishing

This story is about Someone who *did* walk on top of water. One day Peter and the other Apostles were out in their boats fishing again. They were quite far from shore when another terrible storm blew up.

This time Jesus was not with them and they were very much afraid. Suddenly Peter looked out on the lake and saw someone walking toward him on *top* of the water. Can you guess who it was?

2. Jesus Appears and Saves Peter

It was Jesus. Peter was filled with awe when he saw his Lord walking on the waters. He called out to Christ, who told Peter that He was truly Jesus and no vision. Jesus told Peter to walk over the waves too. Peter began to walk on the water, but in a short time his faith failed and he began to sink. He cried out to Jesus for help, and Jesus rescued him, telling Peter that he would not have begun to sink if his faith had remained firm.

3. The Trust We Must Have in Jesus

Jesus wants us to have confidence and faith in Him. He is God — almighty, all-good, and all-merciful. If we have strong faith in Jesus, we can do much good and many great things. We cannot do these things ourselves, but with God's help we can. (Show a picture of the miracle.)

C. Organization

1. Where were the Apostles?
2. What happened when they were on the lake?
3. Were they afraid? Why?
4. What did Jesus say?
5. What did Peter call out?
6. What did our Lord answer?
7. What did Peter do?
8. Why did he begin to sink?
9. How did Jesus help Peter?

D. Virtues and Practices

1. Make simple acts of love.
2. Pray for God's help when you need it.
3. Trust in God and do lovingly what He asks you to do whether it is pleasant or unpleasant.
4. Do not think too much about yourself and what you can do.

IV. SUGGESTED LEARNING ACTIVITIES

A. Discuss the power of God over the elements of nature.

B. Pantomime the story.

C. Discuss the pictures illustrating this miracle.

V. TEACHER REFERENCES

A. Sister Mary, *et al.*, *The Catholic Mother's Helper*, pp. 118–119.

B. Sister Marguerite, *Their Hearts Are His Garden*, pp. 140–141.

LESSON 78

I. SUBJECT MATTER

Raising of Jairus' Daughter to Life

II. OBJECTIVES

A. To foster a growing realization that Jesus is God.

B. To develop habits of gratitude to God for answering our prayers.

III. SUGGESTED PROCEDURE

A. Approach

What were some of the miracles Jesus worked while He was on earth? Could we do these things? Why not?

B. Presentation

1. Jesus Raises Jairus' Daughter to Life

Our story today is about a miracle far greater than the ones you have just mentioned. A Jewish official, named Jairus, had a daughter whom he dearly loved. The girl became very sick, and her father hurried off to find Jesus. While he was pleading with our Lord to come to the girl, a servant came to tell him that his daughter had died. Jairus was grief-stricken, but Jesus told him to have faith. Accompanied by the girl's father and a crowd of people, Jesus went to Jairus' home. He sent the people away and then went to the dead girl. He took her hand and brought her back to life again. Can you imagine how happy her father must have been? What a tremendous miracle! Wasn't Jesus kind to do that for Jairus?

2. How We Should Thank Jesus

Jairus and his entire family believed in Christ. They thanked Him for His great kindness in bringing the daughter back to life. They served Him the rest of their lives. Jesus has been very good to us too. What can we do to thank Him? (Show a picture of the miracle.)

C. Organization

1. Why did Jesus bring Jairus' daughter back to life?
2. Did Jairus really believe that Jesus could help his daughter?
3. How did Jairus and his family thank Jesus?
4. What should we remember to do after Jesus answers our prayers?
5. What does this miracle prove about Jesus?

D. Virtues and Practices

1. Pray for people who are ill, and try to visit them.
2. Send get-well cards to people who are ill.
3. Pray for the dying.
4. Thank God for answering your prayers.

IV. SUGGESTED LEARNING ACTIVITIES

A. Pantomime the story.
B. Illustrate the part liked best.
C. Discuss the picture of this story.
D. Poem: "The Daughter of Jairus," Moran, *Verses for Tiny Tots*, p. 63.

V. TEACHER REFERENCES

A. Sr. Mary, *et al.*, *The Catholic Mother's Helper*, pp. 112–113.
B. Dennerle, *Leading the Little Ones to Christ*, pp. 159–160.
C. Fitzpatrick, *Religion in Life Curriculum, Second Grade Manual*, pp. 61–62.

LESSON 79

I. SUBJECT MATTER

The Raising to Life of the Widow's Son

II. OBJECTIVES

A. To develop a knowledge of the power of God over life and death.

B. To stimulate the desire to imitate Jesus in His compassion for the sorrowful and needy.

III. SUGGESTED PROCEDURE

A. Approach

Do you know what a widow is? Our story today is about a widow whose only son had died.

B. Presentation

1. The Power of Jesus Over Life and Death

We know that Jesus is God. He has absolute power over all the world, over life and death. He is the Supreme Lord and Master, the Creator of heaven and earth, the Source of our life and happiness.

2. Jesus' Compassion for People

A poor widow had lost her only son. She was heartbroken, for her boy had been a good child and was her only support. The people pleaded with Jesus to help the poor woman. Jesus saw her in the funeral procession weeping. He stopped the procession and asked the widow why she was crying. Our Lord felt sorry for the poor widow and immediately stretched out His hand and told the young man to arise. Then Jesus gave the boy back to his mother. Do you think the mother was happy? (Show picture of miracle.)

3. Jesus' Example for Us

Jesus wants us to be kind and merciful just as He is. Many people we know have troubles that bring them sorrow. Can you think of ways to help them? to make them happier?

C. Organization

1. What did Jesus prove when He brought the young man back to life?
2. Why did Jesus work this wonderful miracle?
3. How can we help people who are sad or in trouble?

D. Virtues and Practices

1. Extend sympathy to others in time of sorrow.
2. Pray for people who are sad or lonely.
3. Help others who are in need.

IV. SUGGESTED LEARNING ACTIVITIES

A. Dramatize or pantomime the story.
B. Illustrate the story for a booklet.
C. Poem: "The Son of the Widow of Naim," Moran, *Verses for Tiny Tots,* p. 60.

V. TEACHER REFERENCES

A. Sr. Mary, *et al., The Catholic Mother's Helper,* pp. 111–112.
B. Dennerle, *Leading the Little Ones to Christ,* pp. 160–161.
C. Fitzpatrick, *Religion in Life Curriculum, Second Grade Manual,* pp. 63–64.

LESSON 80

I. SUBJECT MATTER

Raising of Lazarus

II. OBJECTIVES

A. To develop a knowledge of the love of Jesus for those who believe in Him.
B. To develop an attitude of kindness toward those who are more gifted than we are.
C. To love our friends as Jesus did.

III. SUGGESTED PROCEDURE

A. Approach

When Jesus lived on earth many people were very kind to Him and He did not forget their kindness. This is a story about Lazarus and his sisters, Martha and Mary, who were especially kind to Jesus.

B. Presentation

1. The Illness and Death of Lazarus

Lazarus, a special friend of Jesus, was the brother of Martha and Mary. These two women were among the best friends of Jesus. They did all they could to help Jesus and the Apostles, and their brother Lazarus was always happy to be of help. One day Lazarus fell sick.

Shortly afterward he died and was buried. Mary and Martha were very sad and lonely without Lazarus.

2. Jesus' Love for Lazarus and His Friends

When Jesus learned that Lazarus had died, He was also sad. Lazarus had been His friend, and Jesus knew that his death would bring great sorrow to Martha and Mary. He hurried to their home and then went out to Lazarus' grave. Lazarus had already been in the tomb several days, but Jesus ordered the men to roll the stone away. They obeyed, and, with a loud voice, Jesus called Lazarus back to life. What a wonderful miracle this was! Because there were so many people present, and because Lazarus had been dead for some days, this miracle caused many to believe in Christ. It proved once more that Jesus was the Son of God. (Show the picture of the miracle.)

3. The Jealousy of Jesus' Enemies

Some of those who were at this miracle refused to believe their eyes. They were jealous of Jesus and claimed that He used trickery and the help of the devil to perform these wonders. From this day on they looked for a chance to put Jesus to death.

4. Our Attitude Toward Those More Gifted Than Ourselves

Jesus doesn't want us to be jealous of others. He loves us and has given us many wonderful talents. He has given other boys and girls different talents, but He doesn't want any of us to be envious of others. He gives all of us the help we need to get to heaven, and He wants us to love everyone on earth for His sake. One way to show Jesus that we are grateful for all the good things He does for us is to be friendly with our neighbors.

C. Organization

1. Why was Jesus so sad when He heard about the illness of Lazarus?
2. Who were Martha, Mary, and Lazarus?
3. Did Martha and Mary believe that Jesus could help Lazarus?
4. Why did Jesus bring Lazarus back to life again?
5. How did some wicked people feel about this great miracle of Jesus?

D. Virtues and Practices

1. Love those who are kind to you.
2. Hope in your own resurrection.
3. Rejoice in the good done by others.

IV. SUGGESTED LEARNING ACTIVITIES

A. Children retell the story of Lazarus to the class.
B. Pantomime the story.
C. Illustrate the story for a slide show.

V. TEACHER REFERENCES

A. Dennerle, *Leading the Little Ones to Christ.* pp. 160–165.
B. Fitzpatrick, *Religion in Life Curriculum, Second Grade Manual,* pp. 67–68.

LESSON 81

I. SUBJECT MATTER

Cure of the Man Born Blind

II. OBJECTIVES

A. To know that Jesus, because He is God, has power over the body of man.
B. To instill in the children deep reverence toward Jesus because of His power and goodness to mankind.

III. SUGGESTED PROCEDURE

A. Approach

Close your eyes. Can you see anything? Did you ever stop to think what it must be like never to see the beautiful sky, grass, or flowers? Today's story is about a man who was born blind.

B. Presentation

1. The Story of the Man Born Blind

One day Jesus saw a group of Pharisees and others gathered around a blind man. The things they were saying were not very kind. They said the man was blind because he was a sinner. Some said his parents must have been sinners. They looked down upon him because they thought that he was not as good as they were.

The blind man heard Jesus coming and called out to him to have mercy on him. This man had great faith and Jesus rewarded him by curing him of his blindness. Jesus told him to go to a certain pool and bathe his eyes. When he did as Jesus had told him, he could see. Try to picture in your mind how this man felt when he was able to see again. Even after seeing this miracle, some of the enemies of Jesus refused to believe. They pretended that the man had never been blind in the first place. (Show picture of this miracle.)

2. The Cause of Sickness

We know that sickness and death entered the world with Adam's sin. Sickness and death are a punishment on the whole human race for original sin. This does not mean, however, that those who are sick or who suffer are sinners or less good than those of us who have good health. Jesus wanted to show us, in this miracle, that God allows suffering in order to give us some better gift. He gave the blind man the gift of faith and then, miraculously, restored his sight.

3. Our Sight — a Gift of God

Our sight, our hearing, our understanding — all are gifts of God. A special gift we have is the gift of faith — spiritual sight. How thankful we should be to Jesus and His heavenly Father for these precious gifts.

C. Organization

1. How long had the man been blind?
2. Was this man's blindness a punishment for his sins?
3. Could clever doctors make the man see?
4. What is a miracle?
5. Why did Jesus cure the blind man?
6. How did Jesus work this miracle?
7. What other gift did the blind man receive?
8. Why does God sometimes ask good people to suffer?

D. Virtues and Practices

1. Thank God for the gift of sight by using your eyes properly.
2. Do acts of kindness for the afflicted.
3. Suffer willingly for God.

IV. SUGGESTED LEARNING ACTIVITIES

A. Discuss a picture of the miracle.

B. Dramatize the miracle.

C. Discuss proper use and care of the eyes.

D. Poem: "Jesus Heals the Blind Beggar," Moran, *Verses for Tiny Tots*, p. 69.

V. TEACHER REFERENCE

Dennerle, *Leading the Little Ones to Christ*, pp. 126–130.

LESSON 82

I. SUBJECT MATTER

The Cure of the Ten Lepers

II. OBJECTIVES

A. To know that because Jesus is God, He can cure us of every illness, physical and spiritual.

B. To foster an attitude of gratitude to God for His blessings.

III. SUGGESTED PROCEDURE

A. Approach

When someone gives you a present or does a kind deed for you, what should you say? This story is about a group of people who didn't say "Thank You" to Jesus.

B. Presentation

1. Story of the Ten Lepers

Do you know what leprosy is? It is a terrible disease that rots the skin and bones. Many people in our Lord's country had it. There was no one to take care of them because everyone was afraid to catch the disease. They had to go away to live in hills and caves. Many Jews thought leprosy was a punishment for the sins the victim had committed. One day Jesus saw a group of lepers — a name given to these poor people. They asked Jesus to cure them and, in His mercy, He did. He then sent them to a pool to bathe. Only one of the ten returned to thank Him. He said to the one leper, "Were not ten made clean? Where are the other nine?"

2. *We Can Become Sick Both in Body and Soul*

We very often become ill. We get chicken pox, measles, and all kinds of diseases. Worst of all, we commit sins and become spiritually sick or, if we commit very big sins, even lose our spiritual life. Jesus is always ready to bring us back to health. He wants us to be healthy both in body and in soul. If we do get sick and are restored to health, let's be like the one leper who came back to thank Jesus.

C. Organization

1. How many lepers were there?
2. What did they say to Jesus?
3. What did Jesus tell them to do?
4. Were all the lepers cured?
5. What did one man do when he saw that he was cured?
6. Did Jesus expect the lepers to thank Him?
7. Does Jesus expect us to say, "Thank You"?
8. Why do we call sin a leprosy?
9. How is it cured?

D. Virtues and Practices

1. Believe in the power of God.
2. Pray for God's help.
3. Pray together in the home.
4. Thank God for favors received.
5. Say "Thank you" to others.

IV. SUGGESTED LEARNING ACTIVITIES

A. Discuss the picture of the miracle.
B. Compare the forgiveness of sins by the priest with the cleansing of the lepers by Jesus.

V. TEACHER REFERENCE

Sister Mary, *et al., The Catholic Mother's Helper*, pp. 119–120.

LESSON 83

I. SUBJECT MATTER

Cure of the Man at the Pool of Bethsaida

II. OBJECTIVES

A. Knowledge that God knows our needs but wants us to express them.

B. To foster an attitude of patience in time of suffering.

III. SUGGESTED PROCEDURE

A. Approach

Did you ever wait a long time for something you wanted very much? Our story today is about a poor man who waited many years for something he wanted.

B. Presentation

1. *The Man at the Pool of Bethsaida*

The Jews at the time of Christ believed that an angel of God came from time to time and entered the Pool of Bethsaida. The first sick person who entered the pool after the water stirred would be cured from his disease or handicap. The man in our story was paralyzed and could not help himself. He had been lying next to the pool for many years waiting for someone to lift him into the water after the angel's visit. One day Jesus came along and saw the paralytic. He had mercy on the poor man and healed him. He then told him to pick up his bed and walk. (Explain that the "bed" was just a mat.) (Show picture of the miracle.)

2. *The Jews' Anger With Christ*

Jesus worked this miracle on the Sabbath, the day of rest. Many of the Jews, shutting their eyes to our Lord's power and mercy, were angry with Him. They claimed that He broke the Sabbath and dishonored God by working miracles. Jesus told them that the Sabbath or day of rest was meant to help men, not hurt them, and that it was God's will for us to do good on the day set aside for His worship.

C. Organization

1. Where was the sick man?
2. Who saw him there?
3. Did Jesus know how long the sick man had been suffering?
4. What did Jesus tell the man to do?
5. What day was it?

6. Who did not like what Jesus did? Why?

D. Virtues and Practices

1. Practice patience in time of suffering.
2. Help anyone in need.
3. Pray for the crippled and unfortunate.

IV. SUGGESTED LEARNING ACTIVITIES

A. Discuss legitimate work on Sundays.
B. Dramatize the story.

V. TEACHER REFERENCE

Daily Missal — Ember Friday in Lent.

LESSON 84

I. SUBJECT MATTER

Feast of the Purification — February 2

II. OBJECTIVES

A. To give the children some understanding of the meaning of the feast.
B. To foster the imitation of Mary in her obedience to lawful authority.

III. SUGGESTED PROCEDURE

A. Approach

(Show a picture of the Presentation.) Whom do you see in this picture? Where are they? Would you like to know what Mary and Joseph are doing?

B. Presentation

1. The Presentation of Jesus and the Purification of Mary

It was a custom among the Jews to take their young children to the temple to "present" them to God — to offer them to the service of the Lord. Ordinarily, this was done when the mother went to the

171

temple to be "purified" — blessed after having a baby. It really wasn't necessary for Jesus to be "presented" to God, for, after all, He was God and had come from God. It wasn't necessary for Mary to be "purified" after having the Baby Jesus, for she was purified in having Him. Jesus and Mary wanted to give us an example. They wanted to show us how we should give ourselves to God and how we should ask Him for His blessings.

In the picture you noticed an old man. (Present picture again.) His name was Simeon. All his life he had prayed that he would not die until he had seen the Messias. The minute he took Jesus into his arms he knew he was holding the Saviour of the world and now he could die in peace. While he was holding Jesus, he told Mary that a "sword" would pierce her heart. Did he mean a real sword? What do you think Simeon meant?

2. Candlemas Day

On this feast the Church blesses the candles for use in the church during the coming year. It is also on this day that the Church blesses the candles we use in our homes. Do any of you know why we should have blessed candles in our home? Have you ever seen them used?

C. Organization

1. Why did Mary take Jesus to the temple?
2. How old was He?
3. Who was Simeon?
4. Who told Simeon Mary's Baby was God?
5. What did Simeon tell Mary about Jesus?
6. Why do we call Jesus the "Light of the World"?
7. What does the priest bless on this day?
8. Can you tell some times when we use blessed candles?

D. Virtues and Practices

1. Do not think you are better than other children.
2. Obey those who take care of you.
3. Use blessed candles with faith.

IV. SUGGESTED LEARNING ACTIVITIES

A. Discuss the picture of the Presentation.
B. Story: "Ruth's Blessed Candles," *Their Hearts Are His Garden*, pp. 124–125.
C. Poem: "Candles," *Sing a Song of Holy Things*, p. 44.

V

TEACHER REFERENCES

A. Sister Marguerite, *Their Hearts Are His Garden*, pp. 125–126.
B. Fitzpatrick, *Religion in Life Curriculum, First Grade Manual*, pp. 66–68.
C. S.N.D., *Religious Teaching of Young Children*, pp. 30–31.
D. Dennerle, *Leading the Little Ones to Christ*, pp. 103–109.

LESSON 85

I. SUBJECT MATTER

Feast of St. Blaise — February 3

II. OBJECTIVES

A. To celebrate the feast in the proper manner.
B. To foster the proper use of sacramentals.

III. SUGGESTED PROCEDURE

A. Approach

Did you ever have your throats blessed? This is the story of St. Blaise, on whose feast day you have your throats blessed.

B. Presentation

1. Story of St. Blaise

St. Blaise was a bishop in the early Church. He was a very good man and a father-bishop over his flock. In all his actions he imitated our heavenly Father, and he cared for the people in his diocese just as our bishop does. He looked after their health of body and soul. We are told that one day a boy was on the point of death because some food lodged in his throat. Bishop Blaise prayed for the lad and his throat was cleared. Because of this, St. Blaise is the patron who especially protects us from illnesses or injuries of the throat.

2. The Blessing of Throats

On the feast of St. Blaise, the Church likes to give us her blessing. We can go to church and have our throats blessed by the priest. This shows us how much the Church, which Jesus founded, loves us and how well she takes care of us. Because she is like a loving mother, we call the Church "our holy Mother Church."

3. We Must Take Care of Ourselves

We may pray for good health, but we must do something about keeping healthy. Carelessness on our part will not help even though we pray. (Discuss briefly our responsibility in practicing good health rules.)

C. Organization

1. Who is St. Blaise?
2. What did St. Blaise do for the little boy in the story?
3. Who helped St. Blaise do this?
4. When the priest blesses our throats what does he ask St. Blaise to do for us?
5. Does God expect us to take proper care of our health?

D. Virtues and Practices

1. Pray for the sick.
2. Use sacramentals of the Church properly.

IV. SUGGESTED LEARNING ACTIVITIES

A. Story: "The Family Have Their Throats Blessed," *Their Hearts Are His Garden*, pp. 126–127.
B. Practice getting throats blessed.

V. TEACHER REFERENCE

Sister Marguerite, *Their Hearts Are His Garden*, pp. 128–129.

LESSON 86

I. SUBJECT MATTER

Feast of Our Lady of Lourdes — February 11

II. OBJECTIVES

A. To acquaint the children with the story of Our Lady of Lourdes.
B. To foster devotion to Mary under this title.

III. SUGGESTED PROCEDURE

A. Approach

Do you think Mother Mary loves little children? Why?

B. Presentation

1. The Story of Bernadette

There was once a little girl named Bernadette who lived in a small town in France. She was a poor little girl, but she loved the Blessed Virgin very much. One day, while she was out in the woods, Mary appeared to her. How Mary must have loved that little girl! After that first appearance, crowds of people would follow Bernadette to that spot to see if she was telling the truth. Of course, they couldn't see the Blessed Virgin, so some didn't believe her. There were many who did believe in her, however. For those who didn't, Bernadette asked Mary to give them a sign. On one of the visits Mary told the little girl to kneel down and scoop out some dirt from the ground. Bernadette obeyed and a spring of water gushed forth! That same water is still flowing in that same place today. Many sick persons, who bathed in the spring, were cured that day. A grotto was built on the exact spot where Mary had stood and also a great big church called a basilica. The town in which these are built is called Lourdes.

2. Mary Reveals Her Immaculate Conception

During one of her appearances, Mary told Bernadette that she was the Immaculate Conception. She told her to pray and to ask others to pray. At that time many people were trying to deny that the Blessed Virgin had been free from original sin her entire life, and by calling herself the Immaculate Conception, Mary wanted to show us that she really had been free from all stain of sin from the first moment of her life.

3. The Miracles at Lourdes

Soon wonderful cures were given to people who prayed to the Blessed Virgin at the shrine in Lourdes. Many people who didn't believe in God were converted by the miracles worked there, and today the marvelous cures the Blessed Virgin gives to those who visit her shrine strengthen our faith and help us turn our minds to God.

C. Organization

1. Tell the story of Bernadette in your own words.

2. Why do you think our Lady appeared to a little child?
3. What are some of the miracles that have taken place at this shrine?
4. What message did Mary give Bernadette?

D. Virtues and Practices

1. Pray with simplicity and love.
2. Believe as Bernadette did.
3. Foster special devotion to our Lady.

IV. SUGGESTED LEARNING ACTIVITIES

A. Dramatize the story of Lourdes.
B. Story: "Meet Bernadette," Sister Marguerite, *Their Hearts Are His Garden*, pp. 67–70.

V. TEACHER REFERENCE

Sister Marguerite, *Their Hearts Are His Garden*, pp. 70–71.

LESSON 87

I. SUBJECT MATTER

Feast of St. Valentine — February 14

II. OBJECTIVES

A. To acquaint the children with the origin of Valentine's Day.
B. To develop a love for our neighbor.

III. SUGGESTED PROCEDURE

A. Approach

A good friend will let his friends know that he loves him. He will try his best to do something that would make him happy. St. Valentine did exactly that.

B. Presentation

1. Story of St. Valentine

St. Valentine, a very holy priest, lived a long time ago. He was very kind to the people especially to those who were poor and sad. By means of kind and cheery notes, notes telling about God's goodness to them, he made many people happy.

He sent messages of love and cheer even though he was very busy. Father Valentine urged his people to greet one another in Christ's name at all times. He encouraged them, especially by his good example, to be kind to each other.

Father Valentine was cast into prison by those who did not believe in God. Even then he managed to send his cheery notes to his people. He knew that Jesus was Love Itself and that Christian love was the greatest love of all.

Father Valentine was martyred for love of God. (Explain term "martyr.") Now he is a saint in heaven sharing God's happiness for all the kindness he has shown to others for the love of God.

2. *We Imitate St. Valentine*

It is a custom now to send valentines on the feast of this martyr. We should try to remember the spirit of the saint and recall that he wanted us to love all men for Jesus' sake. We should never give valentines that will hurt or make someone sad.

Guide the children toward a better way of honoring the saint, by remembering the missions, the sick or poor thus encouraging a work of mercy for the love of Christ.

C. Organization

1. Who was St. Valentine?
2. What did he do?
3. What do we do on St. Valentine's Day?
4. Why do we send valentines?

D. Virtues and Practices

1. Be kind and loving to all, as St. Valentine was.
2. Be gentle with others.
3. Show your love by acts and not just by words.

IV. SUGGESTED LEARNING ACTIVITIES

A. Send valentines to those who won't receive any.
B. Send only valentines that express love and kindness — not those that will hurt someone.

V. TEACHER REFERENCES

A. *Practical Aids for the Catholic Teacher*, pp. 212–213.
B. Sister Marguerite, *Their Hearts Are His Garden*, pp. 65–67.

UNIT SEVEN

The Greatest Proof of Jesus' Love —
His Passion and Death
Time: 5 weeks

I. INTRODUCTION FOR THE TEACHER

Unit Seven brings home to the child the infinite love of Jesus for him — a love so great that Jesus was willing to die on the cross to open heaven for him. The events of Holy Week are studied in simple detail. Special emphasis is placed on a simple method of making the "Way of the Cross."

II. OBJECTIVES OF THE UNIT

A. To develop the knowledge of the meaning of Lent, and to lead the pupils to a proper observance of this holy season.

B. To develop the knowledge of the infinite love of Christ for us, as shown by His passion and death.

C. To acquaint the child with the events of the passion through studying and making the "Way of the Cross."

D. To develop the knowledge of the great love Jesus manifested for us in the institution of the Holy Eucharist.

E. To foster a deep appreciation of Christ's love.

F. To develop the habit of returning love for love through prayer and little sacrifices.

G. To instill the desire to show gratitude by avoiding whatever displeases Jesus.

H. Teach the articles of the Apostles' Creed. "Suffered under Pontius Pilate, was crucified, died and was buried. He descended into hell."

III. SUBJECT MATTER

A. Meaning of Lent

B. Triumphal entry into Jerusalem

C. Holy Thursday
   1. Washing the Apostles' feet
   2. Institution of the Holy Eucharist

3. The Agony in the Garden
4. Our Lord's arrest and suffering
D. Good Friday
1. Our Lord's trial
2. The Way of the Cross
E. Holy Saturday
F. Liturgical feasts
1. St. Patrick — March 17
2. St. Joseph — March 19

LESSON 88

I. SUBJECT MATTER

Meaning of Lent — Ash Wednesday

II. OBJECTIVES

A. To develop a knowledge of the meaning of Lent and to lead the pupils to a proper observance of this holy season.
B. To foster an appreciation of Christ's love.

III. SUGGESTED PROCEDURE

A. Approach

Do you know what a sacrifice is? It's an offering to someone of an act that we do not like to do. In that act we usually give up something we like or we do some little thing that we find hard to do. The Church has a special season during which we will have many chances to perform these sacrifices.

B. Presentation

1. The Meaning of Lent

You know that Jesus became man to die for our sins and win heaven for us. He loved us dearly, even suffering great torments for us and dying on the cross to show us His love. During the time of Lent, which is that special season, we try to join our sufferings with Christ. We make little sacrifices of our own in order to become more like Him. We want to rejoice with Him and all the angels and saints on Easter, the day of His resurrection. The best way to get ready for that wonderful feast is by making a good Lent.

2. *The Meaning of Ash Wednesday*

Ash Wednesday is the first day of Lent. That is the day the priest puts ashes on our foreheads and reminds us that some day we must die. He reminds us of death, because we are supposed to use our life in order to get ready for death. When we die, we will meet Jesus, who will either welcome us into His heavenly Father's home or will send us away to hell.

The priest gets these ashes by burning the palms from last year's Palm Sunday.

3. *We Can Do Something During Lent*

We, too, can do something special during Lent. We want to go to heaven, so we must learn to do things that are hard, for love of Jesus. We can become more pleasing to God if we can say extra prayers, give up something we like, do something we do not like to do, obey quickly and willingly, say our prayers.

Can you tell what we could practice during Lent?

Guide the children in selecting an appropriate Lenten practice. Lead them toward making the sacrifice a secret with Jesus. Each morning during the religion lesson encourage the children to have a secret talk with Jesus telling Him about the Lenten practice they decided on and how it's progressing.

C. Organization

1. What does the season of Lent mean for us?
2. What takes place on Ash Wednesday?
3. Where does the priest get the ashes?
4. Explain the meaning of the words the priest uses when he blesses us with the ashes.
5. What are some of the things we can do during Lent?

D. Virtues and Practices

1. Make Lenten sacrifices in reparation for our sins.
2. Do little hard things just because you love Jesus.
3. Be mission-minded during Lent.

IV. SUGGESTED LEARNING ACTIVITIES

A. Discuss sacrifices which could be made during Lent.

B. Compose one-sentence prayers telling Jesus what we want to do for Him during Lent.

C. Ejaculation: "We adore Thee, O Christ, and we bless Thee, because by Thy Holy Cross Thou hast redeemed the world" (*Raccolta*, 197).

V. TEACHER REFERENCES

A. S.N.D., *Religious Teaching of Young Children*, pp. 138–139.
B. Sister Marguerite, *Their Hearts Are His Garden*, pp. 142–143.

LESSON 89

I. SUBJECT MATTER

Triumphal Entry Into Jerusalem — Second Passion (Palm) Sunday

II. OBJECTIVES

A. To acquaint the children with the events of this Sunday.
B. To instill in the children a deep sorrow for Christ's suffering.

III. SUGGESTED PROCEDURE

A. Approach

When the President comes to our city all the people are excited. They try to show that they like him and admire him by having a parade in his honor. Today I will tell you about a parade that Jesus' friends had for him when He came to Jerusalem for the last time.

B. Presentation

1. Jesus Arrives in Jerusalem

The Jews in Jerusalem had heard of the wonderful miracles Jesus had worked. They wanted to see this Person who had made a dead man come to life again. They thought He would be a great king who would conquer the world for them and make them a great people. To honor Him as a king they waved palm branches and threw their cloaks on the ground before Him. (Show picture and discuss.)

Jesus was truly a king, but His kingdom was not the kind the Jews were expecting. His kingdom would be in the hearts of men. Jesus cried when He saw that the Jews did not understand what He wanted to do for them.

2. Our Celebration of Palm Sunday

Every year we have a procession on Palm Sunday to honor Jesus as the King of our hearts. The priest blesses palms for us to carry and to keep in our homes to show Him that we want Him to be our King.

3. Holy Week

Palm Sunday was the beginning of the last week of Jesus' life. He had waited and waited for this week to come when He would at last do the great work that God the Father had sent Him to do. That is why this week is called Holy Week.

C. Organization

1. What happened on the first Palm Sunday?
2. What does the priest do on Palm Sunday now?
3. Why should we have a blessed palm in our home?
4. Why is this particular week called Holy Week?

D. Virtues and Practices

1. Rejoice with others who are happy.
2. Use blessed palms reverently.

IV. SUGGESTED LEARNING ACTIVITIES

A. Discuss the attitude of the Jewish priests and the fickleness of the Jewish people.
B. Make little crosses out of blessed palms.
C. Picture study of Christ's entry into Jerusalem.

V. TEACHER REFERENCES

A. S.N.D., *Religious Teaching of Young Children*, pp. 55–56.
B. Dennerle, *Leading the Little Ones to Christ*, pp. 177–181.

LESSON 90

I. SUBJECT MATTER

The Last Supper — Holy Thursday

II. OBJECTIVES

A. To acquaint the children with the events of the Last Supper.

B. To foster the virtue of humility.

III. SUGGESTED PROCEDURE

A. Approach

Suppose you were moving to another city, what are some of the things you would do before leaving? Perhaps some of your neighbors would even have a little good-by party for you. And maybe you would give your little friends a gift so that they would not forget you. When it was time for Jesus to go away, He called His Apostles together to say good-by to them. He gave them a special gift so that they would always remember Him.

B. Presentation

Story of the Last Supper

It was the night before Christ's death. Our Lord wanted to leave His disciples and us a parting gift, the gift of His love. He wanted to teach us that we should love one another just as He loves us. Since He knew that actions speak louder than words, He humbly went about washing the feet of His Apostles. (Discuss our Lord's conversation with Peter.) He did this to show us how much we should respect our neighbors — that is, all men — and how we should imitate His humility. He then spoke to His Apostles, telling them of His great love for all men and of His great love for His heavenly Father. He told them that He and God the Father wanted all men to be united in love. He promised the Holy Spirit, the Spirit of Love, who would come to help us be like Christ and join our hearts in love. (Discuss briefly the sad feeling that overcame Jesus when He thought of Judas and his plan to sell Jesus to the Jews.)

C. Organization

1. Why did our Lord have the Last Supper with the Apostles?
2. Why did He wash their feet?
3. What happened to Peter?
4. How did Judas become such a bad Apostle?
5. Did Jesus know Judas would betray Him?

D. Virtues and Practices

1. Do little tasks that are unpleasant to keep from becoming proud.

183

2. Be kind and helpful toward one another.
3. Be loyal to Christ to make up for Judas' disloyalty.

IV. SUGGESTED LEARNING ACTIVITIES

A. Study the picture of the Last Supper and tell the story of Jesus washing the feet of the Apostles.
B. Discuss little unpleasant things we can do because we want to imitate Jesus.
C. Ejaculation: "O Sacrament most holy, etc." (*Raccolta*, 136).

V. TEACHER REFERENCES

A. Dennerle, *Leading the Little Ones to Christ*, pp. 184–186.
B. S.N.D., *Religious Teaching of Young Children*, pp. 57–59.
C. Sister Mary, *et al.*, *The Catholic Mother's Helper*, pp. 122–124.

LESSON 91 (This lesson may take more than one day.)

I. SUBJECT MATTER

Institution of the Holy Eucharist

II. OBJECTIVES

A. To develop knowledge of the great love of Jesus for us manifested in the institution of the Holy Eucharist.
B. To foster a deep love for the Blessed Sacrament.

III. SUGGESTED PROCEDURE

A. Approach

Recall the events of Jesus' humble washing of the Apostles' feet on Holy Thursday. Jesus did this in preparation for a far more important thing He was to do on the same night.

B. Presentation

1. The Institution of the Eucharist

Before Jesus would die on the cross He wanted to give us a special gift. He wanted to give us Himself, His Body and His Blood. So, at that Last Supper, Jesus took bread into His holy hands, blessed it and said "This is My Body." At once this bread became Jesus' Body. Then Jesus took a cup of wine blessed it and said "This is My Blood." At once the wine became Jesus' precious Blood. Jesus gave His Body and His Blood to the Apostles. They were the first people to receive Holy Communion.

Jesus also said "Do this in My memory." He gave the Apostles the power to do what He did, to change bread into Jesus' sacred Body and to change wine into His precious Blood. The Apostles were made Jesus' first priests. The priests have the power to say Mass and to change bread and wine into Jesus' Body and Blood.

2. Holy Thursday — a Great Day

Holy Thursday is a great day for us. Jesus loved us so much that He wanted to continue to stay with us. So He gave us Himself in the Blessed Sacrament. (Explain — Blessed Sacrament.)

He wanted us to receive Him into our hearts. So He gave the Apostles the power to change bread and wine into His Body and Blood during Holy Mass. Won't it be wonderful when you will go to Holy Communion and receive Jesus into your heart! (Review form of Spiritual Communion.)

C. Organization

1. When was the first Mass offered?
2. Who offered the first Mass?
3. What did Jesus do for the Apostles?
4. Who offers Mass today?
5. When did priests receive the power to offer Mass?
6. What takes place at the Consecration of the Mass?
7. What did our Lord tell the Apostles in His farewell talk?

D. Virtues and Practices

1. Make special visits to church on Holy Thursday to thank Jesus for this great gift of Himself.
2. Be good in church when you make a visit.
3. Assist well at Holy Mass.

IV. SUGGESTED LEARNING ACTIVITIES

A. Tell why Jesus instituted this great sacrament of His love.
B. Explain how to make a Spiritual Communion.

C. Recall proper behavior during the Consecration of the Mass.
D. Make up original prayers for a visit to the Blessed Sacrament.
E. Ejaculation: "My Lord and my God" (*Raccolta*, 133).
F. Filmstrip: "The Mass for Young Children."
G. Story: "Holy Thursday," Sr. Marguerite, *Their Hearts Are His Garden*, pp. 145–146.

V. TEACHER REFERENCES

A. Dennerle, *Leading the Little Ones to Christ*, p. 185.
B. S.N.D., *Religious Teaching of Young Children*, pp. 160–162.
C. Sr. Marguerite, *Their Hearts Are His Garden*, pp. 143–145.

LESSON 92

I. SUBJECT MATTER

The Agony in the Garden

II. OBJECTIVES

A. To know that Jesus suffered for all the sins of all people.
B. To appreciate Jesus' all-embracing love.

III. SUGGESTED PROCEDURE

A. Approach

After our Lord had eaten His Last Supper with His Apostles, He went to a nearby garden, called the Garden of Olives. Jesus was very sad as He entered the garden. Do you know why?

B. Presentation

1. The Agony in the Garden

Jesus went into the Garden of Olives to pray. He took Peter, James, and John with Him. You remember Jesus was true God and true man. As a man, He feared to suffer and die. But He knew that it was God's will that He suffer in order to save us from sin.

When He thought of the terrible death He would die, He became very sad. He asked His Father to spare Him this suffering if possible, but He added, "not my will but yours be done." He was so sad and so heartbroken that all this made Him sweat blood. This was a terrible suffering.

2. Cause of Christ's Suffering

Do you know what made Jesus suffer so much? It was the sins that people commit, the sins that you commit. If Adam had not sinned, if we would be all good, then Jesus would not have had to sweat blood. If we are tempted to do something wrong, think of Jesus in the Garden of Olives.

Would you want to hurt Him?

Jesus didn't want to suffer. But He knew that His heavenly Father wanted Him to die for us. It wasn't easy for Jesus to die for us, but He obeyed, because He loved His Father and He loved us.

He prayed for strength, He wants us to pray too. He asked Peter, James, and John to pray with Him, but they fell asleep. Will you fall asleep or will you pray with Jesus?

C. Organization

1. Where did Jesus go after the Last Supper?
2. What was Jesus' first great suffering?
3. What did Jesus tell Peter, James, and John to do?
4. Did Jesus know all the bad things we would do?
5. Did He know all the pain He would have to suffer?
6. Did He know that many people would never love Him?
7. What happened to Jesus when He became very sad?
8. What did the Apostles do that made Jesus feel sad?
9. Whom did God the Father send to comfort Jesus?
10. Did Jesus want to do what God the Father wanted?
11. What should we think of when something sad happens to us?

D. Virtues and Practices

1. Be sorry because you make Jesus suffer whenever you sin.
2. Thank Jesus for suffering for you.
3. Comfort Jesus by making someone happy.
4. Resign yourself to the will of God in time of suffering.
5. Do nice things to someone who has hurt you.

IV. SUGGESTED LEARNING ACTIVITIES

A. Discuss the cause of Jesus suffering — our sins.
B. Make up original prayers of contrition.

C. Poem: "The Agony in the Garden," Belger, *Sing a Song of Holy Things*, p. 57.

V. TEACHER REFERENCES

A. Dennerle, *Leading the Little Ones to Christ*, pp. 186–188.
B. S.N.D., *Religious Teaching of Young Children*, pp. 60–62.

LESSON 93

I. SUBJECT MATTER

Our Lord's Arrest and Suffering

II. OBJECTIVES

A. To realize that because of His great love for us, Jesus suffered so much to make up for our sins.
B. To love Jesus more and more, because He suffered so much for us.

III. SUGGESTED PROCEDURE

A. Approach

If a child who is a stranger is unkind to you, it makes you feel sad. But, if one of your favorite friends is mean to you, that hurts you even more. Today we shall find out that one of the Apostles hurt Jesus very much.

B. Presentation

1. Judas Arrives With Soldiers

Judas, one of Jesus' own Apostles, now did something very bad. He betrayed Jesus to His enemies in exchange for a few pieces of money. He went to Jesus' enemies and told them he would lead them to Jesus if they would pay him something. They gladly made the bargain with Judas and sent soldiers out to find Christ. Judas even told them how to recognize Jesus. He told them that they should

188

capture the one he would kiss. Just think, a kiss, the sign of love, was used to betray Jesus!

2. Peter's Rashness

When the soldiers came Peter wanted to fight. He drew a sword and cut off the ear of one of the mob with Judas. But Jesus had told us that He did not want us to use violence. He wants us to be peaceful, to have love, not hate, for others. He told Peter to put his sword away, and then, merciful always, He healed the ear of the wounded man. Even in agony Jesus put others first. Don't you want to be as unselfish and generous as Jesus?

3. The Loneliness and Suffering of Jesus

Peter and the other Apostles, His chosen friends, all left Jesus. He was hit by the soldiers and made fun of. They mocked Him, spat upon Him, and beat Him. But Jesus did not get angry. He prayed for those who hurt Him and offered His suffering for us. When you are unjustly treated, think of Jesus. He will give you the strength to carry your sorrow and the grace to forgive your enemies.

C. Organization
1. Who brought the soldiers to the garden?
2. How did Judas let the soldiers know who Jesus was?
3. What did Jesus say to Judas?
4. Would Jesus have forgiven Judas if he had been sorry?
5. What did Jesus say to the soldiers?
6. What happened when Jesus answered the soldiers?
7. What did Peter do?
8. What did Jesus do for the wounded soldier?
9. What did the Apostles do when Jesus was arrested?
10. What would you do if you had been there?

D. Virtues and Practices
1. Try not to hurt the feelings of others.
2. Pray in time of temptation.
3. Be sincere in your expressions of love.

IV. SUGGESTED LEARNING ACTIVITIES

A. Discuss the power of Jesus over His enemies.
B. Tell why the Apostles abandoned Jesus.

C. Discuss the insincerity of Judas and how we should mean what we say to Jesus and others.
D. Compose original prayers of love and compassion.
E. Poem: "My Jesus, Mercy!" Belger, *Sing a Song of Holy Things*, p. 56.

V. TEACHER REFERENCES

A. S.N.D., *Religious Teaching of Young Children*, pp. 60–62.
B. Dennerle, *Leading the Little Ones to Christ*, pp. 188–193.

LESSON 94

I. SUBJECT MATTER

A. Our Lord's Trial Before Annas and Caiphas
B. Denial and Repentance of Peter

II. OBJECTIVES

A. To learn about the unfair trial of Jesus and His patience with His accusers.
B. To realize the necessity of prayer in time of temptation.

III. SUGGESTED PROCEDURE

A. Approach

A real friend is one who will be loyal and "stick up for you" even if you are in trouble. Some of our Lord's friends failed Him when He needed them most of all.

B. Presentation

1. Trial Before Annas and Caiphas

Jesus was led a prisoner before the High Priests Annas and Caiphas. They tried to trap Him, accusing Him of saying false things and of being blasphemous. Jesus kept quiet until asked to speak, and when He spoke He told them that He was truly the Son of God. Because of this, they condemned Him to death.

2. Denial and Repentance of Peter

Peter, the Apostle who always said he would be faithful to Jesus, was very much a coward during Jesus' trial. When he was asked if he knew Jesus, Peter denied ever knowing our Lord. He denied Jesus three times. Then Jesus looked at him, a cock crowed, and Peter left. Outside he wept bitterly because of his cowardice and weakness. From that time on he was a faithful follower of Jesus. He remained true to his Lord, finally dying for Him.

3. Despair of Judas

Judas too, grieved because of his terrible crime. But, unlike Peter, he did not have trust in the mercy and kindness of Jesus. He lost all hope and went out and hanged himself. Whom do you want to follow, Judas or Peter?

C. Organization

1. Had Jesus done anything wrong?
2. Did Jesus say that He is really God?
3. Did the high priests believe Him?
4. What did they say should happen to Jesus?
5. Did the people tell the truth about Jesus?
6. What wrong did Peter do?
7. Was Peter sorry later?
8. Did our Lord forgive Peter?
9. Was Judas sorry for his sin?
10. Did Judas ask Jesus to forgive him?

D. Virtues and Practices

1. Love God and have confidence that He will forgive you.
2. Tell the truth even if you are punished for it.
3. Pray in time of temptation.

IV. SUGGESTED LEARNING ACTIVITIES

A. Contrast the repentance of Peter with the despair of Judas.
B. Discuss how we are dependent upon God's help and not on our own strength in time of temptation.
C. Make up original prayers of sorrow for sin and a firm purpose of amendment.
D. Poem: "My Turn," Belger, *Sing a Song of Holy Things*, p. 58.

V. TEACHER REFERENCES

A. S.N.D., *Religious Teaching of Young Children*, p. 63.
B. Dennerle, *Leading the Little Ones to Christ*, pp. 194–196.

LESSON 95

I. SUBJECT MATTER

Good Friday Morning — Continuation of Our Lord's Trial

II. OBJECTIVES

A. To increase our knowledge of the infinite love of Christ as shown by His suffering.

B. To foster a deeper appreciation of Christ's love.

III. SUGGESTED PROCEDURE

A. Approach

When a prisoner is on trial, the judge must do everything he can to see that it is fair and that the prisoner does not have to suffer more than is necessary. Jesus' trial before Pilate was unfair.

B. Presentation

1. Jesus Before Pilate

The Jews were under Roman rule. Because of this, they could not put a man to death. Thus they sent Jesus to Pilate, the Roman governor, so that he could sentence Him to death. Pilate did not think that Jesus should be killed. He knew that Jesus was not guilty of any crime. But the people were wild and wanted Jesus to die. Pilate was a weak man, and in his fear of the people finally decided to allow an innocent Jesus to suffer the terrible death of crucifixion.

2. Jesus Before Herod

Pilate sent Jesus to Herod, the Jewish leader. This Herod was a relative of the Herod who murdered the Holy Innocents. He was really a man who made fun of religion, even the Jewish religion. He wanted to see Jesus so that he could make fun of Him. He mocked Jesus and had his soldiers hit Him, but all the time Jesus was silent, praying to His Father.

3. The Scourging and Crowning of Thorns

When Jesus returned to Pilate, the Roman governor turned Him over to the soldiers. They put a purple cloak on Him, because purple was the sign of a king and they wanted to make fun of Jesus for saying

192

He was a king. Then they put a crown of thorns on His head and beat the thorns into His head with heavy sticks. How it must have hurt Jesus. Jesus let the soldiers treat His body so cruelly to make up for our sins of impurity.

C. Organization

1. Where was our Lord taken early Friday morning?
2. Did Pilate think Jesus was a bad man?
3. Where did Pilate send Jesus for more questioning?
4. Did Herod send Jesus back to Pilate? Why?
5. Why did Pilate tell the soldiers to scourge Jesus?
6. Why did Jesus receive a crown of thorns?
7. Why did Jesus suffer the terrible pains of the scourging and crowning with thorns?

D. Virtues and Practices

1. Console Jesus by your good life and by detesting sin.
2. Be pure in thought and word and deed.
3. Compose original prayers for purity in thought, word, and act.
4. Wear modest clothing.
5. Offer your little pains to Jesus.
6. Give up little things you like for Jesus.

IV. SUGGESTED LEARNING ACTIVITIES

A. Discuss the sufferings of Jesus to atone for our sins of impurity.
B. Discuss modesty of dress in children.
C. Picture study of Jesus suffering.
D. Asking Jesus to forgive us for causing His sufferings by our sins.

V. TEACHER REFERENCES

A. Dennerle, *Leading the Little Ones to Christ*, pp. 196–199.
B. S.N.D., *Religious Teaching of Young Children*, pp. 63–66.
C. Schumacher, *I Teach Catechism*, Vol. I, pp. 79–80.

LESSON 96

I. SUBJECT MATTER

First Station: Jesus Is Told He Must Die

II. OBJECTIVES

A. To develop a love and compassion for the suffering Jesus.
B. To develop habits of resignation to the will of God as manifested in daily trials.
C. To teach the article of the Apostles' Creed: "Suffered under Pontius Pilate."

III. SUGGESTED PROCEDURE

A. Approach

If someone is called a coward, perhaps it is because that person is afraid to do the right thing. The judge to whom Jesus was brought was a very cowardly man.

B. Presentation

1. Pilate's Cowardice in Sparing Barabbas Instead of Jesus

You remember that Pilate did not like condemning Jesus to death. At that time of the year it was the custom of the Roman governor to release any prisoner the Jews wanted released. Pilate thought that perhaps he might persuade the people to ask for Jesus' release. But the people told him to release a wicked murderer Barabbas instead. Pilate knew that Barabbas was a criminal and he also knew that Jesus was innocent. But still he feared the people. Finally, washing his hands of the whole matter, he set Barabbas free and sent Jesus off to His death. But Pilate could not really wash his hands. He was the one in charge, and he was the one who finally sentenced Jesus to death. (Show picture of the first Station.)

2. Patience and Resignation of Jesus

During all this time Jesus kept silent, praying. He spoke only when Pilate asked Him a direct question. He did not shout and scream, He did not cry, but instead suffered everything for us. What a loving Master, to take all that abuse to show His love for men!

3. Our Patience and Resignation

Jesus wants us to take our crosses too and follow Him. There are many times when we are unjustly accused of something and when we have to suffer. We can bear these trials if we think of Jesus and ask Him for His help.

4. Teach the article of the Apostles' Creed
   "Suffered under Pontius Pilate."

C. Organization

1. Who was Barabbas?
2. Why did the people choose Barabbas instead of Jesus?
3. How did the people make Pontius Pilate say that Jesus must die?
4. What should we do when someone is chosen instead of us?
5. How did Jesus act when He was told that He must die?
6. What can we do when we are blamed for something we did not do?

D. Virtues and Practices

1. Do not show hurt feelings when others are preferred to you.
2. Bear little trials patiently.
3. Do not excuse yourself when you are blamed for something.

IV. SUGGESTED LEARNING ACTIVITIES

A. Study a picture of the first Station.
B. Compose and chart an original prayer for the first Station.
C. Discuss daily activities in which the children can practice patience for the love of Jesus.
D. Poem: "Jesus is Ordered to Die," Belger, *Sing a Song of Holy Things,* p. 61.

V. TEACHER REFERENCES (These will be the same for all Stations).

A. S.N.D., *Religious Teaching of Young Children,* pp. 67–71, 139–142.
B. Religious of the Cenacle — *Stations of the Cross for Children* pp. 139–141.
C. Dennerle, *Leading the Little Ones to Christ,* pp. 199–212.
D. Sister Mary, *et al., The Catholic Mother's Helper,* pp. 120–126.

LESSON 97

I. SUBJECT MATTER

Second Station: Jesus Takes His Cross

II. OBJECTIVES

A. To increase the children's knowledge of our Lord's Passion.
B. To stimulate the children to keep away from sin, which is the cause of Jesus' suffering.

III. SUGGESTED PROCEDURE

A. Approach

It is not easy for your father to work hard every day so that he could buy the things you need, but he does it willingly because he loves you. Jesus loves us and He, too, was anxious and willing to suffer many cruel things so that we could go to heaven. (Show picture of the second Station.)

B. Presentation

1. Jesus Accepts the Cross

Jesus was innocent of any crime, yet He took the cross for us. He knew that He was going to die a terrible death, yet He loved His Father so much that He willingly carried His cross in order to redeem us.

2. Why Jesus' Cross Was Heavy

Jesus' cross was terribly hard to carry. It weighed down on Him and hurt the sores caused by the terrible scourging. The reason Jesus' cross was so heavy was that it represented the sins of men. Our own sins made up the cross, and it was our sins which crushed the back of Jesus.

3. What We Should Do

If we love Jesus, we will try to make His cross lighter by keeping away from sin. Instead, we will try to help Him by carrying a part of it ourselves. We can, if we accept the sorrows we meet in life for love of Jesus. Don't you want to be good and help Jesus? Can you think of ways of carrying the cross?

C. Organization

1. How did Jesus act when the cross was placed upon His shoulder?
2. Why was He glad to carry the cross?
3. What should we do to make up for our sins?
4. Why should we try not to commit sin?

196

D. Virtues and Practices

1. Bear our daily crosses willingly.
2. Try to make Jesus' cross lighter by not committing sin.

IV. SUGGESTED LEARNING ACTIVITIES

A. Discuss daily annoyances that we can put up with, to imitate Jesus.
B. Study the picture of the second Station.
C. Compose and chart a prayer to be said at the second Station.
D. Poem: "Jesus Takes His Cross," Belger, *Sing a Song of Holy Things*, p. 62.

LESSON 98

I. SUBJECT MATTER

Third Station: Jesus Falls the First Time

II. OBJECTIVES

A. To develop a knowledge that Jesus suffered as man.
B. To instill habits of perseverance in trying to do what is right.

III. SUGGESTED PROCEDURE

A. Approach

Is it easy for you to do good *all* the time? Perhaps if you listen to the little story I have to tell you today, you will *never* stop *trying* to be good even when it is hard. (Show picture of the third Station.)

B. Presentation

1. Christ Falls Under the Cross

You know why the cross was so terribly heavy that it forced Jesus to the ground, don't you? Think of how greatly Jesus loves us! Our sins hurt Him and cause Him great pain, but He still loves us and does everything to help us overcome sins and win heaven.

2. The Cruelty of the Soldiers

When Jesus fell to the ground under the cross, the soldiers whipped Him with their lashes and kicked Him. How much that must have hurt

Jesus, for He was already in great pain. When you are tempted to sin, think of how wicked it is to kick a man when he is down. That is just what you do when you sin. You are kicking the fallen Jesus.

3. We Should Rise From Sin

Although He was terribly hurt and in great pain, Jesus bravely rose from the ground, took up His cross, and continued on His way. When we sin, we fall to the ground too. Jesus wanted to give us an example of courage and perseverance. He wanted us to keep on *trying*. Can we follow Him and do only the things He wants us to do?

C. Organization
1. Why did Jesus fall when He was carrying the cross?
2. Could Jesus have kept from falling if He wanted to?
3. Why did Jesus want to suffer so much?
4. What did Jesus want to teach us to do after we fall into sin?
5. Was Jesus angry at the soldiers for hurting Him?
6. How does Jesus want us to act toward people who hurt us?

D. Virtues and Practices
1. Pray for perseverance in trying to be good.
2. Forgive those who hurt you.
3. Be sorry for the suffering of Jesus.
4. Do something good for someone you do not like, for Jesus' sake.

IV. SUGGESTED LEARNING ACTIVITIES

A. Discussion of how we should react to people who are unkind to us.
B. Study the picture of the third Station.
C. Compose and chart an original prayer.
D. Poem: "Jesus Falls the First Time," Belger, *Sing a Song of Holy Things*, p. 63.

LESSON 99

I. SUBJECT MATTER

Fourth Station: Jesus Meets His Mother

II. OBJECTIVES

A. To develop a knowledge of the sufferings of Mary during the passion of Jesus.

B. To encourage the children to keep away from sin, which also caused Mary to suffer.

III. SUGGESTED PROCEDURE

A. Approach

When you are very sick, who stays near you and takes care of you? Why does your mother do all this? Mother Mary saw her Son suffer but she couldn't help Him. (Show picture of fourth Station.)

B. Presentation

1. The Sorrow of Mary

Any mother hates to see her son suffer, especially if her son is innocent of any crime. Mary was the best mother ever, and her Son was the best Son ever, for He was God. Mary knew that Jesus was innocent and that He was suffering all this agony for us. She suffered with Him, and, like her Son, she wants to help us.

2. The Comfort Mary Brought to Jesus

The road to Calvary was very lonely for Jesus. It would have been even lonelier if Mary had not been there with Him. She was Jesus' true friend, who stayed with Him all the time. She could not do anything to help Jesus, but just by being there she gave Him some comfort. Jesus would like us to accompany Him on the road to Calvary too.

3. We Can Comfort Jesus

The best way we can help Jesus is to be like Him and like His mother. Mary was sinless and never hurt God. If we stay away from sin, and if we quickly tell Jesus we are sorry if we ever do hurt Him by sin, we will be giving Him comfort and courage.

C. Organization

1. How did Mary feel when she met Jesus carrying His cross?
2. Were the soldiers very kind to Mary?
3. How did Jesus feel when He met His Blessed Mother on the road to Calvary?
4. How can we make Jesus and Mary happy?

D. Virtues and Practices

1. Pray to Our Lady of Sorrows.
2. Do what your parents wish *before* they ask you to obey.
3. Make your parents happy by showing respect and obedience.

IV. SUGGESTED LEARNING ACTIVITIES

A. Discuss how we can bring joy to the hearts of our parents, especially in time of sorrow and trouble.
B. Study the picture of the fourth Station.
C. Compose and chart an original prayer.
D. Poem: "Jesus Meets His Mother," Belger, *Sing a Song of Holy Things*, p. 64.

LESSON 100

I. SUBJECT MATTER

Fifth Station: Simon Helps Jesus Carry His Cross

II. OBJECTIVES

A. To increase in knowledge of the events of Christ's passion.
B. To develop a desire to be kind to others for the love of the suffering Jesus.

III. SUGGESTED PROCEDURE

A. Approach

When your mother is carrying something heavy, don't you run to help her? Jesus' cross was very heavy, but the soldiers wouldn't let anyone help Him.

B. Presentation

1. The Weakness of Jesus

By now our Saviour was terribly weak. He had lost a great amount of blood and His entire body ached from the wounds He had received. He could barely move. Yet He was struggling on, for He knew that His heavenly Father willed that He suffer death on Calvary for our sins. (Show picture of fifth Station.)

2. Simon Is Forced to Help Jesus

The soldiers were now afraid that Jesus might not make it to Calvary. They therefore forced Simon, a man from Cyrene, to help Jesus carry the cross. At first Simon was unwilling to help our Lord, but one glance from Jesus told him how much Jesus was suffering and how much He would appreciate any help. Because he helped to carry the cross, Simon received the gift of faith and became one of Jesus' followers.

3. How We Can Help

We can, like Simon, help Jesus carry His cross. We can help Him by taking the little crosses He sends us. We can be good and uncomplaining. If we are hurt or suffer something, we can offer this to God and forgive all those who hurt us.

C. Organization

1. Why did the soldiers force Simon to help Jesus carry His cross?
2. Why didn't Simon want to help Jesus at first?
3. What made Simon happy to help Jesus?
4. How can we help Jesus carry the cross?

D. Virtues and Practices

1. Show kindness to others for the love of Jesus.
2. Be a cheerful giver by offering to help others before you are asked to do so.

IV. SUGGESTED LEARNING ACTIVITIES

A. Discuss the daily acts of kindness we can perform for others.
B. Study the picture and discuss.
C. Compose and chart an original prayer for the fifth Station.
D. Poem: "Simon Helps Jesus Carry His Cross," Belger, *Sing a Song of Holy Things*, p. 65.

LESSON 101

I. SUBJECT MATTER

Sixth Station: Veronica Wipes the Face of Jesus

II. OBJECTIVES

A. To develop the knowledge of the infinite love of Christ as shown by His Passion.

B. To promote a desire to return love for love through our sacrifices.

III. SUGGESTED PROCEDURE

A. Approach

On the road to Calvary one good woman did a very brave act of kindness for Jesus.

B. Presentation

1. Jesus, a Man of Sorrows

With Simon's help Jesus continued on His way to Calvary. By this time He was extremely exhausted. His body was covered with wounds and sores. His feet were torn and cut. Blood from the wounds in His head flowed down His face. Sin had done its work; it had made the God-Man physically weak and utterly exhausted. (Show picture of sixth Station.)

2. Veronica's Kind Deed

A good woman named Veronica then did a very kind thing for Jesus. Touched with pity, she took a cloth and wiped the blood from His poor face. To reward her for her good deed, Jesus left a picture of Himself in the cloth. How Veronica must have treasured this.

3. Ways We Can Imitate Veronica

Can you think of any ways we can imitate Veronica's kindness? We too can help our suffering Jesus. We can soothe Him in His sorrows by wiping away the sins that keep us from Him. We can be kind and good and grateful.

C. Organization

1. How did Jesus' face look while carrying the cross?
2. Did anyone feel sorry for Jesus?
3. What did Veronica do?
4. Was she afraid of the soldiers?
5. How did Jesus feel after Veronica did this kind deed?
6. How did Jesus show His thanks for the act of kindness?

202

D. Virtues and Practices

1. Be helpful at home, especially when your parents are tired.
2. Do something kind to someone at home, and in school today.

IV. SUGGESTED LEARNING ACTIVITIES

A. Discuss ways in which we can show that we are good Catholic children.
B. Picture study of the sixth Station.
C. Compose and chart an original prayer.
D. Poem: "Veronica Wipes the Face of Jesus," Belger, *Sing a Song of Holy Things*, p. 66.

LESSON 102

I. SUBJECT MATTER

Seventh Station: Jesus Falls the Second Time

II. OBJECTIVES

A. To develop the knowledge of Christ's love for us as shown by His suffering.
B. To instill a desire of showing our love by prayers and sacrifices.

III. SUGGESTED PROCEDURE

A. Approach

Did you ever fall in the school yard or on the street? Of course you did — many times. Did it hurt? Jesus fell a second time on the way to Calvary. (Show picture of seventh Station.)

B. Presentation

1. Jesus Very Weak and Tired

Even though Simon and Veronica tried to help Jesus, He was now completely worn out. You know how tired you are after a long day. Just think of how worn out Jesus must have been. He had suffered the agony in the Garden; the soldiers had scourged Him with their whips and had pierced His head with the crown of thorns. He had been carrying the cross a long time over a rough road, and the soldiers had been beating Him all the time. It is no wonder that He fell to the ground again.

2. *Why Jesus Fell Again*

Jesus fell again because our sins are so terrible. Even after Jesus forgives us, we go out and sin again. These terrible sins of ours are the real reason why Jesus had to suffer so much; they are the blows that forced Him to the ground a second time.

3. *We Must Rise From Sin*

Jesus gave us an example all His life. He now got up again and continued on His journey, because He wanted to teach us that, no matter how often we fall into sin, we should rise again. When we sin, we should go at once to Jesus to ask Him for forgiveness. We should then do all we can to keep away from sin.

C. Organization

1. Why did Jesus fall the second time?
2. Was this fall harder than the first one?
3. Did anyone help Jesus get up?
4. What did the soldiers do?
5. What can we do to help Jesus today?

D. Virtues and Practices

1. Have pity on those who are suffering.
2. Do not complain when unable to do something — try again.

IV. SUGGESTED LEARNING ACTIVITIES

A. Discuss how we can keep praying and trying to do what God wants.
B. Picture study of the seventh Station.
C. Compose and chart an original prayer.
D. Poem: "Jesus Falls the Second Time," Belger, *Sing a Song of Holy Things*, p. 67.

LESSON 103

I. SUBJECT MATTER

Eighth Station: Jesus Speaks to the Holy Women

II. OBJECTIVES

A. To develop an appreciation of and gratitude for the love of Jesus as manifested in His suffering.

B. To foster a keen desire of imitating Jesus' virtue of kindness.

III. SUGGESTED PROCEDURE

A. Approach

Many of the people who followed Jesus to His crucifixion were His friends. They were sorrowful because they knew Jesus was innocent and should not have to suffer this way. (Show picture of eighth Station.)

B. Presentation

1. The Women

Jesus continued His way to Calvary. A group of women were crying along the road, because they were grieved to see someone suffer as much as Jesus was suffering.

2. What Jesus Told the Women

Jesus was grateful to these holy women. But He wanted to let them know the chief cause for His suffering. He told them not to weep for Him, but for themselves and for their sins. He was God, and He chose to suffer to save us. But He wants us to root out the cause of His suffering — our sins, the only things that can keep us from Him and keep us out of heaven.

3. What Jesus Wants Us to Do

Jesus wants us to weep for our sins by doing penance for them. He wants us to stay close to Him. He died for us, but His death will have been in vain if we refuse to follow Him, if we prefer our own sins to Him. What will you choose — Jesus or sin?

C. Organization

1. Who felt sorry for Jesus carrying the heavy cross?
2. What were the women doing?
3. Why were they crying?
4. What did Jesus tell the weeping women?
5. What does Jesus want us to do?

D. Virtues and Practices

1. Be truly sorry for sin.
2. Speak kindly to others.
3. Do not talk unnecessarily in school.

IV. SUGGESTED LEARNING ACTIVITIES

A. Discuss how we can encourage others to be good, especially by our good example.
B. Picture study of the eighth Station.
C. Compose and chart an original prayer.
D. Poem: "Jesus Comforts the Women," Belger, *Sing a Song of Holy Things,* p. 68.

LESSON 104

I. SUBJECT MATTER

Ninth Station: Jesus Falls the Third Time

II. OBJECTIVES

A. To become acquainted with the incidents of the Way of the Cross.
B. To foster a desire of returning love for love by our sacrifices and prayers.

III. SUGGESTED PROCEDURE

A. Approach

(Show picture of ninth Station.) Look what happened to Jesus again. How many times did He fall before this? Why did He fall so often?

B. Presentation

1. Jesus Falls the Third Time

Once more Jesus falls to the ground. This shows us how horrible our sins are and how terrible we are when we keep on sinning. For our sins are the real reasons why Jesus had to suffer and why He fell three times on His way to Calvary.

2. *Jesus' Example*

Jesus got up still a third time. He did this to show us that we must be brave and strong. We must rise each time we fall into sin. He will give us His hand to help us. When He stretches out His arm to lift us from sin, will we refuse?

C. Organization

1. What happened to Jesus now?
2. Why did Jesus fall again?
3. Did the soldiers help Jesus get up?
4. How can we help Jesus?

D. Virtues and Practices

1. Persevere in doing your work well.
2. Avoid discouragement.

IV. SUGGESTED LEARNING ACTIVITIES

A. Discuss ways in which we can comfort the suffering Jesus.
B. Picture study of the ninth Station.
C. Compose and chart an original prayer.
D. Poem: "Jesus Falls the Third Time," Belger, *Sing a Song of Holy Things*, p. 69.

LESSON 105

I. SUBJECT MATTER

Tenth Station: Jesus Is Stripped of His Garments

II. OBJECTIVES

A. To develop a deep appreciation of Christ's love for us as shown by His Passion.
B. To foster a desire of imitating Jesus' virtues.

III. SUGGESTED PROCEDURE

A. Approach

When you have a cut on your finger you usually put a bandage on it. What happened when you tried to take the bandage off? That's what happened to Jesus when they pulled His garments off. The soldiers did this cruel act at the end of Jesus' sorrowful journey. (Show picture of Tenth Station.)

B. Presentation

1. Jesus Reaches Mount Calvary

At last Jesus comes to the end of the sorrowful road. He has reached the hill where He will be crucified. He has just about finished the work His heavenly Father gave Him.

2. Jesus Is Stripped of His Garments

The soldiers then pull the clothes off Jesus' body. When they do, they rip off the scabs that had begun to form over the wounds in Jesus' poor sides. Those wounds were reopened and began to bleed again. How much this must have hurt Jesus. But He suffered it all for us.

C. Organization

1. Where did Jesus finally come?
2. What was to happen there?
3. What did the soldiers do to Jesus?
4. How did Jesus feel?
5. For whom was Jesus suffering this shame?

D. Virtues and Practices

1. Dress modestly.
2. Give up little pleasures.
3. Be pure in thought, word, and deed.
4. Be willing to give up what keeps us from Jesus, and Jesus from us.

IV. SUGGESTED LEARNING ACTIVITIES

A. Picture study of the tenth Station.
B. Compose and chart an original prayer.
C. Poem: "Jesus Is Stripped of His Garments," Belger, *Sing a Song of Holy Things*, p. 70.

LESSON 106

I. SUBJECT MATTER

Eleventh Station: Jesus Is Nailed to the Cross

II. OBJECTIVES

A. To further the knowledge that Jesus suffered for our sins.

B. To foster an attitude of sympathy for Jesus and a desire to make up to Him.

III. SUGGESTED PROCEDURE

A. Approach

Did you ever prick your finger with a pin? It hurts, doesn't it? Can you imagine how the nails must have hurt Jesus? Look at this picture. What do you see? (Show picture of eleventh Station.)

B. Presentation

1. Jesus Is Nailed to the Cross

The soldiers are very rough. They stretch out Jesus' arms and legs and drive nails through His hands and feet. What terrible agony that must have been for Jesus. You know how much it hurts when you stick your finger with a pin or needle. Think of how much the nails must have hurt your Jesus.

2. Jesus' Forgiveness

Jesus was kind and forgiving all His life, even when He lay dying. He did not curse the soldiers or us, but instead asked His heavenly Father to forgive us our sins. We are the ones who made Jesus suffer; we crucify Jesus each time we commit a big sin and we hurt Him every time we do anything bad. But Jesus still loves us and wants to forgive us. All He asks of us is for us to be good. Is this too much to ask?

C. Organization

1. Where is Jesus now?
2. What are the men going to do to Him?
3. Why did Jesus suffer this pain?
4. Were any of Jesus' friends with Him? Who?
5. Could they do anything to help Him?
6. What can we do to make up to Jesus?

D. Virtues and Practices

1. Be patient in suffering any pain.
2. Be grateful to Jesus for suffering for you.

3. Obey your parents and teachers.
4. Forgive those who injure us.

IV. SUGGESTED LEARNING ACTIVITIES

A. Retell the suffering of Jesus to someone at home.
B. Discuss the picture of the station.
C. Compose and chart an original prayer.
D. Poem: "Jesus Is Nailed to the Cross," Belger, *Sing a Song of Holy Things*, p. 71.

LESSON 107

I. SUBJECT MATTER

Twelfth Station: Jesus Dies on the Cross

II. OBJECTIVES

A. To further the knowledge that Jesus died for our sins.
B. To foster a hatred of sin.
C. To foster a spirit of forgiveness.

III. SUGGESTED PROCEDURE

A. Approach

How much do you love your father and mother? Show us with your arms. (Allow children to extend their arms.) Show picture of twelfth Station. This picture shows how much Jesus loves each one of us.

B. Presentation

1. Jesus on the Cross

For three long hours Jesus was on the cross. People cursed Him, spat on Him, and mocked Him all that time. Even one of the criminals hanging next to Him cursed Him. But Jesus did not complain. He suffered all in silence, speaking only a few times, and then only to ask His Father to forgive us or to say something kind and thoughtful. He loved all men — think of it, all men — even to the point of dying for them on the cross.

2. *Jesus' Words to Mary*

Once Jesus spoke to Mary His mother and to St. John the Apostle. He asked John to take care of His mother and He asked Mary to take care of John and of all of us. How thoughtful Jesus was. Even while dying He gives us a present — His own mother.

3. *Jesus Dies*

Finally the moment comes when Jesus offers His life for us. He tells His Father that His work is finished, and He dies, offering Himself as a victim for sins to God the Father. Jesus has finished the work of Redemption. Will we let Jesus come to us so that He can give us the merits of His death, or will we prefer sinful, selfish lives?

C. Organization

1. How long did Jesus suffer on the cross?
2. Whom was Jesus thinking about when He was suffering?
3. What did Jesus say about His enemies?
4. What did He say to the good thief?
5. What did He say to Mary? To St. John?
6. What frightened the enemies of Jesus?
7. What happened at three o'clock on Good Friday?
8. Why do we call this day Good Friday?
9. What do we do every Friday to make up for Jesus' suffering?

D. Virtues and Practices

1. Kiss the crucifix with devotion.
2. Forgive those who offend you.
3. Thank God for suffering for you.

IV. SUGGESTED LEARNING ACTIVITIES

A. Discuss the picture of the twelfth Station.
B. Compose and chart an original prayer.
C. Discuss the liturgy on Good Friday — organ, bells, empty tabernacle.
D. Poems: "Jesus Dies on the Cross," Belger, *Sing a Song of Holy Things*, p. 72; "Jesus Dying on the Cross," Schumacher, *I Teach Catechism*, Vol. I, p. 82.
E. Stories: "Good Friday," Sister Marguerite, *Their Hearts Are His Garden*, pp. 146–147; "The Good Thief," Sister Mary, *et al.*, *The Catholic Mother's Helper*, pp. 127–128; "Mary, Our Mother," *ibid.*, p. 128.

LESSON 108

I. SUBJECT MATTER

Thirteenth Station: Jesus Is Taken Down From the Cross

II. OBJECTIVES

A. To know that Jesus by His suffering and death fulfilled the promise of God to mankind.

B. To foster devotion to our Sorrowful Mother.

III. SUGGESTED PROCEDURE

A. Approach

A man named Joseph of Arimathea went to Pilate and asked if he could bury Jesus in his own newly cut tomb. Permission given, Joseph and some of his friends went back to Calvary to take Jesus down from the cross. (Show picture of thirteenth Station.)

B. Presentation

1. Jesus Is Taken Down From the Cross

Mary and Jesus' friends then take the body of our crucified Redeemer down from the cross. You can imagine how much care they took of His body. How they must have touched it tenderly and lovingly. They could see the terrible wounds in His hands and feet and side. They could see how much sin had hurt Him.

2. Sorrow of Mary

As Mary, the Mother of God, held the body of her Son, she must have been terribly sad. She had never sinned, but she knew how terrible sin must be to cause such torment. But she was not angry at us for our sins. Like Jesus, she forgave us and wants to help us. She knew that Jesus loves us and that He died to save us, and she is ready to help us go to Him. Ask her for her help. She will never refuse.

C. Organization

1. Who took the body of Jesus down from the cross?
2. To whom did they give Jesus?
3. How did they prepare the body of Jesus for burial?
4. How did Mother Mary feel when she saw Jesus' body?

D. Virtues and Practices

1. Tell Mary that you are sorry she had to suffer.
2. Pray for those who are in sorrow.
3. Give comfort to those in sorrow.

IV. SUGGESTED LEARNING ACTIVITIES

A. Make a visit to the church on Good Friday to adore the Cross.
B. Study and discuss the picture of the Station.
C. Compose and chart an original prayer.
D. Poem: "Jesus Is Taken Down From the Cross," Belger, *Sing a Song of Holy Things*, p. 73.

LESSON 109

I. SUBJECT MATTER

Fourteenth Station: Jesus Is Buried

II. OBJECTIVES

A. To further the knowledge of the events of Holy Week.
B. To foster the habit of returning love for love through prayer and sacrifice.
C. To teach the article of the Apostles' Creed: "Was crucified, died and was buried."

III. SUGGESTED PROCEDURE

A. Approach

After Jesus died, who do you suppose was there to take care of His dead body? (Show picture of fourteenth Station.)

B. Presentation

1. Mary and the Holy Women Prepare Jesus for Burial

Mary and the holy women who had followed Jesus now took His body. With tender love they made it ready for burial. How tenderly they must have handled His sacred body. What thoughts must have passed through their minds as they recalled His kindness and goodness and the terrible suffering He accepted for our sins.

2. *Jesus Is Buried*

Finally Mary and others put Jesus' body in a tomb. The tomb is not His own; He had no place to rest His head either in life or in death. He even had to borrow a tomb from a friend. Won't you open your hearts to Jesus, to give Him a place to rest? He will bless you very much if you do.

3. *Teach the Article of the Apostles' Creed*

"Was crucified, died and was buried."

C. Organization

1. Who prepared the body of Jesus for burial?
2. Where was Jesus buried?
3. How long did Jesus tell His enemies He would remain in the grave?
4. Did the Jews believe Him?

D. Virtues and Practices

1. Tell Jesus you believe in Him.
2. Take your sorrows to Mary.
3. Love to make the "Way of the Cross."

IV. SUGGESTED LEARNING ACTIVITIES

A. Discuss the picture.
B. Compose and chart original prayer.
C. Visit the church and make the "Stations of the Cross."
D. Poem: "Jesus Is Laid in the Tomb," Belger, *Sing a Song of Holy Things*, p. 74.

LESSON 110

I. SUBJECT MATTER

Holy Saturday

II. OBJECTIVES

A. To review the events of Holy Saturday.
B. To instill in the children a love for Jesus, hatred for sin, and a desire to live a holy life.

214

C. To teach the article of the Apostles' Creed: "He descended into hell."

III. SUGGESTED PROCEDURE

A. Approach

The Jews never wanted to believe the things Jesus promised He would do. After He was buried, the Jews began to worry that one of His big promises might come true.

B. Presentation

1. "I Will Rise Again"

Jesus was dead. He had been placed in a tomb. But the story of Jesus is not finished. For He had promised His disciples that He would rise from the dead. He claimed to be God, and to prove that He was He would rise from the tomb.

2. The Guards at the Tomb

Because Jesus had promised to rise from the dead, the Jews asked Pilate to station guards in front of the tomb. They did not want to take any chances. They did not want Jesus' followers to steal His body and then claim that He had risen from the dead.

3. He Descended Into Hell

While His body lay in the tomb, Jesus' soul went to Limbo. There the good men who had lived during all the time between Adam and Jesus were waiting for Him. They could not enter into heaven until Jesus rose from the dead. How happy they must have been to see Jesus, for they knew that He had died for their sins and that soon He would lead them into heaven.

4. How the Church Celebrates Holy Saturday

Holy Saturday is a great feast in the Church. On this day the Church welcomes new members by giving them the sacrament of Baptism. She recalls the death of Jesus and His victory over sin. The long season of Lent, the time of penance, is about to end and the glorious time of Easter is about to begin. For the Church knows that on Holy Saturday night Jesus fulfilled His great promise. He arose from the dead and showed men that He is truly God.

5. Teach the article of the Apostles' Creed

"He descended into hell" (Limbo).

C. Organization

1. What did Jesus tell the people before He died?
2. Did the Jews believe Him?
3. What did the Jews do?
4. Where was the body of Jesus all day Holy Saturday?
5. Where was His soul?
6. Who were waiting in Limbo for Jesus? Can you name some of these people?
7. What made them very happy?

D. Virtues and Practices

1. Be good so you can be with Jesus someday.
2. Hate sin because it alone can keep you from being with Jesus.

IV. SUGGESTED LEARNING ACTIVITIES

A. Dramatize the meeting of Jesus and St. Joseph in Limbo.
B. Discuss liturgy of Easter Vigil.

V. TEACHER REFERENCES

A. Sister Mary, *et al., The Catholic Mother's Helper*, p. 129.
B. *Daily Missal* — Holy Saturday.

LESSON 111

I. SUBJECT MATTER

Feast of St. Patrick — March 17

II. OBJECTIVES

A. To acquaint the children with the story of this great saint.
B. To foster perseverance in prayer.

III. SUGGESTED PROCEDURE

A. Approach

When you see a picture of a saint on a holy card, it looks as though he did nothing but pray to God all day. But there is another side of that saint's life that we sometimes forget. The saints spent most of their time working for God.

B. Presentation

1. Story of St. Patrick

When he was a little boy, Patrick was kidnaped by some pirates. They sold him as a slave to some pagans in Ireland, where he stayed for several years. Finally, he escaped from Ireland and went to Rome. There he became a priest and later on a bishop. He remembered the good traits of the Irish people and was on fire with the desire to bring them to Christ. He returned to Ireland, now a bishop, and went from one end of the little isle to the other, preaching Jesus. The people heard Patrick's words and were touched by God's grace. By the time Patrick died, almost all of Ireland was Catholic.

2. How We Can Imitate Patrick

We can imitate Patrick by learning more about our faith, by praying for those who do not have this precious gift, and by helping the missionary priests and Sisters.

C. Organization

1. What happened to Patrick after he was kidnaped?
2. Did he stop praying when he was sold as a slave?
3. How did he escape from Ireland?
4. What did he do then?
5. Why did he come back to Ireland?
6. Why does Ireland honor him as their great saint?

D. Virtues and Practices

1. Persevere in prayer.
2. Give good example to non-Catholics.
3. Pray every day to know your vocation.

IV. SUGGESTED LEARNING ACTIVITIES

A. Dramatize scenes from the life of St. Patrick.
B. Recording: "Story of St. Patrick," *Catholic Children's Record Club.*

V. TEACHER REFERENCE

Aurelia-Kirsch, *Practical Aids for Catholic Teachers*, pp. 213–214.

LESSON 112

I. SUBJECT MATTER

The Feast of St. Joseph — March 19

II. OBJECTIVES

A. To increase in love for St. Joseph, and to strive to imitate his virtues.

B. To appreciate more and more St. Joseph's place in our own lives and in the life of the Church.

III. SUGGESTED PROCEDURE

A. Approach

Who is the head of this family? (Show a picture of Holy Family.) Because St. Joseph is such a great saint, the Catholic Church celebrates a special feast day in his honor.

B. Presentation

1. Joseph the Head of the Holy Family

Review the story of St. Joseph giving good leads pertinent to his life. (See Lesson 61, p. 129.)

2. The Greatness of St. Joseph

Joseph is one of the greatest of God's saints. He is foster father of Jesus, the protector of the Holy Family. He is the patron of God's family on earth today, the Catholic Church. He is also the special patron of fathers and workingmen because he worked hard to support Jesus and Mary and he knows what a big job fathers have.

3. St. Joseph, Patron of a Happy Death

How fortunate Joseph was. He had a very happy death, for he died in the arms of Jesus and Mary. For this reason, he is the patron of a happy death. He wants us to die happily, that is, die with God living in us. Let us pray to St. Joseph for a happy death and he will do all he can to help us.

C. Organization

1. Why was St. Joseph chosen to take care of Jesus and Mary?
2. Tell some of the things St. Joseph did for Jesus and Mary.

218

3. Why do some parents name their children in honor of St. Joseph?
4. Why do we call St. Joseph, Patron of Happy Death?
5. Why do we call St. Joseph the Protector of the Catholic Church?

D. Virtues and Practices

1. Ask St. Joseph to help your father in his work.
2. Pray to St. Joseph every day asking him for a happy death.

IV. SUGGESTED LEARNING ACTIVITIES

A. Dramatize incidents from the life of St. Joseph.
B. Prayer: "Jesus, Mary, and Joseph, I give you my heart and my soul" (*Raccolta*, 636).

V. TEACHER REFERENCES

A. Schumacher, *I Teach Catechism*, Vol. I, p. 125.
B. Aurelia-Kirsch, *Practical Aids for Catholic Teachers*, pp. 215–216.
C. Fitzpatrick, *Religion in Life Curriculum, First Grade Manual*, pp. 38–39.

UNIT EIGHT

The Resurrection and Ascension of Jesus

Time: 2 weeks

I. INTRODUCTION FOR THE TEACHER

Unit Eight is concerned with the events of our Lord's glorious Resurrection and Ascension. Accounts of the appearance of Jesus to His Apostles and others after the Resurrection are also included in this unit.

II. OBJECTIVES OF THE UNIT

A. To teach a fuller realization of the meaning of our Lord's Resurrection — a Christian interpretation of Easter.

B. To develop the knowledge that the Resurrection and the Ascension prove Jesus is God and show He is the Victor over death.

C. To rejoice in the knowledge that Jesus arose from the grave and that one day we will do the same.

D. To acquaint the children with some incidents in our Lord's life after His Resurrection.

E. To foster a deep appreciation of the power given to priests to forgive sins.

F. To develop habits of good Christian living.

G. To teach the articles of the Apostles' Creed: "the third day He arose again from the dead. He ascended into heaven, sitteth at the right hand of God the Father Almighty, from thence He shall come to judge the living and the dead."

III. SUBJECT MATTER

A. The Resurrection — Early Easter morning

B. Appearance to the disciples on the way to Emmaus

C. Appearance to the Apostles

D. Appearance on the Sea of Tiberius

E. Resurrection of our bodies

F. The work of our Lord during the forty days after Easter

G. The Ascension of our Lord into heaven

LESSON 113

I. SUBJECT MATTER

Jesus Christ's Resurrection

II. OBJECTIVES

A. To develop the knowledge that the Resurrection proves Jesus is God and shows He is Victor over death.

B. To foster a feeling of gratitude and joy in the glorious victory of our risen Saviour.

C. To teach the article of the Apostles' Creed: "The third day He arose again from the dead."

III. SUGGESTED PROCEDURE

A. Approach

Do you remember what Jesus did to prove that He was God? (Recall briefly some miracles.) Jesus did something else that was even more wonderful and showed that He is really God.

B. Presentation

1. The Resurrection

After His friends put Jesus in the tomb a big stone was put in front of the opening. The Jews thought that Jesus' Apostles would come and steal His body and then say He had risen from the dead so they had Pilate put some soldiers there to keep watch that no one would come near. All Friday night, all day Saturday, and part of Sunday morning Jesus' body lay in the tomb.

Early Easter morning Jesus came out of the tomb. A bright and shining light blinded the guards and they fell backward. (Show picture of Resurrection.)

2. The Arrival of Jesus' Friends

Early Easter morning Mary Magdalene and other holy women came to Jesus' tomb because they loved Him. They were very surprised when they arrived there because the heavy stone was rolled back from the tomb. (Show picture.) An angel told them not to be fearful because he had good news for them. The angel told that "Jesus is not here any more. He has come back to life again."

How happy the women were when they heard this. The angel also told them to go and tell the good news to the Apostles. On the way the women said "Now we know Jesus is God. Only God could come back to life again."

Mary Magdalene stayed behind and cried, thinking that someone had stolen Jesus' body. Seeing a gardener she asked him if he saw anyone take Jesus' body. But the gardener just said "Mary." At once Mary knew that it was Jesus Himself. She fell on her knees and adored Him.

Peter and John ran to the tomb to see for themselves and found only a linen cloth in the tomb. They said "Truly Jesus is God. He is risen as He said." Jesus made His friends believe in Him more than they ever did because He showed them that He is God. How happy this made them!

3. The Resurrection, a Proof of Christ's Divinity

Jesus showed that He is true God and true man by rising from the dead. He had suffered for all of our sins and the sins of all people from the beginning to the end of the world. Jesus died for you and for me. He suffered to show us how much He loves us.

Christ rose from the dead the third day after He died and opened the gates of heaven for us. At the end of the world Jesus will bring my body to life again and I will be with God forever in heaven if I keep loving Him here on earth, keep His laws called the ten commandments, and keep myself close to Jesus.

4. Teach the Article of the Apostles' Creed

"The third day He arose again from the dead."

C. Organization

1. How long did our Lord's body stay in the grave?
2. What happened on Sunday, the third day after His death?
3. Who rolled the stone away from the tomb?
4. How did the soldiers behave?
5. Why did Jesus rise from the dead?
6. What was His body like now?
7. Did anyone help Jesus rise from the dead?
8. Why were the women going to the tomb?
9. What did the angel tell them?
10. What did Mary Magdalene do when she saw the tomb empty?

11. What did the gardener say to Mary Magdalene?
12. Why did John and Peter hurry to the tomb?

D. Virtues and Practices

1. Tell Jesus that you believe that He is God.
2. Cheer someone by sharing your joys with him.

IV. SUGGESTED LEARNING ACTIVITIES

A. Dramatize the story of the Resurrection.
B. Recording: "The Resurrection," *Catholic Record Club.*
C. Poem: "He is Risen," Belger, *Sing a Song of Holy Things,* pp. 75–76.
D. Story: "Easter Sunday," Sister Marguerite, *Their Hearts Are His Garden,* p. 147.

V. TEACHER REFERENCES

A. Sister Mary, *et al., The Catholic Mother's Helper,* pp. 129–131.
B. S.N.D., *Religious Teaching of Young Children,* pp. 72–75.
C. Sister Marguerite, *Their Hearts Are His Garden,* pp. 148–149.
D. Dennerle, *Leading the Little Ones to Christ,* pp. 215–217.

LESSON 114

I. SUBJECT MATTER

Appearance to the Disciples on the Way to Emmaus

II. OBJECTIVES

A. To acquaint the children with one of the incidents which occurred after the Resurrection.
B. To appreciate more fully our wonderful gift of faith.

III. SUGGESTED PROCEDURE

A. Approach

When Jesus called Mary Magdalene's name, she knew this was no gardener but her Jesus. Mary fell on her knees. She must have been so happy and told Jesus how much she loved Him. Soon after that Jesus showed Himself to two of His disciples. Would you like to know how and when He did this?

B. Presentation

1. Appearance of a Stranger to Two Disciples

On Easter day, two of Jesus' disciples were walking along the road to a town called Emmaus, feeling very sad because they knew Jesus died on the cross. They thought this was the end of everything because their friend was gone from them. As they walked along another man asked if he might join them as he was going the same way. The stranger asked them what they were speaking about. The disciples said, "You mean to say that you haven't heard that Jesus died on the cross?" The stranger seemed not to have heard and listened to the disciples speak of Jesus whom they loved and felt they had lost.

The stranger asked, "Doesn't the bible say that one man must die for the sins of the people?" The disciples still could not understand.

2. The Disciples Recognize Christ

When the three men came into the town of Emmaus, it was late and they knew the stranger had not eaten so they invited him to have lunch with them. As the stranger picked up the bread he blessed it and broke it. It made them think of the Last Supper, when Jesus gave them His own Body to eat. It was then that they knew Jesus was with them. They knew Jesus was truly God and that He had risen from the dead. Then Jesus disappeared.

Jesus is with us, but we cannot see Him now but we will be able to see Him when we go to heaven.

C. Organization

1. Why were the disciples so sad?
2. How did they show courtesy to Jesus?
3. How did the disciples discover that the stranger was Jesus?
4. What did Jesus do as soon as the disciples recognized Him?

D. Virtues and Practices

1. Be kind to others by trying to make them happy.
2. Thank God for the gift of faith.

IV. SUGGESTED LEARNING ACTIVITIES

A. Discuss the joy of the two disciples in seeing Jesus again.
B. Dramatize the story of the journey to Emmaus.
C. Story: "The Two Disciples at Emmaus," *Catholic Mother's Helper*, pp. 131–132.

V. TEACHER REFERENCES

A. Sister Mary, *et al.*, *The Catholic Mother's Helper*, pp. 131–132.

B. Dennerle, *Leading the Little Ones to Christ*, pp. 217–218.

LESSON 115

I. SUBJECT MATTER

Appearance to the Apostles

II. OBJECTIVES

A. To further the knowledge that the Resurrection is a proof of the divinity of Jesus.

B. To foster a deep appreciation of the power given to priests to forgive sin.

C. To rejoice in the thought of our own resurrection.

III. SUGGESTED PROCEDURE

A. Approach

The only thing the Apostles could remember was how Jesus suffered. This made them very sad. They were afraid, too, of what the bad men might do to them since they had killed their leader. So they went to the upper room and locked the door. But Jesus wouldn't leave them alone and sad. Would you like to know how Jesus made the Apostles happy again?

B. Presentation

1. Jesus Appears to the Apostles

Suddenly Easter day Jesus was there with the Apostles. He did not open the door. He did not open the windows. He was just there. He came right through the door like the sun comes through a window. The Apostles were afraid. Was it a ghost? Jesus smiled at them. He held out His hands to them and what did they see? (Show picture.) The marks of the nails were in His hands, the wound was in His side, but they were not bleeding now.

Then Jesus said, "Peace be to you! It is I; do not be afraid." And they were no longer afraid. They knew it was really and truly Jesus.

225

Joy filled their hearts and the Apostles fell down at Jesus' feet. Their Jesus was alive. He had risen from the dead. He showed He was truly God.

2. *Thomas Did Not Believe*

One of the Apostles named Thomas wasn't in the room when Jesus came the first time. When the others told Thomas, "We have seen the Lord," he wouldn't believe. He said, "I won't believe until I put my fingers into the wounds of Jesus' hands, feet, and side."

It wasn't long after that Jesus came again, and Thomas was with the others. He went up to Thomas and told him to put his fingers into His wounds. Thomas fell at Jesus' feet and said, "My Lord and my God." Now he believed. Jesus said, "Because you have seen me, Thomas, you believe — blessed are those who have not seen and believe." Christ meant us — we haven't seen Jesus' wounds but we believe He died for our sins and will give us heaven if we love Him.

3. *Jesus Gave Us an Easter Gift*

Jesus didn't forget us that Easter day. He gave us the wonderful sacrament of Penance, sometimes called "Confession."

Jesus breathed on His Apostles and then He said, "Receive the Holy Spirit. Whose sins you shall forgive, they are forgiven." The Apostles then had the power to forgive sins, just as Jesus did. With these words Jesus gave us confession. Why? To make us happy. We are only happy when we are free from sin.

The priest has the same power of forgiving our sins because the priest is a servant of Jesus, just like the Apostles. Jesus gave us this wonderful Easter gift to make us happy.

C. Organization

1. When did Jesus go to see His Apostles?
2. What did He say to them?
3. What did the Apostles think Jesus was?
4. What did Jesus show His friends?
5. How did our Lord's wounds look now?
6. What wonderful power did Jesus give to the Apostles that night?
7. Does anyone have the same power today?
8. Who was not in the upper room when Jesus came?
9. Did Thomas believe what the Apostles told him?
10. Why did Jesus come back again when Thomas was there?

11. What did Thomas say to our Lord?
12. What did Jesus say to Thomas?

D. Virtues and Practices

1. Tell Jesus that you believe in Him.
2. Thank God for the sacrament of Penance.

IV. SUGGESTED LEARNING ACTIVITIES

A. Discuss the Apostles' power to forgive sins.
B. Explain Thomas' profession of faith. Learn: "My Lord and my God."
C. Story: "Jesus Visits His Friends After Easter," Sister Marguerite, *Their Hearts Are His Garden,* pp. 150–151.

V. TEACHER REFERENCES

A. Schumacher, *I Teach Catechism,* Vol. I, p. 85.
B. S.N.D., *Religious Teaching of Young Children,* p. 84.
C. Dennerle, *Leading the Little Ones to Christ,* pp. 219–224.
D. Sr. Mary, *et al., The Catholic Mother's Helper,* pp. 132–134.

LESSON 116

I. SUBJECT MATTER

Appearance of Jesus at the Sea of Tiberias

II. OBJECTIVES

A. To know some of the events pertaining to the foundation of the Church.
B. To instill love and respect for our Holy Father as successor to St. Peter.

III. SUGGESTED PROCEDURE

A. Approach

Remember how happy the Apostles were when Jesus came to them Easter Sunday? This wasn't the only time Jesus visited them. He surprised them again.

B. Presentation

1. The Apostles Fishing

One day after the Resurrection, the Apostles were out fishing. The Apostles knew a lot about fishing. Although they fished all night, they did not catch any fish.

2. Jesus Appears on the Shore

As they returned Jesus stood on the shore of the lake. He knew that the Apostles worked hard with no success. Then Jesus' voice came out over the water to them, "Put your nets on the other side of the boat." The Apostles obeyed, and immediately they caught so many fish that the net was breaking. Peter called out "It is the Lord."

Wasn't Jesus good to them? He is good to us, too, when we are obedient.

3. Jesus Prepares a Meal

The Apostles were tired and hungry after the night's work. How thankful they were when they reached the shore and saw that Jesus had prepared a meal for them. Jesus always thought of others first. He did all He could to take care of His Apostles.

4. Jesus' Love for Peter

Jesus loved all the Apostles, but He loved Peter very much. He asked Peter three times whether or not he loved Him. Each time Peter said, "Yes, Lord I love You." Then Jesus said, "Feed My sheep, feed My lambs." What Jesus meant was for Peter to take care of everyone in His Church.

5. Peter — The Head of the Church

Jesus made Peter the head of the church — the first pope. The other Apostles would help Peter teach.

Peter is not living on earth now, he is a saint in heaven with God. But we have someone who takes his place as pope. (Show picture.) He is head of all the priests and bishops and everyone in Jesus' Catholic Church. He loves us and takes care of us even though he lives in Rome.

C. Organization

1. Why did the Apostles go to the Sea of Tiberius?
2. What were the Apostles doing when they saw Jesus?

3. How was the obedience of the Apostles rewarded?
4. What other kind thing had Jesus done for His tired and hungry friends?
5. How many times did Jesus ask Peter if he loved Him?
6. Which Apostle was chosen by Jesus to be head of the Church?
7. Who takes Peter's place now?

D. Virtues and Practices

1. Obey at once as the Apostles did.
2. Show love and respect for the Holy Father.
3. Pray for the Pope.
4. Show respect and loyalty to your parish priests.
5. Pray for the priests of your parish.

IV. SUGGESTED LEARNING ACTIVITIES

A. Discuss the beginnings of the Church.
B. Discuss the position of Peter as visible head of the Church.
C. Discuss briefly the position of the Pope today.

V. TEACHER REFERENCE

Sister Mary, *et al.*, *The Catholic Mother's Helper*, pp. 105–107.

LESSON 117

I. SUBJECT MATTER

Resurrection of the Body

II. OBJECTIVES

A. To know that some day our bodies and souls will be reunited.
B. To prepare each day for a glorious resurrection at the end of the world.

III. SUGGESTED PROCEDURE

A. Approach

On Easter Sunday, Jesus arose from the dead, glorious and immortal, never to die again. Do you know that some day we will rise from the dead, too?

B. Presentation

1. Death and Burial of Our Bodies

We know that everyone must die someday. This is a punishment for the sin of Adam and Eve. We are the children of Adam and Eve so we, too, must die. Remember what the priest said on Ash Wednesday when he put the ashes on our foreheads? "Remember, man, that thou art dust and unto dust thou shalt return."

2. The Immortality of the Soul

Although we must die, our souls will live forever. Our soul is immortal. That means it will never die, it will live forever with God.

3. The Resurrection of Our Body

Jesus arose from the dead. We, too, like Christ, will rise from the dead on the last day. God will give us back our bodies. Whether or not we will rise glorious, as Jesus did, is up to us. If we want our bodies to arise glorious we will have to obey God's laws while on earth, while we are living. Only those who know, love, and serve God faithfully will rise glorious.

Let us keep ourselves so clean and holy that the Blessed Trinity will always stay within us. Then we will rise gloriously as Christ did.

4. Jesus as Judge

Jesus is merciful and just. He will judge us according to our deeds. If we have obeyed and loved Him here, He will reward us with His heavenly home. There we will not only be with God, face to face, but we will be with Mother Mary and all the saints. How happy we will be to see and speak to our patron saints and our guardian angel who helped us to get to heaven. This will be our reward.

Those who have known but have not loved or obeyed Christ here on earth will have to go to the fires of hell forever and ever.

C. Organization

1. What happens to our bodies when we die?
2. What happens to our souls?
3. What will happen to our souls and bodies at the end of the world?
4. Who told us that we shall rise from the dead?
5. Who will be our judge?
6. What will happen to the good people?
7. How long will they be happy in heaven?

8. What will happen to the bad people?
9. How long will they have to suffer in hell?
10. What makes heaven such a happy place?

D. Virtues and Practices

1. Be happy that some day your body will rise from the dead.
2. Live a good life so you can get to heaven.

IV. SUGGESTED LEARNING ACTIVITIES

A. Discuss the resurrection of our bodies.
B. Discuss the beauty of our heavenly home.
C. Make up original prayers of hope.
D. Poem: "How God Will Reward Me," Belger, *Sing a Song of Holy Things,* pp. 100–101.

V. TEACHER REFERENCES

A. S.N.D., *Religious Teaching of Young Children,* pp. 103–109.
B. Dennerle, *Leading the Little Ones to Christ,* pp. 223–224, 282–283.

LESSON 118

I. SUBJECT MATTER

The Work of Our Lord During the Forty Days After Easter

II. OBJECTIVES

A. To develop a knowledge of the work assigned by Jesus to the Apostles before His Ascension.
B. To foster an attitude of willingness to help spread the kingdom of Christ on earth.

III. SUGGESTED PROCEDURE

A. Approach

Remember when Jesus made Peter the first pope? Jesus is also getting the Apostles ready to carry on the work of His Church.

231

B. Presentation

1. Jesus Prepares the Apostles

Jesus came to the Apostles often during the forty days after His Resurrection. He wanted to make them so strong in their faith that they would know just how to teach other people to believe in Him. He reminded them of all the truths He had taught them. He showed them why He had to suffer and die. Jesus wanted to get the Apostles ready to continue His work among men. He also wanted to strengthen Peter so that he could be a strong and brave leader of the Church. Finally, Jesus wanted to prepare the Apostles for the coming of the Holy Spirit.

2. Jesus' Promises

Jesus promised His Apostles to be with His Church always. He was going to send them through the whole world to do His work, and He promised His Apostles that the Holy Spirit would give them great strength so that they would be able to "Go and teach all nations, baptizing them in the name of the Father, and of the Son, and of the Holy Spirit."

Jesus also promised the Apostles that He would get a place ready for them in heaven and we know that He will have one ready for us, too, if we love Jesus and do what He wants us to do.

C. Organization

1. What did Jesus do during the forty days after Easter?
2. Why did Jesus appear to His friends?
3. How were the Apostles to carry on Christ's work after the Ascension?
4. What did Jesus promise to do for them in heaven?
5. Whom did Jesus say He would send to help the Apostles do His work?
6. How did the Apostles work for Jesus?
7. Who does the work of the Apostles today?

D. Virtues and Practices

1. Imitate the risen Christ by being kind to others.
2. Believe in God's promises.
3. Pray for missionaries.
4. Listen reverently when a priest talks to you in church.
5. Be a little missionary by giving good example.

232

IV. SUGGESTED LEARNING ACTIVITIES

A. Compose original prayers for the spread of Christ's kingdom.

B. Discuss ways in which we can be little missionaries.

C. Discuss the work of the Catholic priest, especially his mission to teach and baptize.

D. Compose a prayer to the Holy Spirit, asking His assistance in doing the work of God.

V. TEACHER REFERENCES

A. Dennerle, *Leading the Little Ones to Christ*, pp. 224–226.

B. Schumacher, *I Teach Catechism*, Vol. I, pp. 84–86.

LESSON 119

I. SUBJECT MATTER

The Ascension of Our Lord Into Heaven

II. OBJECTIVES

A. To acquaint the children with the events surrounding our Lord's Ascension into heaven.

B. To foster an attitude of hope that some day we too will be taken up into heaven.

C. To teach the articles of the Apostles' Creed: "He ascended into heaven, sitteth at the right hand of God, the Father Almighty, from thence He shall come to judge the living and the dead."

III. SUGGESTED PROCEDURE

A. Approach

Jesus told the Apostles that He would be with them and with His Church always. He was telling His Apostles good-by, but He promised that He would send down the Holy Spirit to help them. Jesus was getting ready to go to His Father in heaven.

B. Presentation

1. *Jesus and His Apostles on Mount Olivet*

Jesus and His Apostles went to a place called Mount Olivet. The place was to be a scene of Christ's glory, a proof of Christ's divine power. When they reached the Mount, Jesus and His Apostles climbed to the top. Jesus told them that His work on earth was done.

2. The Ascension

Once more Jesus reminded them to go and teach all nations. He then raised His hand, blessed them and slowly, very slowly, began to rise from the ground. (Show picture.)

The Apostles were silent. As Jesus was ascending a cloud hid Him and soon He disappeared. Jesus had gone to His heavenly Father.

3. The Message of the Angels

While the Apostles were still looking up, two angels appeared. They said "Men of Galilee, why do you stand looking up into heaven? This Jesus, who has been taken up from you into heaven, shall come in the same way as you have seen Him going up to heaven." (Explain.)

4. The Return to Jerusalem

The Apostles, with Mary, returned to Jerusalem. They went to the upper room and prayed. They were getting ready for the Holy Spirit to come to them as Jesus has promised. They had much work to do. The Holy Spirit would make them strong and brave soldiers of Christ.

5. Jesus Thinks of Us

When Jesus ascended into heaven, He thought of us, too. He wants us to come to heaven, and He is always helping us to get there. We, too, must pray to Jesus and ask for a deep faith to keep loving Him, so that one day we can go to heaven and live with Him.

6. Teach and explain a part of the Apostles' Creed

"He ascended into heaven, sitteth at the right hand of God, the Father Almighty, from thence He shall come to judge the living and the dead."

C. Organization

1. What did Jesus prove when He ascended into heaven?
2. What did the Apostles do as Jesus rose from the ground?
3. What did the angel tell them to do?
4. Why did the Apostles need the Holy Spirit?
5. How did they get ready for the coming of the Holy Spirit?
6. What is Jesus always doing for us in heaven?

7. How did Mary help the Apostles get ready for the coming of the Holy Spirit?

D. Virtues and Practices

1. Always hope that you will be in heaven some day.
2. Don't give up hope when you pray.
3. Trust in Mary's power to help you.
4. Pray often to the Holy Spirit.

IV. SUGGESTED LEARNING ACTIVITIES

A. Study the picture of the Ascension.
B. Discuss the significance of the extinguishing of the Paschal Candle during the Mass on Ascension Thursday.
C. Discuss the obligation of assisting at Mass and abstaining from servile work on Ascension Day.
D. Recording: "The Ascension," *The Catholic Children's Record Club.*
E. Poem: "The Ascension," Belger, *Sing a Song of Holy Things,* pp. 84–85.

V. TEACHER REFERENCES

A. Dennerle, *Leading the Little Ones to Christ,* pp. 226–227.
B. Schumacher, *I Teach Catechism,* Vol. I, pp. 86–88.
C. Sister Marguerite, *Their Hearts Are His Garden,* pp. 151–152.
D. Sister Mary, *et al., The Catholic Mother's Helper,* pp. 134–135.
E. *Religious Teaching of Young Children,* pp. 76–78.

UNIT NINE

God the Father and God the Son Show Their Love by Sending the Holy Spirit

Time: 2 weeks

I. INTRODUCTION FOR THE TEACHER

The subject matter of Unit Nine is concerned with the part the Holy Spirit plays in the life of Christ, in the life of the Catholic Church, and in our lives. The work of St. Peter and the Apostles in spreading the true Church is compared with the work of our present Pope, bishops, and priests. The sacraments of Baptism, Penance, and Holy Eucharist are mentioned and emphasized.

II. OBJECTIVES OF THE UNIT

A. To develop the knowledge that the Holy Spirit is God.

B. To teach the prayer: "Glory be to the Father . . ."

C. To develop a knowledge of the truths concerned with Pentecost, the "birthday of the Church."

D. To love God the Holy Spirit and the Catholic Church through which He teaches us and makes us holy.

E. To develop an appreciation of the need of the Holy Spirit in our daily lives and to foster devotion to Him.

F. To develop a knowledge of the effects of sin upon our life of grace.

G. To inspire the children with gratitude to God for the graces of the true faith and to profess it by being good Catholics.

H. To teach the remaining articles of the Apostles' Creed: "I believe in the Holy Ghost, the Holy Catholic Church, the communion of saints, the forgiveness of sins, the resurrection of the body and life everlasting. Amen."

III. SUBJECT MATTER

A. The Holy Spirit in the life of Jesus Christ

B. The Holy Spirit in the Catholic Church
   1. Pentecost Sunday

2. The Catholic Church and its rulers
3. Jesus helps us gain heaven through the Catholic Church
C. The Holy Spirit in the life of each of us

LESSON 120

I. SUBJECT MATTER

The Holy Spirit in the Life of Jesus Christ

II. OBJECTIVES

A. To develop the knowledge of the part played by the Holy Spirit in the life of Jesus.

B. To foster devotion to the Holy Spirit.

III. SUGGESTED PROCEDURE

A. Approach

Let us make the Sign of the Cross. We mentioned the names of the Three Persons of the Blessed Trinity. Name them again. What name do we give to the third Person? The Holy Spirit is true God.

B. Presentation

1. The Holy Spirit at the Annunciation

When the Angel Gabriel told Mary that God had chosen her to be the Mother of the Redeemer, Mary wondered how this could be, because she had made a promise to God. It was then that Angel Gabriel told her that God the Holy Spirit would take care of her promise. And this He did. God the Holy Spirit helped Mary become the Mother of the Saviour.

2. The Holy Spirit in the Life of Christ

All through the life of Jesus, while He was here on earth, the Holy Spirit was with Him. When Jesus was baptized, the Holy Spirit came down on Him in the form of a dove. Before He began to teach the Holy Spirit led Him into the desert where He prayed and fasted.

3. The Holy Spirit in Us

Just as the Holy Spirit was with Jesus always, so He is with us. He comes to us at Baptism, and brings us courage and wisdom, helping us to know what is right and giving us the strength to do it. He will come to us again in the sacrament of Confirmation.

4. Prayer in Honor of Holy Spirit

The Holy Spirit is truly God, just as truly as God the Father and God the Son. That is why we say in a special prayer honoring the Blessed Trinity — "Glory be to the Father and to the Son and to the Holy Spirit." (Teach the prayer "Glory Be . . .")

C. Organization

1. Who helped Mary become the Mother of the Saviour?
2. What form did the Holy Spirit take at the baptism of Jesus?
3. Did the Holy Spirit play an important part in the life of Jesus?
4. Does the Holy Spirit do anything for us?

D. Virtues and Practices

1. Do everything for God, not for praise or reward.
2. Ask the Holy Spirit to be near you at all times.

IV. SUGGESTED LEARNING ACTIVITIES

A. Recall the story of the Annunciation, using a picture.
B. Have a picture study of the baptism of Jesus.
C. Explain the symbol of the Holy Spirit — the dove; have children make symbols.

V. TEACHER REFERENCES

A. Dennerle, *Leading the Little Ones to Christ*, pp. 121–124.
B. S.N.D., *Religious Teaching of Young Children*, pp. 19–42, 101–102.

LESSON 121

I. SUBJECT MATTER

The Holy Spirit in the Catholic Church

II. OBJECTIVES

A. To develop the knowledge of the truths concerned with Pentecost, the "birthday of the Church."

B. To love God the Holy Spirit and the Catholic Church through which He teaches us and makes us holy.

C. Teach the last part of the Apostles' Creed: "I believe in the Holy Ghost, the Holy Catholic Church, the communion of saints, the forgiveness of sins, the resurrection of our body and life everlasting. Amen."

III. SUGGESTED PROCEDURE

A. Approach

Before Jesus went back to heaven on Ascension Day, He made a promise to His mother and Apostles. Do you remember what it was? Mary and the Apostles returned to the upper room to await the Holy Spirit.

B. Presentation

1. The Descent of the Holy Spirit

The Apostles were very much afraid of the Jews. They were afraid that they, too, would be taken prisoners and punished like Jesus. For nine days Blessed Mother and the Apostles prepared and prayed for the coming of the Holy Spirit. On the tenth day, a sound of a loud wind was heard and soon the Apostles saw a flame of fire, shaped like tongues, over the head of each one present there. That was the form in which the Holy Spirit descended upon Mary and the Apostles. Everyone, filled with the Holy Spirit, began to praise and thank God.

2. Effects of the Holy Spirit

The Holy Spirit brought the Apostles and Mary the light to remember, to know and to understand the things that Jesus had taught them. The Holy Spirit filled them with a burning love for Jesus that no trouble, sorrow, or suffering could ever change. Fire is red. Red is the color of strength and the Holy Spirit gave them the strength to do God's work despite all danger, all trouble.

3. Pentecost, the Birthday of the Church

After the Holy Spirit came upon the Apostles they spoke in languages they never learned before. They received the gift of tongues. Peter, strengthened and brave, now, opened the door and taught the thousands of people who had gathered there. Three thousand were baptized that day. The day the Holy Spirit came upon the Apostles is called Pentecost, because it is the fiftieth day after Easter. It is the birthday of the Church, for on this day the Church Jesus founded really came to life. The Holy Spirit is the life of the Church. He works in the Church and keeps it alive even today.

4. Teach the last part of the Apostles' Creed

"I believe in the Holy Spirit, the Holy Catholic Church, the communion of saints, the forgiveness of sins, the resurrection of the body, and life everlasting. Amen."

C. Organization

1. Why did the Apostles lock themselves in the upper room?
2. What happened while they were in the room?
3. Were the Apostles afraid after the Holy Spirit descended upon them?
4. What form did the Holy Spirit take?
5. What did they do after the descent of the Holy Spirit?
6. Why is Pentecost called the birthday of the Church?

D. Virtues and Practices

1. Love the Catholic Church by trying to be a good Catholic.
2. Help God save souls as the Apostles did.

IV. SUGGESTED LEARNING ACTIVITIES

A. Discuss the meaning of Pentecost.
B. Illustrate the story of Pentecost.
C. Compose original prayers to the Holy Spirit for light, strength, and love.

V. TEACHER REFERENCES

A. Dennerle, *Leading the Little Ones to Christ*, pp. 232–235.
B. S.N.D., *Religious Teaching of Young Children*, pp. 76–78.
C. Sister Mary, *et al.*, *The Catholic Mother's Helper*, pp. 135–136.
D. Sister Marguerite, *Their Hearts Are His Garden*, pp. 152–153.

LESSON 122

I. SUBJECT MATTER

The Catholic Church

II. OBJECTIVES

A. To develop the knowledge that the Catholic Church founded by Jesus Christ is the true Church.

B. To instill in the children love for the Church, and its members.

III. SUGGESTED PROCEDURE

A. Approach

Do you remember what happened on Pentecost Sunday? It was on that day the Catholic Church really became alive.

B. Presentation

1. Jesus Started the Catholic Church

When Jesus was here on earth He taught the people and the Apostles what they should believe and do to be able to go to heaven. He wanted His teaching to continue and go on until the end of the world. He was returning to heaven so He started the Catholic Church to continue His work.

2. The Apostles Were the First Priests

Those who knew Jesus best and had been with Him every day for three years were the Apostles. Jesus made them bishops and priests of the Church when He gave them the power to change bread and wine into His Body and Blood. Jesus chose Peter to be the head of the Catholic Church, the pope. All the other friends and people who loved and followed Jesus and believed in Him, even the Blessed Mother, were the first Catholics.

3. The Catholic Church Today

Today the bishops take the place of the Apostles. Their leader is still the Pope, the head of the Catholic Church. Our priests try to show us the way to heaven. We are also the members of Christ's Body — the Church. (Present pictures and discuss: Our Holy Father, our Bishop, our Pastor and Assistants.)

4. The Catholic Church Is the Only True Church

There is only one Church which Jesus founded. That Church is the one to which we belong, the Roman Catholic Church. The Church has been working for Christ ever since Pentecost and it will continue to do Christ's work until the end of the world. Jesus promised that He would stay with the Church and He does.

5. The Church Is Our Mother

The Church is a loving Mother. She watches over us and gives us divine life. She teaches us through the Pope, the bishops, and the priests. We the Catholics of today, are her children. Our Mother Church cannot teach us anything wrong, for Jesus is still the real Leader, the invisible Head of the Church.

6. Respect and Obedience We Owe

Because the Pope, bishops, and priests try to show us the way to heaven, the way Jesus taught, we should love and respect them always and try to do everything they tell us. Through them Jesus is speaking to us today, as He did when He lived on earth.

C. Organization

1. Who started the Catholic Church?
2. When is the "birthday of the Catholic Church"?
3. Who were the first priests?
4. Who was the head of the Catholic Church at that time?
5. Who were the first Catholics?
6. Who takes the place of the Apostles now?
7. Who is the head of all the bishops?
8. Do we belong to the Church?
9. Is the Church our Mother?
10. How can we help the Pope? our bishop? our priests?

D. Virtues and Practices

1. Thank God for letting you belong to the Catholic Church.
2. Thank God for priests.
3. Help our Holy Father by your prayers and sacrifices.
4. Obey and serve Holy Mother Church.

IV. SUGGESTED LEARNING ACTIVITIES

A. Compose an original prayer to the Holy Spirit asking Him to make our faith strong.

242

B. Make a chart with a picture of our Lord at the top. Stemming from this have pictures of the Apostles, St. Peter, our present Pope, and the faithful. Discuss the chart.

C. Present a picture of: our Pope, our Bishop, and of our pastor. Discuss how each one helps in the Catholic Church.

V. TEACHER REFERENCES

A. Dennerle, *Leading the Little Ones to Christ*, pp. 236–241.
B. Schumacher, *I Teach Catechism*, Vol. I, pp. 87–88.

LESSON 123

I. SUBJECT MATTER

Jesus Helps Us to Gain Heaven Through the Catholic Church

II. OBJECTIVES

A. To develop a knowledge of how to gain heaven through the help of the priests of the Church and the use of the means of grace.

B. To inspire in the children gratitude to God for His help in getting to heaven.

C. To instill reverence for the Catholic Church — its teachings, its rulers (bishops and pastors), and its means of grace.

III. SUGGESTED PROCEDURE

A. Approach

The Catholic Church does God's work and will continue to do so until the end of the world. The Catholic Church, like a loving Mother, watches over us from birth until death helping us to gain heaven.

B. Presentation

1. Jesus Helps Us Through His Priests and Bishops

Jesus loves us and wants us so very much in heaven that He gave us some special helpers to help us along the way. The bishops and priests, God's special helpers, have the same power Jesus gave the Apostles, namely, the power to change bread and wine into His Body and Blood at Mass and give us Jesus in Holy Communion.

243

It is the priest who baptizes us so we can become children of God. It is the priest, who, like Jesus, is merciful and forgives us our sins in confession. And when we die, it will be the priest who will help us get ready to meet God. We need the help of these friends who guide and inspire us to do good to gain heaven.

2. *Jesus Helps Us Through the Sacraments*

Jesus provides for us the means or ways of getting grace through the sacraments. Jesus Himself confers on us the sacraments through His priests and bishops. All the sacraments give us special graces and bring us closer to Jesus so that we may be happy and have the strength to be good. (Show pictures of seven sacraments, mentioning briefly what each does for us. Emphasize the sacraments of Baptism, of Penance, and of the Holy Eucharist.)

We became children of God and members of the Catholic Church when we were baptized. In the sacrament of Penance our sins will be forgiven by the priest. Jesus Himself comes to us in the sacrament of Holy Eucharist. Through these sacraments we receive many, many graces for our salvation. (Explain term *salvation*. No formal instruction on the sacraments is necessary at this stage.)

3. *The Church Is Our Mother*

The Church, as a loving Mother, watches over us and gives us divine life. Through the Church we receive God's life in Baptism. The Church gives us Jesus Himself in Holy Communion. When we sin, the Church forgives us our sins in confession. She is ready to give us strength in the sacrament of Extreme Unction when we die. The Church brings God to us, to our families, and to others. The Church loves us as a true mother and is ever ready to help us. How happy and grateful we ought to be that Jesus gives us the help to do His will and to come and live with Him in heaven.

C. Organization

1. How does Jesus help us to get to heaven?
2. Why must we believe the things that the pope, bishops, and priests tell us about God?
3. Why must we obey the leaders of the Church?
4. What can our priests do for us to help us get to heaven?
5. What do the sacraments do for us?
6. What sacrament have you already received?

D. Virtues and Practices

1. Believe everything that your priest teaches you about God and His holy Church.
2. Love, obey, and respect all members of the Catholic Church, especially those who take the place of Christ and His Apostles.
3. Be polite to the priests at all times.
4. Thank God for His wonderful sacraments.

IV. SUGGESTED LEARNING ACTIVITIES

A. Practice the proper way to greet and speak to priests.
B. Discuss how the pastor and priests work for the Church.
C. Discuss briefly the sacraments of Penance and Holy Eucharist, which will be received next year.

V. TEACHER REFERENCES

A. Dennerle, *Leading the Little Ones to Christ*, pp. 278–284.
B. Schumacher, *I Teach Catechism*, Vol. I, pp. 93–94.

LESSON 124

I. SUBJECT MATTER

The Coming of the Holy Spirit at Baptism

II. OBJECTIVES

A. To develop the knowledge of the work of the Holy Spirit in us.
B. To develop the knowledge that the Holy Spirit dwells in us through the sacrament of Baptism.
C. To foster a devotion to the Holy Spirit living in us.

III. SUGGESTED PROCEDURE

A. Approach

Jesus left us His Church and His sacraments to help us get to heaven. He also gave us Someone to help us. He sent the Holy Spirit to each one of us, just as He did to the Apostles and to Mary.

B. Presentation

1. The Holy Spirit Comes to Live in Us at Baptism

The Holy Spirit is a very important Person in our life. Jesus sends Him to us just as soon as He can. When we were baptized and received sanctifying grace, we became God's child and we became the special child of the Holy Spirit. On our baptismal day we began a new life, the life of God. It is on that great day that the Holy Spirit begins to dwell within us. He makes us the living temples of the Blessed Trinity. What a glory we have, to be so closely united to God.

2. The Holy Spirit Does Many Wonderful Things for Us

When we were baptized, the Holy Spirit brought many wonderful gifts with Himself. He gave us the gift of faith, hope, and charity. He gave us the grace to believe the truths Jesus taught His Apostles that we may believe in Him and love Him more and more. This is the greatest work of the Holy Spirit — to help us love Jesus and love all men.

3. Respect We Should Have for Ourselves

We call the Church and the Tabernacle holy because God lives in them. Because the Holy Spirit and the other Persons of the Blessed Trinity live in us and we are the temples of God, we should have a respect for what we are. God wants us to be His images. Your body is holy too, because God chose to live within you. How happy you should be that your body is God's house. And how careful we should be of that house. We should try never to lose the presence of the Blessed Trinity within us by doing something very wrong.

4. Respect We Should Have for Others

The Blessed Trinity lives in a special way within all baptized people. God wants to live in all men because they are holy and pleasing to Him. Because of this privilege we should show respect and kindness to others. We should realize that God loves them dearly and that He wants us to love them just as He does.

C. Organization
1. When does the Holy Spirit come to live in us?
2. What does the Holy Spirit do for us?
3. How does the Holy Spirit help us to keep away from sin?
4. How does the Holy Spirit help us to become holy?
5. Why do we call our souls "Temples of the Holy Spirit"?

D. Virtues and Practices

1. Remember that the Holy Spirit is living in your soul.
2. Thank the Holy Spirit for coming to live with you.
3. Act at all times and in all places as a child of God should act.
4. Often say the prayer "Glory Be" to the Blessed Trinity living in you.

IV. SUGGESTED LEARNING ACTIVITIES

A. Discuss simply the life of grace in the soul resulting from the reception of Baptism.
B. Compose original prayers of gratitude for our life of grace.

V. TEACHER REFERENCE

Schumacher, *I Teach Catechism*, Vol. I, pp. 93–94.

LESSON 125

I. SUBJECT MATTER

The Effect of Sin Upon the Life of Grace

II. OBJECTIVES

A. To know how sin affects the life of grace.
B. To show gratitude to God for His love and mercy by striving to avoid sin.

III. SUGGESTED PROCEDURE

A. Approach

Sanctifying grace makes us so beautiful that God is pleased to live within us. We sometimes call this "the life of grace."

B. Presentation

1. Sin Offends God

Baptism took away original sin and gave us the life of grace because it gave us sanctifying grace, the key of heaven. But the evil spirit does not want us to go to heaven. He tries to take away that grace. He tempts us to commit sin, mortal sin, so that God will have to take sanctifying grace away from us.

Sin is an offense against God. It is any thought, word, or deed which hurts God. Jesus suffered greatly because of sin. If we truly love Jesus we will not hurt Him by sinning.

2. The Effect of Sin

Sin crucified Jesus. Mortal sin hurts God grievously. (Explain term *grievously*.) and kills the life of grace in us. It robs us of the presence of the Holy Spirit and His wonderful gifts. It keeps us from our divine Redeemer and closes the gate of heaven for us. We lose the friendship of God. Knowing this, how can we ever sin and hurt God?

3. Sacrament of Penance — A Means of Removing Sin

Jesus knew that just as Adam and Eve listened to the devil, we, too, are weak and sometimes we would give in to temptation. That is why He gave us the wonderful sacrament of Penance on Easter Sunday. If we are really sorry for our sins the priest can remove them in the sacrament of Penance. God is so good and merciful. He not only gives the priest power to remove sin but through this sacrament, God gives back to us sanctifying grace.

Once again, He lives in us and we are His temples.

We could try to make up for our sins by doing something hard for Jesus, by doing some little penances, or by saying some extra prayers. Kind Jesus wants us to keep the "life of grace" until we die.

C. Organization

1. When did you receive the life of grace?
2. What will take away the life of grace?
3. If you commit a big sin and lose the life of grace, how can you get your grace back?
4. How can you thank God for the wonderful sacrament of Penance?
5. How can you find out your sins?
6. Will your sins be taken away if you are not sorry for them?

D. Virtues and Practices

1. Tell God you are sorry when you offend Him by committing sin.
2. Ask forgiveness when you hurt someone; forgive those who hurt you.
3. Thank God for His love and mercy.

248

IV. SUGGESTED LEARNING ACTIVITIES

A. Explain how the Holy Spirit helps us get ready for confession.

B. Discuss God's goodness and love in giving us the sacrament of Penance.

C. Make a simple examination of conscience and act of sorrow every night before going to bed.

D. Make up original acts of sorrow.

V. TEACHER REFERENCES

A. S.N.D., *Religious Teaching of Young Children*, pp. 148–160.

B. Schumacher, *I Teach Catechism*, Vol. I, pp. 64–70.

C. Dennerle, *Leading the Little Ones to Christ*, pp. 53–55, 124–125, 281–282.

UNIT TEN

Mary, Our Heavenly Mother   *Time: 5 weeks*

I. INTRODUCTION FOR THE TEACHER

Unit Ten presents a simple explanation of Mary's life from her childhood to her coronation in heaven. The mysteries of the rosary studied incidentally throughout the year are reviewed by recalling the role played by Jesus and Mary in each mystery. The story of Fatima is also introduced in this unit.

II. OBJECTIVES OF THE UNIT

A. To develop a knowledge of the life of Mary with reference to Jesus as depicted in the mysteries of the rosary.

B. To inspire reverence and love toward Mary, our Heavenly Mother.

C. To develop the practice of thanking God, our Father, for giving us the Blessed Virgin as our Mother.

D. To foster a desire to honor Mary every day of our lives and to imitate her virtues.

E. To acquaint the children with the story of Fatima.

III. SUBJECT MATTER

A. Mary, our Mother
   1. Love and care of our earthly mother
   2. Love and care of our heavenly Mother

B. Our Lady of Fatima

C. The story of Jesus and Mary in the mysteries of the rosary
   1. Joyful Mysteries
   2. Sorrowful Mysteries
   3. Glorious Mysteries

D. Liturgical Feasts
   1. Corpus Christi — Thursday after the Òctave of Pentecost
   2. Sacred Heart — Friday after the Octave of Corpus Christi
   3. Assumption of the Blessed Virgin — August 15

LESSON 126

I. SUBJECT MATTER

Mary, our Mother
1. Love and care of an earthly mother
2. Love and care of our heavenly Mother

II. OBJECTIVES

A. To inspire the children with reverence and love toward Mary our heavenly Mother.

B. To develop the practice of thanking God, our Father, for giving us the Blessed Virgin to be our Mother.

III. SUGGESTED PROCEDURE

A. Approach

Do you remember who was God's special chosen creature? Mary was extraordinary from the time of her birth. (Recall briefly some chief facts in the early childhood of Mary — freedom from original sin at birth, freedom from all other sin, obedient life in the temple, etc.)

Of all His creatures, Jesus loves Mary most of all, just like we love our mothers the best of all. That is why we honor in a special way these two Mothers during the beautiful month of May.

B. Presentation

1. Love and Care of Our Earthly Mother

Every one of you knows how wonderful your mothers are. Just think, how hard they work for you, fixing your food, cleaning your home, and making you as happy as possible. Mother loses a lot of sleep when you are sick caring for you. How eagerly they give up little things for you just to make you happy. You know too, how happy and proud mothers are when you do little things to help them and when you are kind to them. We love and honor our mothers every day. Can you tell why?

2. Love and Care of Our Heavenly Mother

Mary is our Mother also. Jesus gave her to us as our Mother, and He gave us to Mary as her children when He was dying on the cross. Now Mary is our heavenly Mother. She is also our protector and our guardian. Mary wants all of us to love Jesus so that we can live with Him in heaven some day. She is especially interested in helping us keep pure and pleasing to God. She presents our petition to her Son and begs Jesus to bless us during our lives.

3. We Honor Mary as Our May Queen

Because Mary loves us, we should love her, pray to her, and honor her, too. May, the most beautiful month of the year, is set aside for honoring Mary in a special way.

A most beautiful way of honoring Mary is to be good boys and girls, trying to imitate her kindness to everyone, obedience at home and school, praying with love especially saying her favorite prayer, the rosary.

Mary is the Queen of heaven and earth. The angels and saints honor and praise Mary as their Queen in heaven. We, too, can honor and praise Mary as our Queen. Can you tell what we can do to honor Mary as our May Queen? (Discuss — May Devotions, May Crowning, Rosary, May altars, etc.)

C. Organization

1. How can we show our mothers that we really love them?
2. What does the Blessed Mother do for us every day?
3. How can we show that we love Mary, our heavenly Mother?
4. How can we help others to know and love Mary?
5. Why do we have May altars at school and at home?

D. Virtues and Practices

1. Show love for your mother by being kind to her and helping her cheerfully.
2. Make every day "Mother's Day."
3. Thank your heavenly Mother for taking care of you.
4. Say the "Hail Mary" devoutly and often.
5. Make extra visits to Mary's altar.
6. Tell others about Mary. Use Mary's name reverently.
7. Try to imitate Mary's purity and patience.

IV. SUGGESTED LEARNING ACTIVITIES

A. Illustrate various scenes showing how you can make your mother happy.
B. Compose original prayers to Mary our heavenly Mother.

252

C. Make a May altar at home and in school.

D. Say a decade of the rosary every day and sing a class hymn to Mary.

E. Children take daily turns crowning Mary as May Queen.

F. Stories: "A Good Mother," Sister Marguerite, *Their Hearts Are His Garden*, pp. 8–10; "Mary, Our Heavenly Mother," *ibid.*, pp. 10–11; "The Lost Child," *Going His Way*, pp. 49–51.

G. Poems: "Mothers," *A Lovely Gate Set Wide*, p. 19; "Dear Mother Mary," Fitzpatrick, *Religious Poems for Little Folk*, p. 38; "To the Blessed Mother," Thayer, *Child on His Knees*, p. 81; "My Mother Mary," Belger, *Sing a Song of Holy Things*, p. 25.

V. TEACHER REFERENCES

A. Aurelia-Kirsch, *Practical Aids for Catholic Teachers*, pp. 138–142.

B. Sister Mary, *et al.*, *The Catholic Mother's Helper*, p. 128.

C. S.N.D., *Religious Teaching of Young Children*, p. 143.

LESSON 127

I. SUBJECT MATTER

Our Lady of Fatima

II. OBJECTIVES

A. To acquaint the children with the events surrounding the apparitions of Our Lady of Fatima.

B. To develop the practice of reciting the family rosary daily.

III. SUGGESTED PROCEDURE

A. Approach

Have you ever heard of these children, Lucy, Jacinta, and Frances to whom Mother Mary appeared? (Show picture of Our Lady of Fatima.) Don't you wish you had been one of them?

B. Presentation

1. The Blessed Virgin Appears to the Children

The three children loved Mother Mary very much. They prayed to her often. In 1917, when the world was at war, the Blessed Virgin appeared to these children at Fatima, in Portugal. She appeared to them six times and each time Mary encouraged them to say the rosary. She told the children that she was God's Mother and that she wants to shower her blessings upon earth. But they must pray, pray much, especially, say the rosary and make sacrifices for sinners. Mary also told the children that she would take them to heaven some day. What happy and good news for the children! They were to be in heaven with Mary.

2. Mary's Message

The Blessed Virgin told the children that people must do penance for their sins. The people will suffer much because of their sins, but Mary promised that she would always be ready to help them. She asked the children, especially, to spread devotion to her rosary — everyone should say the rosary. Mary promised special blessings to the family that says the rosary together. Mary also promised special blessings for those who would honor her on the first Saturday of each month, receiving her Son in Holy Communion and praying for all the world.

If we pray hard enough and do sacrifices, Mary promises to send peace and blessings into the world.

3. The Rosary — Mary's Favorite Prayer

The rosary is a powerful prayer. It pleases Mary very much when we say it well. It is made up of special prayers in honor of Jesus and Mary. (Show and explain the parts of the rosary and prayers said on each part.)

C. Organization
1. Why did our Lady appear to the three simple shepherd children?
2. What did our Lady tell these little children to do?
3. Did everyone believe the children when they told the story?
4. What message did our Lady have for all the people?
5. What does our Lady want families to do?
6. How can we help to keep world peace?

D. Virtues and Practices
1. Encourage and suggest the practice of the family rosary in the home.
2. Make sacrifices and pray for world peace as the children of Fatima did.

254

IV. SUGGESTED LEARNING ACTIVITIES

A. Children retell the story of Fatima.
B. Pantomime or dramatize incidents from the story.
C. Show a filmstrip or movie of the story of Fatima.
D. Learn how to say the rosary correctly — think of Jesus and Mary as we say the prayers.
E. Poem: "Our Lady's Rosary," Belger, *Sing a Song of Holy Things,* p. 15.

V. TEACHER REFERENCE

Windeatt, M. F., *Children of Fatima,* p. 155.

LESSON 128

I. SUBJECT MATTER

The story of Jesus and Mary in the Mysteries of the Rosary — (to be used as a review of the year's work and not to be taught formally as mysteries)

The First Joyful Mystery — The Annunciation

II. OBJECTIVES

A. To recall the events of the story of the Annunciation.
B. To encourage the children to imitate Mary's humility and obedience.

III. SUGGESTED PROCEDURE

A. Approach

The children of Fatima said the rosary every day as the Blessed Virgin told them to do. The children loved Mary very much. Not only did they say the rosary well but they thought of some things that happened in the life of Jesus and Mary. Thinking about Mary and praying to her made the children love her more and more.

B. Presentation

1. Mysteries of the Rosary

We do not understand all the things we see around us — how a bird knows just how to build a nest, or how the animals know where to look for food. These are mysteries, things we do not fully understand.

In the life of Jesus and Mary many things happened that we do not understand, but we believe. They are the mysteries that we think about when we say the rosary. Some of the things that happened to Jesus and Mary were joyful. We call them the Joyful Mysteries. Sometimes the things that happened were sad. We call them the Sorrowful Mysteries. And some things were glorious. We call them the Glorious Mysteries.

2. The First Joyful Mystery — The Annunciation

One of the joyful things that happened to Mary was when the Angel Gabriel announced the wonderful news that she was to be the Mother of the Saviour. We call this joyful mystery the Annunciation. (Show picture of the Annunciation.) You remember the story from an earlier lesson. Children retell the story of the Annunciation.

3. Recite the Decade of the Rosary — Ask for Help

Mary was very humble when the angel told her the message from God. She did not think too much of herself — she was a handmaid of the Lord. She did not boast or show off. We too can be like Mary, humble at all times. (Relate a few examples of humility as can be detected in the life of the child.)

When we say the decade of the rosary let us ask Mary to help us be humble and kind at all times.

C. Organization

1. What do we mean by a mystery?
2. What does joyful mean?
3. What happy news did the angel tell Mary?
4. Why didn't Mary think she was good enough to be God's mother?
5. Whom did the angel say would help Mary become God's mother?
6. What did Mary say when she heard that the Holy Spirit would help her?
7. Who is the Holy Spirit?

D. Virtues and Practices

1. Do not think you are better than others.
2. Obey quickly your parents' orders.

IV. SUGGESTED LEARNING ACTIVITIES

A. Picture study of the Annunciation.
B. Discussion of how we can imitate Mary in this mystery.
C. Compose a co-operative prayer to Mary to be used for a rosary booklet or a series of charts on the mysteries of the rosary.

V. TEACHER REFERENCES

A. Dennerle, *Leading the Little Ones to Christ*, pp. 73–76.
B. Schumacher, *I Teach Catechism*, Vol. I, pp. 47–48, 259.
C. Sister Mary, *et al.*, *The Catholic Mother's Helper*, pp. 61–63.

LESSON 129

I. SUBJECT MATTER

The Second Joyful Mystery — The Visitation

II. OBJECTIVES

A. To recall the joys in the life of our Blessed Mother.
B. To foster devotion to the rosary as a means of honoring Mary.
C. To foster a desire to imitate Mary in her charity to her neighbor.

III. SUGGESTED PROCEDURE

A. Approach

You remember the story of the Angel Gabriel coming to the Blessed Virgin. What a joyful event for Mary when she heard the message from God. Because of this message another joyful visit happened.

B. Presentation

1. Second Joyful Mystery — The Visitation

The Angel Gabriel told Mary the good news about her cousin Elizabeth. Mary, filled with the Holy Spirit and love for her cousin, decided to visit Elizabeth. (Show picture of the Visitation.) What a wonderful meeting of Mary and her cousin. Both were happy, both had a secret. This is another Joyful Mystery called the Visitation. Can you tell the joyful part of this visit?

Children retell the story of the Visitation.

2. Recite a Decade of the Rosary — Ask for Help

Mary was kind and helpful to her cousin Elizabeth. She did not think of herself only, but of others. When we are charitable and kind to others we serve Jesus who is in their hearts. We want to be like Mary, thinking of others more than of ourselves and helping them every chance we get.

When we recite the decade of the rosary, the Visitation, we will ask Mary to help us be like she was, kind and helpful to everyone.

C. Organization

1. What did the angel tell Mary about her cousin Elizabeth?
2. What did Mary do?
3. What did Elizabeth say when she saw Mary?
4. What did Mary say about herself?
5. What do you think Mary did for her cousin during her visit?

D. Virtues and Practices

1. Show kindness to others.
2. Help others who need assistance, the sick, the aged, etc.

IV. SUGGESTED LEARNING ACTIVITIES

A. Picture study of the Visitation.
B. Dramatize the meeting of Mary and Elizabeth.

V. TEACHER REFERENCES

A. Fitzpatrick, *Religion in Life Curriculum, First Grade Manual,* pp. 50–52.
B. S.N.D., *Religious Teaching of Young Children,* pp. 22–23.

LESSON 130

I. SUBJECT MATTER

The Third Joyful Mystery — The Nativity

II. OBJECTIVES

A. To recall the joy of Mary at the birth of Jesus.
B. To foster devotion to the rosary as a means of honoring Mary.

III. SUGGESTED PROCEDURE

A. Approach

Joyful Mysteries are the wonderful and joyful things that happened to Jesus and Mary. One of the most joyful events happened on Christmas Day — the birth of our Lord.

B. Presentation

1. *Third Joyful Mystery — The Nativity*

Jesus was God. He could have been born with all the riches in the world. But He chose a poor place for His home when He came upon earth as God and Man. What a joyful event for Mary and Joseph! It was joyful for us, too, to have God become Man and choose to live among us, to show us the way to heaven. The birth of our Lord, called the Nativity, is the third Joyful Mystery.

Children retell the story of the Nativity and all related events.

2. *Recite the Decade of the Rosary — Ask for Help*

The first Christmas day was a joyful day to Mary and Joseph. Holding the greatest treasure, Jesus, kneeling and adoring Him made them happy. They did not mind the poor stable and the poor objects in it. They had love for each other. Riches don't make us happy. We should be satisfied with what we have and serve God with love.

When we recite the decade of the rosary, let us ask Mary to help us love Jesus more than anything else and to make us satisfied with what we have.

C. Organization

1. Why did Mary and Joseph go to Bethlehem?
2. Why did they make the stable their home?
3. What wonderful thing happened that night in the stable?
4. What did Mary and Joseph do to show they knew Jesus was God?
5. Who came from the hillside to adore Jesus?

D. Virtues and Practices

1. Believe that Jesus is God.
2. Thank God the Father for sending His Son to us.

IV. SUGGESTED LEARNING ACTIVITIES

A. Read the Christmas story from a classroom reader.
B. Encourage the family rosary in the home.

V. TEACHER REFERENCES

A. S.N.D., *Religious Teaching of Young Children*, pp. 24–29.
B. Fitzpatrick, *Religion in Life Curriculum Manual, First Grade Manual*, pp. 53–66.
C. Sister Mary, *et al., The Catholic Mother's Helper*, pp. 71–79.

LESSON 131

I. SUBJECT MATTER

The Fourth Joyful Mystery — The Presentation

II. OBJECTIVES

A. To further the knowledge of Mary's virtues as shown in this mystery.
B. To foster the desire to imitate Mary in these virtues.

III. SUGGESTED PROCEDURE

A. Approach

When you were a little baby the first place your father and mother took you was to church to be baptized. Do you remember what Mary and Joseph did when they took Jesus to the temple? (Present picture of the Presentation.)

B. Presentation

1. Fourth Joyful Mystery — The Presentation

It was a Jewish custom that the parents present their child in the temple and offer him up to God. St. Joseph and Mary knew that Jesus was not an ordinary Child like the others. He was the Son of

God, God Himself. He did not need to be presented in the temple. But Mary and Joseph were always obedient. Even now, they obeyed the law, presented Jesus in the temple, and made their offering. Do you recall the joyful feeling Simeon had when He recognized the Saviour? This is the fourth Joyful Mystery of the rosary called the Presentation.

Do you remember all that happened and all that was said at the Presentation?

Children retell the story of the Presentation.

2. *Recite the Decade of the Rosary — Ask for Help*

What wonderful obedience of the Holy Family! They always wanted to please God by doing His will. They obeyed the laws of God and the laws of the town. Sometimes we do not want to obey, we do what we feel like doing instead of what is right.

Think, do you then really feel happy? If we obey willingly and cheerfully at home and in school we may be sure that God loves us more and is very pleased with us. (Develop specific points in obedience: work, companions, food, modesty.)

When you recite the decade of the rosary, ask Jesus and Mary to make you an obedient child.

C. Organization
1. Why did Mary take Jesus to the temple?
2. Why was Simeon so very happy to see Jesus?
3. What did he tell Mary about her Baby?
4. What did Anna tell her?
5. Who do you think told Simeon to go to the Temple that day?

D. Virtues and Practices
1. Obey those in authority.
2. Be humble in imitation of Mary.
3. Do good when something inside of you tells you to do the good thing.
4. Offer all we do and have to God, as Mary did.

IV. SUGGESTED LEARNING ACTIVITIES

A. Discuss what gifts children can offer daily to Jesus.
B. Dramatize the story.

V. TEACHER REFERENCES

A. Dennerle, *Leading the Little Ones to Christ,* pp. 105–108.
B. Schumacher, *I Teach Catechism,* Vol. I, pp. 53–54.
C. Fitzpatrick, *Religion in Life Curriculum, First Grade Manual,* pp. 66–68.

LESSON 132

I. SUBJECT MATTER

The Fifth Joyful Mystery — The Finding of Jesus in the Temple

II. OBJECTIVES

A. To further the knowledge of Mary's virtues as shown in this mystery.
B. To foster the imitation of Mary's perseverance in prayer.
C. To foster the imitation of Jesus in His obedience to His parents.

III. SUGGESTED PROCEDURE

A. Approach

When Jesus was twelve years of age, the Holy Family went to Jerusalem to celebrate a great feast. It was a great celebration which ended sadly. Do you recall why? (Show picture — Jesus in the Temple.)

B. Presentation

1. Fifth Joyful Mystery — Finding of Jesus in the Temple

Every year Mary and Joseph went to Jerusalem to celebrate the Jewish feast. This time Jesus went, too. They stayed there several days. While Mary and Joseph were returning home they noticed Jesus missing. What a sad feeling, Jesus was lost. After three days of searching they found Him in the temple amidst doctors. How surprised these men were! If they only knew that they were talking to a little Boy who was God, Himself. What a joy for Joseph and Mary to find their Son!

That is the last Joyful Mystery, called the Finding of Jesus in the Temple. Can you tell what Mary said to Jesus?

Children retell the facts of finding Jesus in the Temple.

2. *Recite the Decade of the Rosary — Ask for Help*

Like Mary and Joseph we too must search for Jesus every day and remain close to Him. Jesus will be very pleased if we go along with Him on our voyage leading us to heaven. With Jesus and Mary at your side you will love Him more and never want to hurt Him.

When you recite the decade of the Rosary, ask Jesus and Mary to keep you as their closest friend.

C. Organization

1. Why did the Holy Family go to the temple?
2. What did Jesus do when it was time to go home?
3. When did Mary and Joseph know that Jesus was not in the group?
4. Did Jesus know that His absence would make Mary and Joseph suffer?
5. Why did He stay in the temple?
6. How long did Mary and Joseph look for Jesus?
7. What reason did Jesus give His mother for remaining in the temple?
8. How did Jesus obey His mother?
9. How do we lose our friendship with Jesus?
10. What must we do to make Jesus our Friend again?

D. Virtues and Practices

1. Keep saying your daily prayers.
2. Obey your parents and those in authority.
3. Pay attention during religious instructions, in church, in school, at home.
4. Tell Jesus you are sorry after you commit sin.

IV. SUGGESTED LEARNING ACTIVITIES

A. Discuss reason why Jesus let His parents suffer.
B. Pantomime this mystery.

V. TEACHER REFERENCES

A. Sister Mary, *et al., The Catholic Mother's Helper,* pp. 92–95.

B. Sr. Marguerite, *Their Hearts Are His Garden,* pp. 131–133.
C. S.N.D., *Religious Teaching of Young Children,* pp. 37–39.
D. Dennerle, *Leading the Little Ones to Christ,* pp. 110–117.

LESSON 133

I. SUBJECT MATTER

The First Sorrowful Mystery — The Agony in the Garden

II. OBJECTIVES

A. To become acquainted with the sorrowful mysteries of the rosary
B. To foster sorrow for sin.

III. SUGGESTED PROCEDURE

A. Approach

Jesus came on earth to suffer and die for us, so He could open the gates of heaven again. When we think of all the things Jesus suffered for us we are sad and sorrowful. We call those mysteries of the rosary which remind us of Jesus' sufferings the Sorrowful Mysteries.

B. Presentation

1. The First Sorrowful Mystery — The Agony in the Garden

After Jesus ate the Last Supper with His Apostles and after He gave us a gift of Himself in the Holy Eucharist, He went to the Garden of Olives to pray. (Show picture — Agony in the Garden.) Jesus was very sad, for He knew that He was going to suffer a great deal and die on the cross. How Jesus' heart hurt to see the many sins that people commit because they do not love Him. This Sorrowful Mystery is called the Agony in the Garden. Can you tell other sad things that happened in the Garden of Olives? Children relate the story of the "Agony in the Garden."

2. Recite the Decade of the Rosary — Ask for Help

When we see Jesus suffer such great agony it makes us feel sad, too. Our sins did that to Jesus. Mother Mary is sad too, when she sees how we hurt her Son, Jesus. Tell Jesus how sorry you are and promise to remain close to Him. We need help to be faithful to Jesus. We must watch and pray.

When you say the decade of the rosary ask Mary to help you remain good and please Jesus in all you do and say.

C. Organization

1. How did Jesus pray in the garden?
2. What caused the bloody sweat?
3. What did the Apostles do while our Lord prayed?
4. What did Jesus say to them?
5. Do we always do as Jesus wants us to?

D. Virtues and Practices

1. Accept whatever God sends.
2. Be sorry for your sins.
3. Try to make Jesus happy today by being good.

IV. SUGGESTED LEARNING ACTIVITIES

A. Retell the story of the agony in the garden.
B. Discuss the cause of Jesus' sufferings and how we can please Him by doing good.

V. TEACHER REFERENCES

A. S.N.D., *Religious Teaching of Young Children*, pp. 60–61.
B. Schumacher, *I Teach Catechism*, Vol. I, pp. 76–78.
C. Dennerle, *Leading the Little Ones to Christ*, pp. 186–188.

LESSON 134

I. SUBJECT MATTER

The Second Sorrowful Mystery — Scourging at the Pillar.

II. OBJECTIVES

A. To become acquainted with the second sorrowful mystery of the rosary.
B. To renew our love for our crucified Saviour.
C. To foster a spirit of patient suffering for Christ.

III. SUGGESTED PROCEDURE

A. Approach

Jesus was always kind to the people. He blessed them with many miracles, but they were not kind to Him. They were ungrateful.

B. Presentation

1. The Second Sorrowful Mystery — The Scourging at the Pillar

After Jesus finished praying in the Garden of Olives, He was seized by the soldiers and put into prison. All night long He was mistreated by them. (Show picture of the Scourging at the Pillar.) Look, poor Jesus, our King, is being whipped, and drops of blood are streaming down His body.

This scourging at the pillar is a Sorrowful Mystery. How Jesus was able to endure all that, no one can understand. But He took it all in silence for love of you and me.

Can you tell some things that happened during the night?

Review and discuss the sad treatment Jesus received during the night.

2. Recite the Decade of the Rosary — Ask for Help

Jesus was silent, He never uttered a word of complaint for the injustice and mistreatments toward Him. How often we cry, pout, complain, and pity ourselves when we are sick or when something happens to us.

Little sacrifices and offering of our pain and sorrow as our penance will console us and make us resemble Jesus more.

When we say this decade of the rosary, we should ask for the grace to be patient and silent during our sickness and not to complain when we can't have something we want.

C. Organization

1. Why was our Lord taken to Pontius Pilate's palace?
2. Why was Pilate afraid to set Jesus free?
3. How was Jesus scourged?
4. Why did Jesus permit Himself to be scourged?

D. Virtues and Practices

1. Do hard things for the love of God.
2. Do little penances to make up for your sins.
3. Do not complain about our little aches and pains.

IV. SUGGESTED LEARNING ACTIVITIES

A. Retell the story of the scourging.

B. Discuss the heroic patience of Jesus and tell how we can imitate Him in our little everyday trials.

V. TEACHER REFERENCES

A. S.N.D., *Religious Teaching of Young Children*, pp. 65–66.

B. Schumacher, *I Teach Catechism*, Vol. I, p. 79.

C. Dennerle, *Leading the Little Ones to Christ*, p. 198.

LESSON 135

I. SUBJECT MATTER

The Third Sorrowful Mystery — The Crowning With Thorns

II. OBJECTIVES

A. To become acquainted with the third sorrowful mystery of the rosary.

B. To foster an appreciation of the sufferings of our Lord.

III. SUGGESTED PROCEDURE

A. Approach

While the soldiers of Pilate had Jesus, they did something very cruel to Him. (Show picture — Crowning With Thorns.) It was a very painful thing that they did to Jesus.

B. Presentation

1. The Third Sorrowful Mystery — The Crowning With Thorns

Jesus had once said that He was the King of the Jews. Now the soldiers made fun of Him for claiming to be a king. Look at the crown of thorns on His head. What a terrible thing to do to Jesus! How painful it must have been!

This Sorrowful Mystery is known as the Crowning With Thorns. Jesus, who had done only good and kind things to others, is now treated shamefully by the rough soldiers who thought they were playing a joke and having fun. How Jesus must have suffered for us. Children relate other sad events of this night.

2. *Recite the Decade of the Rosary — Ask for Help*

Pilate was a coward. Being afraid of the people, he let Jesus suffer at the hands of his soldiers. He feared to do what is right.

Sometimes, we, too, say and do things because we are afraid of people.

Jesus and Mary want us to be brave and always do what is right no matter what it costs us. When you say the decade of the rosary ask Jesus and Mary to help you be brave and always do what is right.

C. Organization

1. Why did the soldiers crown Jesus?
2. How was the crown made?
3. How was it put on Jesus' head?
4. What other cruel things did the soldiers do to our Lord?
5. Why did Jesus suffer like this?

D. Virtues and Practices

1. Do not show hurt feelings when others are preferred to you.
2. Think beautiful and pure thoughts.
3. Suffer with Jesus for sinners.

IV. SUGGESTED LEARNING ACTIVITIES

A. Retell the story of the crowning with thorns.
B. Discuss how Jesus made up for our sins of pride by being crowned with thorns.

V. TEACHER REFERENCES

A. S.N.D., *Religious Teaching of Young Children*, pp. 65–66.
B. Schumacher, *I Teach Catechism*, pp. 79–80.
C. Dennerle, *Leading the Little Ones to Christ*, pp. 198–199.

LESSON 136

I. SUBJECT MATTER

The Fourth Sorrowful Mystery — The Carrying of the Cross

II. OBJECTIVES

A. To become acquainted with the fourth sorrowful mystery of the rosary.

B. To foster a sincere sympathy for those who suffer.

III. SUGGESTED PROCEDURE

A. Approach

The cross on which Jesus was to die was very heavy. It was made not only of wood, but also of something that only He could see — the sins of the people.

B. Presentation

1. The Fourth Sorrowful Mystery — Jesus Carries the Cross

Pilate was weak and cowardly, He gave Jesus to the Jews. They decided to crucify Jesus on the cross. Jesus had to carry the heavy cross up the steep hill to Mount Calvary. (Show picture — Jesus carries the Cross.)

How terribly He suffered on the long journey up the hill. The Carrying of the Cross, another Sorrowful Mystery, was hard and agonizing. Jesus endured many hardships as He went along. How the cross must have hurt Jesus as He dragged it over the rough streets. It dug deeper into His shoulder wounded from the scourging. As He went along the Way of the Cross, other sad events happened. Can you tell about them?

Children retell about some events that occurred along the Way of the Cross, particularly those that emphasized kindness.

2. Recite the Decade of the Rosary — Ask for Help

Jesus met a few kind people along the road of suffering. They were not afraid to show their kindness to Jesus. Whenever we see someone in trouble let us be kind to them and help if we can. Being kind to others is really being kind to Jesus.

When you recite the decade of the rosary, ask Jesus and Mary to keep you close to them by being kind to others.

C. Organization

1. Why was a cloak put on Jesus?
2. Why did Pilate show our Lord to the people?
3. What did the people cry out?

4. What kind of cross did they make Jesus carry?
5. Was the cross heavy on Jesus' shoulder?

D. Virtues and Practices

1. Bear your own troubles patiently.
2. Help others who have crosses to bear.

IV. SUGGESTED LEARNING ACTIVITIES

A. Retell the story of the carrying of the cross.
B. Recall the stories of the Way of the Cross.
C. Discuss how God sometimes asks us to carry little crosses in imitation of Jesus.

V. TEACHER REFERENCES

A. S.N.D., *Religious Teaching of Young Children*, pp. 67–68.
B. Sr. Mary, *et al.*, *The Catholic Mother's Helper*, pp. 126–127.
C. Dennerle, *Leading the Little Ones to Christ*, pp. 199–200.

LESSON 137

I. SUBJECT MATTER

The Fifth Sorrowful Mystery — The Crucifixion

II. OBJECTIVES

A. To realize more fully the sufferings of Jesus.
B. To ask Mother Mary to help us thank Jesus again and again for suffering so much for love of us.

III. SUGGESTED PROCEDURE

A. Approach

As we come to the last of our Lord's suffering and the Fifth Sorrowful Mystery, we see again and again how good and how patient Jesus was. He suffered all the pain and agony for love of us.

B. Presentation

1. The Fifth Sorrowful Mystery — The Crucifixion

How much Jesus must want us to be with Him, for He suffered very much to re-open the gates of heaven. After suffering a great deal, Jesus was nailed to the cross, arms outstretched to embrace us and the world. The Blessed Virgin suffered with Him in her heart. What sorrow for a Mother to see her Son suffer so much. A sword of sorrow, likewise, pierced her heart as Jesus hung in agony.

You remember the kind words Jesus uttered from the cross. Even then Jesus showed us how good and kind He was.

Children retell the events of the Crucifixion.

2. Recite the Decade of the Rosary — Ask for Help

Who else but God loved us enough to suffer so much for us? Who else but God could have thought of giving us Mary to be a Mother to pray with us to Jesus? Let us love Joseph and Mary very much and try to make up for all they suffered by being good.

As you recite the decade of the rosary, ask Jesus and Mary to help you keep away from sin and not hurt them any more.

C. Organization
1. What made our Lord suffer so much?
2. Will praying help us to keep from sin?
3. When did Jesus give us to the Blessed Mother as her children?
4. When did Jesus give the Blessed Mother to us as our heavenly Mother?
5. Will the Blessed Mother give our prayers to Jesus if we ask her?

D. Virtues and Practices
1. Thank Jesus for dying on the cross for you.
2. Try to obey God perfectly today.

IV. SUGGESTED LEARNING ACTIVITIES

A. Discuss the meaning of the seven last words pronounced by our Lord on the cross.
B. Discuss ways in which we can show our love for Jesus by prompt obedience.

V. TEACHER REFERENCES

A. S.N.D., *Religious Teaching of Young Children*, pp. 69–70.
B. Dennerle, *Leading the Little Ones to Christ*, pp. 200–205.
C. Sister Mary, *et al., The Catholic Mother's Helper*, p. 128.

LESSON 138

I. SUBJECT MATTER

The First Glorious Mystery — The Resurrection

II. OBJECTIVES

A. To realize more fully that our Lord's Resurrection proved that He is God.

B. To rejoice with the Blessed Mother in the Resurrection.

III. SUGGESTED PROCEDURE

A. Approach

Jesus died in the most shameful way anyone could die — nailed to a cross. But that cross has become a glorious sign that helps Him prove that He is truly God.

B. Presentation

1. The First Glorious Mystery — The Resurrection

Jesus' body was taken off the cross reverently and placed into a tomb. Soldiers guarded it for fear that someone might steal Jesus' body. On Easter Sunday morning, you remember, a great surprise happened. (Show picture — The Resurrection.) Jesus rose gloriously from the dead. This greatest miracle, called the Resurrection, is the first Glorious Mystery of the Rosary.

Mary suffered with Jesus but, on the first Easter Day, her suffering turned into joy at the Resurrection of her Son.

Let the children review the story of the Resurrection and Jesus' appearances to His friends.

2. Recite the Decade of the Rosary — Ask for Help

Jesus rose from the dead in glory to teach us that we, too, will rise from the dead. But only those who served Jesus faithfully will share in His glory. When you say the decade of the rosary, ask Jesus and Mary to help you live so well that we may enjoy them in eternity.

C. Organization

1. What happened on Easter Sunday morning?
2. Whom do you think our Lord appeared to first?

272

3. How did Jesus rise from the dead?
4. Why did Jesus rise from the dead?

D. Virtues and Practices

1. Faith — I believe that Jesus is God.
2. Rejoice in Christ's victory over death.

IV. SUGGESTED LEARNING ACTIVITIES

A. Picture study and discussion of the Resurrection.
B. Story: "The Resurrection," Sister Mary, *et al.*, *The Catholic Mother's Helper*, pp. 129–131.

V. TEACHER REFERENCES

A. S.N.D., *Religious Teaching of Young Children*, pp. 72–75.
B. Dennerle, *Leading the Little Ones to Christ*, pp. 215–223.
C. Schumacher, *I Teach Catechism*, Vol. I, pp. 83–84.
D. Sr. Mary, *et al.*, *The Catholic Mother's Helper*, pp. 129–131.

LESSON 139

I. SUBJECT MATTER

The Second Glorious Mystery — The Ascension

II. OBJECTIVES

A. To realize more fully that we shall all go to heaven if we follow the good example of Jesus and Mary.
B. To increase our desire to gain a high place in heaven.

III. SUGGESTED PROCEDURE

A. Approach

Jesus had finished God's will here on earth and now it was time for His Apostles to carry on His work. He knew that if He stayed here they would never get started.

B. Presentation

1. The Second Glorious Mystery — The Ascension

When Jesus rose from the dead, He knew the Apostles were not ready to take care of His Catholic Church. After His resurrection, Jesus spent forty days upon earth instructing them and preparing them for their mission. On the fortieth day Jesus took His Apostles and friends to a high mountain. He gave them their last lesson. Suddenly, as He spoke, He lifted from the ground and began rising up until He was hid by a cloud. What a glorious moment! This glorious mystery is called the Ascension. As the Apostles stood, looking up to heaven, two angels told them that Jesus has gone into heaven and will some day come back again.

2. Recite the Decade of the Rosary — Ask for Help

Jesus ascended into heaven to prepare a place for you and me. It is up to us to get there. With Jesus' and Mary's help we can travel safely along the road until the happiness of heaven will be ours.

When you recite the decade of the rosary, ask Mother Mary to help you be good so that some day she can take you to heaven to her Son.

C. Organization
1. What happened on the third day after Jesus was buried?
2. How did Jesus rise from the dead?
3. How long did Jesus stay on earth?
4. What did Jesus do during the forty days?
5. What happened on the fortieth day?
6. Who took care of the Blessed Mother after Jesus ascended into heaven?

D. Virtues and Practices
1. Show by your actions that you want to go to heaven.
2. Be happy when you think of the place that is waiting for you in heaven.

IV. SUGGESTED LEARNING ACTIVITIES
A. Picture study and discussion of the Ascension.
B. Draw pictures illustrating the event of the Ascension.

V. TEACHER REFERENCES
A. S.N.D., *Religious Teaching of Young Children*, pp. 76–78.
B. Dennerle, *Leading the Little Ones to Christ*, pp. 224–227.

C. Sr. Mary, *et al., The Catholic Mother's Helper*, pp. 134–135.

D. Schumacher, *I Teach Catechism*, Vol. I, pp. 86–87

LESSON 140

I. SUBJECT MATTER

The Third Glorious Mystery — The Descent of the Holy Spirit

II. OBJECTIVES

A. To increase in love for the Holy Spirit.

B. To beg graces from the Holy Spirit through the intercession of our Blessed Mother.

III. SUGGESTED PROCEDURE

A. Approach

Jesus had promised to send the Holy Spirit to the Apostles. They knew that Jesus would never break a promise, so they prayed and waited until the promise was fulfilled.

B. Presentation

1. *The Third Glorious Mystery — The Descent of the Holy Spirit*

For nine days Mary and the Apostles prepared by prayer for the coming of the Holy Spirit. On the tenth day a glorious event occurred. (Show picture — Descent of the Holy Spirit.) A strong wind sounded from heaven and suddenly above each one present in the room stood a flame of fire. The Holy Spirit descended upon the Apostles and Mary in the form of fire. The Descent of the Holy Spirit upon the Apostles is one of the glorious mysteries.

The Apostles filled with the Holy Spirit were no longer afraid. Now they had the courage, wisdom, and powers to go out and teach the people about God. You remember what Peter did.

Children review the events that occurred on Pentecost Day.

2. *Recite the Decade of the Rosary — Ask for Help*

God the Holy Spirit descended upon us at the moment we were baptized. He chose us as a dwelling place, His tabernacle. We became

Temples of the Holy Spirit. We must try every day to please God so that He will never leave us.

When you recite the decade of the rosary, ask Mary to keep you a pure temple of the Holy Spirit.

C. Organization

1. Where did the Apostles go after our Lord went up to heaven?
2. How long was it before the Holy Spirit came to them?
3. In what form did the Holy Spirit come?
4. What did the Apostles do after the Holy Spirit came?
5. Who fills our souls with grace when we obey God's law?

D. Virtues and Practices

1. Think often of the Holy Spirit living in your soul.
2. Thank the Holy Spirit for His gifts.
3. Be brave in telling others you believe in God.

IV. SUGGESTED LEARNING ACTIVITIES

A. Discuss how the Holy Spirit confirmed the faith of the Apostles.
B. Discuss Mary's intercessory power.

V. TEACHER REFERENCES

A. Dennerle, *Leading the Little Ones to Christ*, pp. 232–240.
B. S.N.D., *Religious Teaching of Young Children*, pp. 76–78.
C. Sr. Mary, *et al.*, *Their Hearts Are His Garden*, pp. 152–153.
D. Sister Marguerite, *The Catholic Mother's Helper*, pp. 135–136.

LESSON 141

I. SUBJECT MATTER

The Fourth Glorious Mystery — The Assumption

II. OBJECTIVES

A. To develop the knowledge of the Assumption of the Blessed Virgin.
B. To increase in love for Mary and in the desire for a happy death.

III. SUGGESTED PROCEDURE

A. Approach

When Jesus went back to heaven He left the Apostles to continue His work. He also left Mother Mary to help them and pray for them.

B. Presentation

1. The Fourth Glorious Mystery — The Assumption

Mary was happy because Jesus went back to His heavenly Father, but she missed Him very much. How she would have loved to go to heaven with Him! But she knew that as long as He left her here on earth, there was some work He wanted her to do for Him, and as always, she wanted what God wanted. For many years Mary lived with St. John, helping the Apostles, telling them things about Jesus they might have forgotten, giving them courage or help when it seemed that they would have to give up. Most of all, she prayed for them.

Oh, how Mary prayed for them and the whole world! But all the time her heart was longing to see Jesus again, waiting for the time when He would call her to heaven with Him. And one day, that is exactly what happened. God called Mary, and she went to heaven to be with Him. Because of Mary's holiness God took her to heaven, soul and body. (Show picture — The Assumption.) This glorious mystery is called the Assumption, that means that Mary was assumed (taken) into heaven, body and soul.

When Mary entered heaven the angels and saints gave her a glorious greeting. The Blessed Trinity greeted and rewarded her.

2. The Assumption — A Holyday of Obligation

The Catholic Church celebrates Mary's Assumption on August 15. It is a holyday of obligation. (Explain.)

3. Recite the Decade of the Rosary — Ask for Help

From her place in heaven Mother Mary is looking upon us, listens to our prayers, asks Jesus to grant our petition. She wants us in heaven with her Son.

When you recite the decade of the rosary, ask Mary to help you along life's way to do what is right.

She is your good Mother, always ready to help.

C. Organization

1. Did Mary feel lonely when Jesus ascended into heaven?
2. Why did she feel that way?
3. How did Mary help the Apostles?
4. What was Mary's greatest wish?
5. Where did the Apostles put Mary's body after her death?
6. What happened to Mary's body?
7. When do we celebrate the Feast of the Assumption?

D. Virtues and Practices

1. Rejoice with the angels at Mary's entrance into heaven.
2. Raise our thoughts to Mary often during the day and ask her to take you to heaven when you die.

IV. SUGGESTED LEARNING ACTIVITIES

A. Tell the story of the Assumption.
B. Stress the fact that the Feast of the Assumption, a holyday of obligation, occurs during vacation time.
C. Discuss a picture of the Assumption.

V. TEACHER REFERENCES

A. Sister Mary, *et al.*, *The Catholic Mother's Helper*, pp. 132–136.
B. Sister Marguerite, *Their Hearts Are His Garden*, pp. 153–154.

LESSON 142

I. SUBJECT MATTER

The Fifth Glorious Mystery — The Coronation of the Blessed Virgin

II. OBJECTIVES

A. To increase in love for Mary and her rosary.
B. To foster the desire of imitating Mary's virtues, thus adding joy to her coronation as Queen of heaven and earth.

III. SUGGESTED PROCEDURE

A. Approach

All the angels and saints in heaven rejoiced when the Mother of God arrived "home." They praised her for her goodness and for her greatness. Jesus had a special way of saying "Thank you" to His Mother for all she had done.

B. Presentation

1. The Fifth Glorious Mystery — The Coronation

Here on earth a sword of sorrow pierced Mary's heart because of the many things that had happened to Jesus. Now in heaven Jesus had a special honor He wanted to bestow upon Mary. Jesus was King of heaven and earth. He wanted His mother to be the Queen. (Show picture — The Coronation.)

He placed on her head a most beautiful crown — the crown He had made for her because of her obedience to God's will and the great love she had for Him. Mary was crowned as Queen of heaven and earth. This is a glorious mystery called the Coronation.

Jesus, the Son of Mary, gave His mother all the joy, all the happiness that only heaven could give her, for heaven meant being with Him again. For all eternity she sits beside her divine Son — His mother and our mother. And just as our mother, always busy, she is taking our prayers to Jesus and asking Him for the graces we ask.

2. Recite the Decade of the Rosary — Ask for Help

Let us love our Lady, our Mother, our Queen very much and turn to her always in every joy and every need. She will never refuse to hear our prayer and like all mothers, she will be happy with our love.

When you recite the decade of the rosary, ask Mother Mary to help you remain good so that some day she may come for you at your death, and take you to heaven with Jesus and herself.

C. Organization

1. Why were the angels and saints so happy?
2. Was Mary happy to be again with her Son?
3. What did Jesus do to Mary?
4. Did Mary deserve this honor?
5. Whose Queen did Mary become?

279

6. Is Mary our Queen, too?

7. What can we do to show our Queen our true love?

D. Virtues and Practices

1. Do good to others.
2. Say your prayers fervently at all times.
3. Pray three "Hail Marys" daily for a happy death.
4. Ask Mary to help you to be her faithful child.

IV. SUGGESTED LEARNING ACTIVITIES

A. Tell the story of the Coronation of Mary.

B. Sing songs in honor of Mary.

V. TEACHER REFERENCE

Sister Mary, *et al.*, *The Catholic Mother's Helper*, p. 137.

LESSON 143

I. SUBJECT MATTER

Feast of Corpus Christi — Thursday After the Octave of Pentecost

II. OBJECTIVES

A. To foster great love for Jesus in the Blessed Sacrament, and to appreciate His presence more and more.

B. To increase the desire to visit Jesus in the Blessed Sacrament more frequently.

III. SUGGESTED PROCEDURE

A. Approach

On Ascension day Jesus went to heaven. However, before He went to His heavenly Father, He thought of a good plan to stay with us upon earth. Only God could be wise enough to think of so wonderful a plan.

B. Presentation

1. Jesus Instituted the Holy Eucharist

The night before Jesus died, He left us a wonderful gift at the

Last Supper. (Review the events of the Last Supper.) Jesus gave the Apostles the power of changing water and wine into His Sacred Body and Precious Blood. He told them to use this power in memory of Him.

The priest offers Mass every day and uses this miraculous power during Consecration.

After the Consecration, Jesus is really present on our altar, under the form of bread and wine. Isn't this kind of Jesus to want to stay with us all the time?

The white Host is really Jesus. It is always present in the tabernacle. Jesus' presence in the tabernacle is called the Blessed Sacrament.

2. Purpose of the Feast of Corpus Christi

Jesus instituted the Holy Eucharist on Holy Thursday which comes during Lent. This is a very sad time of the Church year. The Church could not joyously enough celebrate the institution of the Blessed Sacrament. Therefore, every year after Lent and Easter, we have a special feast on which we honor the Body and Blood of Jesus in the Blessed Sacrament of the Altar. This day is called "Corpus Christi" which means Body of Christ.

3. We Can Honor the Body and Blood of Jesus

How can we honor the Body and Blood of Jesus on this day? We can assist at Mass. We can take part in procession and sing hymns in honor of Jesus. During the day we can visit Jesus in the Blessed Sacrament. We can tell Jesus how much we love Him and thank Him for the wonderful gift of His Body and Blood. Also, tell Jesus how happy you will be when you receive Him in Holy Communion.

Ask Jesus to come into your heart now. (Review and make a Spiritual Communion.) Then speak to Jesus and tell Him your little secrets. But best of all, keep telling Him how much you love Him and how good you are going to be to prove your love.

C. Organization
1. When did Jesus eat His Last Supper with the Apostles?
2. What great gift did Jesus give on the same night?
3. Why did Jesus wish to remain with us?
4. Why do we celebrate the Feast of Corpus Christi?
5. What can we do to show our appreciation for this great gift?
6. How can we honor the Blessed Sacrament?

D. Virtues and Practices

1. Make frequent visits to the Blessed Sacrament.
2. During the day make spiritual communions.

IV. SUGGESTED LEARNING ACTIVITIES

A. Learn the ejaculation: "Jesus in the Blessed Sacrament have mercy on us" (*Raccolta*, 134).
B. Learn a hymn in honor of the Blessed Sacrament.
C. Take part in the procession on the feast.

V. TEACHER REFERENCE

Dennerle, *Leading the Little Ones to Christ*, pp. 181–183.

LESSON 144

I. SUBJECT MATTER

Feast of the Sacred Heart — Third Friday After Pentecost

II. OBJECTIVES

A. To foster love and devotion to the Sacred Heart.
B. To increase the desire to imitate the virtues of the Sacred Heart of Jesus.

III. SUGGESTED PROCEDURE

A. Approach

After Jesus returned to heaven no one could see Him upon earth any more. But, sometimes, Jesus appears upon earth to someone who is unusually good and loves Him very much. As He does appear, He usually has a special message for them. (Show picture of St. Margaret Mary and the Sacred Heart.)

B. Presentation

1. Jesus Appears to St. Margaret Mary

Sister Margaret Mary loved Jesus so much that she prayed very often before the Blessed Sacrament. One day, while she was at prayer, Jesus appeared to her. He was very sad. He told Sister Margaret Mary that He loves all men, but they love Him so little in return. Jesus also told Margaret to spread special devotion to His Sacred Heart. That Heart burns with love for all, but is so often hurt by our sins.

2. *Jesus' Promises*

Jesus made twelve promises to those who would love and honor His Sacred Heart. One promise was that they would have their names written in His heart. Another promise was that those who received Jesus in Holy Communion on First Friday of 9 months would be given the grace to win heaven. Many people go to Holy Communion on the first Friday because of this promise. Jesus promised special blessings upon everything we do if we do it for love of Him. (Discuss briefly some of the other promises.)

3. *Ways We Can Show Love for the Sacred Heart*

How can you show your love for the Sacred Heart? First, by visiting Jesus in the Blessed Sacrament and telling Him you love Him. Visit Him often, talk to Him in the Blessed Sacrament, not only as your God, but as your very best Friend. After you receive your first Holy Communion, you may receive Jesus every First Friday. Talk about the Sacred Heart at home. Tell your family how much He loves us and wants us to love Him. Many people offend the Sacred Heart by their sins. You can make up for them by praying to and loving the Sacred Heart more and more.

C. Organization

1. Whom did St. Margaret Mary love very much?
2. Where was her favorite place to pray?
3. Who appeared to St. Margaret Mary while she was praying?
4. What did Jesus say to her?
5. What did Jesus say makes Him very sad?
6. What did Jesus promise to those who pray to Him and show Him their love?

D. Virtues and Practices

1. Whisper little acts of love to Jesus during the day.
2. Do kind favors to someone in honor of the Sacred Heart.

IV. SUGGESTED LEARNING ACTIVITIES

A. Discuss the picture showing the Sacred Heart speaking to St. Margaret Mary.

B. Learn a hymn in honor of the Sacred Heart.

C. Learn and recite before doing something.
"All for Thee Most Sacred Heart of Jesus" (*Raccolta*, 234).

D. Poem: "The Sacred Heart of Jesus," Belger, *Sing a Song of Holy Things*, pp. 106–108.

V. TEACHER REFERENCE

Lord, Daniel, A., *The Story of the Sacred Heart*.

Units for Preparation of First Holy Communion

HOW GOD PARDONS SIN

Unit One. Subject Matter*

* For fuller detail see Units IV and V of the Pupil Text and of the Teacher's Manual for *Jesus Comes* (Grade 2) of *Our Holy Faith* Religion Series (Bruce).

A. How God in His mercy takes away original sin.

   1. General instructions on the seven sacraments:
      a) what they are
      b) where they come from
      c) how many
      d) brief explanation of "grace"

   2. The sacrament of Baptism:
      a) what it is
      b) what it does
         1) takes away original sin
         2) makes us children of God
      c) why we need the sacrament of Baptism
      d) renewal of the baptismal promises

B. How God in His mercy takes away our own sins (actual sins).

   1. Sin is disobedience to God's laws:
      a) sin offends God
      b) story of Cain and Abel

   2. Kinds of actual sin:
      a) mortal sin:
         1) what it is
         2) what it does
      b) venial sin:
         1) what it is
         2) what it does
      c) conditions necessary:
         1) mortal sin
         2) venial sin

   3. Jesus forgave the people's sins when they were sorry:
      a) story of Mary Magdalene
      b) story of the Good Thief

4. Jesus gave His power of forgiving sins to His Apostles and to all priests — the institution of the sacrament of Penance:
   a) what it is
   b) what it does
   c) why we need it

C. What I must do to receive the sacrament of Penance worthily.
   Introduction: Story of the Prodigal Son
   1. Before confession pray to the Holy Spirit:
      a) to find out your sins
      b) to be sorry for your sins:
         1) sorrow for sin because of God's goodness to us:
            (a) creation (b) providence (c) redemption
         2) sorrow for sin because of God's just punishment:
            (a) purgatory: a place of punishment to clean us of venial sins
            (b) hell: a place of everlasting suffering for those who die in mortal sin
      c) to make up your mind not to sin again:
         1) pray for God's help
         2) resolve not to sin again
   2. In the confessional:
      a) go into the confessional and kneel
      b) tell your sins to the priest
      c) suggested formula for the confession of sins:
         1) make the sign of the cross and say: "Bless me, Father, for I have sinned" (after first confession — "My last confession was . . . weeks ago.")
         2) tell your sins (begin with "I" and end with . . . "times.")
         3) be sorry for these and all the sins of your past life, "I am sorry for . . ."
         4) listen to the talk the priest gives you.
         5) listen to the penance the priest gives you.
         6) say the Act of Contrition loud enough for the priest to hear you
         7) leave the confessional after the priest has said, "God bless you," telling him "Thank you, Father."
   3. After Confession:
      a) do or say the penance that the priest gives you;

1) when it is to be done
2) what should be done if the penance is forgotten
3) prayer of thanksgiving
4) prayer of petition to help us keep our promises

b) The Seal of Confession
1) how the priest keeps it a secret
2) how we must keep it a secret

Immediate Preparation for Confession

HOW GOD CARES FOR US THROUGH THE HOLY EUCHARIST

Unit Two. Subject Matter

A. Jesus promises to give us food for our supernatural life.

1. The miraculous multiplication of the loaves and fishes:
    a) Jesus showed His love and kindness
    b) Jesus showed His great power
2. The promise of the Holy Eucharist:
    a) Jesus promised a new bread
    b) Jesus, the Bread of Life

B. Jesus keeps His promise.

1. The first Mass — the institution of the Holy Eucharist:
    a) The Last Supper
    b) the words used by Jesus to change bread and wine into His Body and Blood
    c) the meaning of this Sacrament
2. The Apostles receive their First Holy Communion
3. Jesus makes the Apostles His first priests:
    a) Jesus gave the Apostles power to change bread and wine into His Body and Blood
    b) all priests have this power
    c) they use this power at Holy Mass
4. Why Jesus gave us the Eucharist:
    a) to help us love God — in the Mass we offer Him to God
    b) to come to us in Holy Communion
    c) to remain with us in the Blessed Sacrament — He is our Friend in the Tabernacle

C. The Mass: We offer Jesus to God, His heavenly Father
1. What the Mass is:
   a) Christ offered Himself at the Last Supper
   b) Christ offered Himself on the cross
   c) Christ offers Himself in every Holy Mass
2. What we do at Mass: The three principal parts:
   a) The Offertory:
      1) the priest offers gifts to God — bread and wine
      2) we offer gifts to God: ourselves, our prayers, our good deeds
   b) The Consecration and the Elevation:
      1) what the priest does:
         (a) the priest changes bread into the Body of Jesus with the words, "This is My Body"
         (b) the priest changes wine into the Blood of Jesus with the words, "This is My Blood"
         (c) Jesus is present in every part of the consecrated host; He is present in every part of the consecrated wine
      2) what we do:
         (a) we look at the Sacred Host and say, "My Lord and my God"
         (b) we look at the chalice and say, "My Lord and my God'
      3) what Jesus does:
         (a) Jesus offers Himself to His heavenly Father
         (b) we offer Jesus to His heavenly Father through the priest
   c) The Communion:
      1) what the priest does:
         (a) the priest receives Jesus in his heart
         (b) the priest gives Jesus in Holy Communion to the people
      2) what should we do:
         (a) we should receive Jesus in Holy Communion
         (b) we should make a spiritual communion when we are not able to receive sacramentally

D. Holy Communion: Jesus is the "Bread of Life."

288

1. How to prepare for Jesus' first visit: remote preparation:
   a) by prayer: Acts of Faith, Love, and Desire
   b) by making little sacrifices
   c) by visiting Jesus in the Blessed Sacrament
   d) by keeping free from sin
   e) by being obedient, kind, truthful, etc.
   f) by imitating other first communicants
2. Holy Communion: What it means to me:
   a) who comes to me in Holy Communion:
      1) the Sacred Host is Jesus; Jesus is God
      2) the Sacred Host looks and tastes like bread
   b) who Jesus is (approachableness of Jesus):
      1) Jesus the friend of little children
      2) stories that exemplify this love: tell a story each day during the preparatory period
         (a) Blessed Imelda — *Mine* magazine (Two), May, 1954
         (b) St. Tarciscius — This is Our Town (*Third Reader*), pp. 297–304
         (c) Little Nellie — "True stories for First Communion," *Jr. Cath. Mess.*, May, 1953, p. 8
         (d) St. Gerard — *Mine* magazine (Three), April, 1949
         (e) Pius X — *Mine* magazine (Two), June, 1954
   c) what Jesus does for me in Holy Communion:
      1) Jesus lives in me and gives me grace to live a holy life
      2) He strengthens me against temptation
   d) why I want to receive Jesus:
      1) good motives
      2) unworthy motives
3. What I must do to receive Holy Communion:
   a) prepare for His coming:
      1) be free from mortal sin
      2) say prayers before Holy Communion
      3) fast — 3 hours from solid food; 1 hour from liquids except water
      4) be neat and clean
   b) at the altar:
      put head back slightly; open mouth moderately, wet the

tongue; extend the tongue out a bit and rest it on the lower lip; draw the tongue back carefully; close the mouth; if the host sticks to the roof of the mouth use the tongue to get it down; swallow the Sacred Host as soon as possible being careful never to touch it

    c) return to your place with hands folded, eyes looking down and begin prayers of thanksgiving immediately

4. What I should do after Holy Communion:
    a) talk with Jesus:
        1) tell Jesus that you believe He is in your heart (Faith)
        2) tell Jesus how much you love Him (Adoration)
        3) thank Jesus for coming to you (Thanksgiving)
        4) tell Jesus that you are sorry for all your sins (contrition)
        5) ask Jesus to help you and others (Petition)
        6) promise Jesus to be good (Resolution)

5. First Communion Day:
    a) at home:
        1) think of Jesus and make the sign of the cross when you wake up
        2) say your morning prayers
        3) keep the fast
    b) on the way to church:
        1) say prayers to Jesus
        2) think of stories about Jesus
    c) in church:
        1) pray
        2) listen to the sermon
        3) receive Holy Communion with love
        4) say prayers of thanksgiving

Subject to local customs:

Renewal of baptismal vows (sometimes made at the conclusion of the study of the sacrament of Baptism)

Enrollment in the Scapular

HOW WE CAN SHOW OUR LOVE OF GOD — PRACTICE OF RELIGION

Unit Three. Subject Matter

A. Prayer and Devotional Practices
  1. Prayers to God: review new prayers taught during the year
  2. Devotional practices:
     a) First Friday
     b) use of sacramentals: meaning
  3. Prayers to our Blessed Mother:
  4. Devotional practices to our Blessed Mother:
     a) May altar
     b) May devotion and Crowning
     c) First Saturday: Story of Our Lady of Fatima
     d) use of sacramentals:
        scapular and medals
     e) novenas
  5. Prayers to the angels and saints
  6. Devotional practices to the angels and the saints:
     a) meaning and use of relics
     b) use of sacramentals:
        1) medals
        2) statues and pictures of the angels and the saints

B. Obedience to God's laws in imitation of our Blessed Mother
  1. Our Blessed Mother prayed: First Commandment:
     a) how Mary honored God through prayer
     b) things Mary prayed for:
        1) to do God's will
        2) to love God above all things
        3) to love God's creatures
  2. Our Blessed Mother loved and honored God's name: Second Commandment
     a) how Mary loved the names given to Jesus, the Son of God and her Son
     b) how Mary loves the beautiful names we give to her:
        1) Mother of God
        2) Queen of the Angels and Saints
        3) Refuge of Sinners
        4) Comforter of the Afflicted

     5) Our Lady of the Blessed Sacrament

     6) Queen of Peace

3. Our Blessed Mother worshiped God in the Temple: Third Commandment

   a) Mary's Presentation in the Temple

   b) Mary's Presentation of the Child Jesus in the Temple

   c) Mary's attendance at Jewish ceremonies in the Temple and in the Synagogue

4. Our Blessed Mother always did God's will: Fourth Commandment

   a) Mary obeyed God and all those who took God's place

   b) Mary's reward for her life of perfect obedience to God's will:

     1) life with Jesus: sorrow and joys:

       (*a*) seven sorrows of Mary

       (*b*) five joys of Mary

     2) Mother of the Church

       First Novena: Story of Pentecost

5. Our Blessed Mother is kind to everyone: Fifth Commandment

   a) Mary showed kindness to everyone when she lived here on earth

   b) Mary shows kindness to everyone from her throne in heaven today

6. Our Blessed Mother is the purest of all God's creatures: Sixth and Ninth Commandments:

   a) Mary's freedom from all sin — original and actual

   b) Mary's reward for her purity

7. Our Blessed Mother's love for honesty and justice: Seventh and Tenth Commandments:

   a) Mary showed contentment and satisfaction:

     1) in suffering: the loss of Jesus in the temple

     2) in poverty: the flight into Egypt

   b) Mary is generous now in obtaining graces for all men:

     1) Mary, the Mediatrix of all graces

     2) Mary, the Queen of the Holy Rosary

8. Our Blessed Mother is most loving and most true. Eighth Commandment:

   a) how Mary showed her loving thoughtfulness and considerations for others at all times: wedding feast at Cana

b) Mary is faithful now in keeping her promises and helping those who pray to her:
   1) all priests
   2) her children: the faithful

C. Faithful attendance at holy Mass.
   1. Why we should be faithful
   2. When we should be faithful

D. Frequent reception of the sacraments of Penance and Holy Eucharist.
   1. When we should receive these sacraments
   2. Why we should want to receive these sacraments often

First Communion Catechism

LESSON 1

The Purpose of Man's Existence

1. **Who made you?**

   God made me.

2. **Did God make all things?**

   Yes, God made all things.

3. **Why did God make you?**

   God made me to show His goodness and to make me happy with Him in heaven.

4. **What must you do to be happy with God in heaven?**

   To be happy with God in heaven I must know Him, love Him, and serve Him in this world.

LESSON 2

God and His Perfections

5. **Where Is God?**

   God is everywhere.

6. **Does God know all things?**

   Yes, God knows all things.

7. **Can God do all things?**

   Yes, God can do all things.

FOOTNOTES FOR PARENTS AND TEACHERS

2. The teacher should relate how God created all things out of nothing. An account of the creation of the angels and their fall should be given. See question 23 of this Catechism. (See also Catechism No. 2: Questions 2, 8 to 10, 35, 36.)

4. The teacher should explain that we *know* God from reason and revelation; we *love* and *serve* God by doing what He wants us to do, that is, by keeping the Ten Commandments. (See Catechism No. 2: Questions 5, 6, 22, 23, 188 to 190, 195, 196.)

5. (See Catechism No. 2: Questions 16 to 18.)

6. (See Catechism No. 2: Question 15.)

8. Did God have a beginning?

No, God had no beginning; He always was.

9. Will God always be?

Yes, God will always be.

LESSON 3

The Unity and Trinity of God

10. Is there only one God?

Yes, there is only one God.

11. How many Persons are there in God?

In God there are three Persons — the Father, the Son, and the Holy Ghost.

12. What do we call the three Persons in one God?

We call the three Persons in one God the Blessed Trinity.

13. How do we know that there are three Persons in one God?

We know that there are three Persons in one God because we have God's word for it.

LESSON 4

The Incarnation

14. Did one of the Persons of the Blessed Trinity become man?

Yes, the Second Person, the Son of God, became man.

15. What is the name of the Son of God made man?

The name of the Son of God made man is Jesus Christ.

---

8. (See Catechism No. 2: Questions 10, 13.)

13. Children may be told that they show their belief in the Blessed Trinity every time they make the sign of the cross or recite the "Glory be, etc." (See Catechism No. 2: Questions 33, 34, 487 to 489.)

15. Children should be taught to bow their heads reverently whenever the Sacred Name of Jesus is mentioned.

16. When was Jesus born?

Jesus was born on the first Christmas Day, more than nineteen hundred years ago.

17. Who is the Mother of Jesus?

The Mother of Jesus is the Blessed Virgin Mary.

18. Is Jesus Christ both God and man?

Yes, Jesus Christ is both God and man.

LESSON 5

The Redemption; the Church

19. Why did God the Son become man?

God the Son became man to satisfy for the sins of all men and to help everybody to gain heaven.

20. How did Jesus satisfy for the sins of all men?

Jesus satisfied for the sins of all men by His sufferings and death on the cross.

21. How does Jesus help all men to gain heaven?

Jesus helps all men to gain heaven through the Catholic Church.

LESSON 6

Sin; Original Sin

22. What is sin?

Sin is disobedience to God's laws.

---

16. The account of Our Lord's birth should be told to the children. (See Catechism No. 2: Questions 86 to 89.)

18. (See Catechism No. 2: Questions 79 to 85.)

19. (See Catechism No. 2: Question 90.)

20. Our Lord's suffering and death should be explained, stressing the love of God for us. (See Catechism No. 2: Questions 91 to 94.)

21. (See Catechism No. 2: Questions 136 to 169.)

23. **Who committed the first sin?**

The bad angels committed the first sin.

24. **Who committed the first sin on earth?**

Our first parents, Adam and Eve, committed the first sin on earth.

25. **Is this sin passed on to us from Adam?**

Yes, this sin is passed on to us from Adam.

26. **What is this sin in us called?**

This sin in us is called original sin.

27. **Was anyone ever free from original sin?**

The Blessed Virgin Mary was free from original sin.

LESSON 7

Actual Sin

28. **Is original sin the only kind of sin?**

No, there is another kind of sin, called actual sin.

29. **What is actual sin?**

Actual sin is any sin which we ourselves commit.

30. **How many kinds of actual sin are there?**

There are two kinds of actual sin: mortal sin and venial sin.

31. **What is mortal sin?**

Mortal sin is a deadly sin.

---

23. Parents and teachers should again remind children about the creation of the angels and the fall of the bad angels. Children should be told about their guardian angels and how they help them. (See Catechism No. 2: Questions 36 to 46.)

24. (See Catechism No. 2: Questions 51 to 56.)

25. (See Catechism No. 2: Question 57.)

26. (See Catechism No. 2: Questions 59 to 61.)

27. (See Catechism No. 2: Question 62.)

28. (See Catechism No. 2: Question 64.)

31. For example, it is a mortal sin to commit murder, or to miss Mass on Sunday through one's own fault. (See Catechism No. 2: Question 66.)

32. **What does mortal sin do to us?**

Mortal sin makes us enemies of God and robs our souls of His grace.

33. **What happens to those who die in mortal sin?**

Those who die in mortal sin are punished forever in the fire of hell.

34. **What is venial sin?**

Venial sin is a lesser sin.

35. **Does venial sin make us enemies of God or rob our souls of His grace?**

No, venial sin does not make us enemies of God or rob our souls of His grace.

36. **Does venial sin displease God?**

Yes, venial sin does displease God.

LESSON 8

The Sacraments; Baptism, Confirmation

37. **How does the Catholic Church help us to gain heaven?**

The Catholic Church helps us to gain heaven especially through the sacraments.

38. **What is a sacrament?**

A sacrament is an outward sign, instituted by Christ to give grace.

39. **What does grace do to the soul?**

Grace makes the soul holy and pleasing to God.

---

32. (See Catechism No. 2: Questions 67 to 69.) See also question 39 on page 7 of this Catechism.

33. It should be explained simply that those who die in the state of grace go to heaven, where they see God and are happy forever, while those who die with mortal sin on their souls go to hell, where they never see God and where they suffer the pains of fire and torments that will never end. (See Catechism No. 2: Question 185.)

34. For example. it is a venial sin to lie or to disobey one's parents. (See Catechism No. 2: Questions 70 to 72, 184.)

39. (See Catechism No. 2: Questions 109 to 117.)

40. What sacrament have you received?

I have received the sacrament of Baptism.

41. What did Baptism do for you?

Baptism washed away original sin from my soul and made it rich in the grace of God.

42. Are you preparing to receive other sacraments?

I am preparing to receive the sacraments of Confirmation, Penance, and Holy Eucharist.

43. What will Confirmation do for you?

Confirmation, through the coming of the Holy Ghost, will make me a soldier of Jesus Christ.

LESSON 9

Penance

44. What is the sacrament of Penance?

Penance is the sacrament by which sins committed after Baptism are forgiven.

45. What must you do to receive the sacrament of Penance worthily?

To receive the sacrament of Penance worthily I must:
1. Find out my sins.
2. Be sorry for my sins.
3. Make up my mind not to sin again.
4. Tell my sins to the priest.
5. Do the penance the priest gives me.

---

40. Questions 40, 42, and 43 presuppose that the child has not been confirmed before First Communion.

41. (See Catechism No. 2: Questions 315 to 317.)

43. (See Catechism No. 2: Questions 330 to 342.)

44. (See Catechism No. 2: Questions 379 to 383.)

45. Children need to be helped in preparing for confession. They should be taught how to examine their consciences, etc. (See Catechism No. 2: Questions 384 to 420.)

LESSON 10

How to Make a Good Confession

46. How do you make your confession?

I make my confession in this way:

1. I go into the confessional and kneel.
2. I make the sign of the cross and say: "Bless me, Father, for I have sinned."
3. I say: "This is my first confession" (or, "It has been one week, or one month, since my last confession").
4. I confess my sins.
5. I listen to what the priest tells me.
6. I say the act of contrition loud enough for the priest to hear me.

47. What do you do after leaving the confessional?

After leaving the confessional, I say the penance the priest has given me and thank God for forgiving my sins.

LESSON 11

The Holy Eucharist

48. What is the sacrament of the Holy Eucharist?

The Holy Eucharist is the sacrament of the body and blood of Our Lord Jesus Christ.

49. When does Jesus Christ become present in the Holy Eucharist?

Jesus Christ becomes present in the Holy Eucharist during the Sacrifice of the Mass.

---

46. (See Catechism No. 2: Questions 426 to 433.)
47. (See Catechism No. 2: Question 434.)
48. (See Catechism No. 2: Questions 343 to 347.)
49. The mystery of the Real Presence may be stated briefly. At Mass the host is ordinary bread before consecration. But when the priest pronounces the words of consecration, bread and wine are changed into the living body and blood of Christ. The Host, therefore, is Jesus Christ Himself and no longer ordinary bread, though it appears as such to our sight, taste, and touch. Hence, we should assist at Mass and visit Our Lord present in the Blessed Sacrament on the altar whenever we can. Children should be taught to genuflect whenever they come into the presence of the Blessed Sacrament. Whenever they pass a Catholic Church, boys should reverently raise their hats and girls should bow their heads. (See Catechism No. 2: Questions 347 to 365.)

50. Do you receive Jesus Christ in the sacrament of the Holy Eucharist?

I do receive Jesus Christ in the sacrament of the Holy Eucharist when I receive Holy Communion.

51. Do you see Jesus Christ in the Holy Eucharist?

No, I do not see Jesus Christ in the Holy Eucharist because He is hidden under the appearances of bread and wine.

52. What must you do to receive Holy Communion?

To receive Holy Communion I must:

1. Have my soul free from mortal sin.
2. Not eat anything for three hours before Holy Communion or drink anything for one hour. But water may be taken at any time before Holy Communion.

53. What should you do before Holy Communion?

Before Holy Communion I should:

1. Think of Jesus.
2. Say the prayers I have learned.
3. Ask Jesus to come to me.

54. What should you do after Holy Communion?

After Holy Communion I should:

1. Thank Jesus for coming to me.
2. Tell Him how much I love Him.
3. Ask Him to help me.
4. Pray for others.

---

51. (See Catechism No. 2: Questions 348 to 352.)
52. (See Catechism No. 2: Questions 367 to 371.)
53. (See Catechism No. 2: Question 373.)
54. (See Catechism No. 2: Question 374.)

Bibliography

TEACHER REFERENCES*

1. Aurelia, Sister Mary, and Kirsch, F., *Practical Aids for Catholic Teachers* (New York: Benziger Bros., 1928).
2. Bandas, R., *Catechetics in the New Testament* (Milwaukee: Bruce, 1935).
3. Bedier, Julie, *Lots of Sisters and Brothers* (New York: Macmillan, 1949).
4. ——— *My Book About God* (New York: Macmillan, 1948).
5. Brennan, Gerald, *Angel City* (Milwaukee: Bruce, 1946).
6. ——— *Angel Food* (Milwaukee: Bruce, 1948).
7. ——— *God Died at Three O'Clock* (Milwaukee: Bruce, 1947).
8. ——— *Going His Way* (Milwaukee: Bruce, 1946).
9. ——— *For Heaven's Sake* (Milwaukee: Bruce, 1946).
10. *A Catholic Catechism*, American Edition (New York: Herder, 1957).
11. *Dennerle, George, *Leading the Little Ones to Christ* (Milwaukee: Bruce, 1944).
12. Doane, Pelagie, *A Small Child's Bible* (New York: Oxford University Press, 1946).
13. Dorcy, Sister Mary Jean, O.P., *Mary, My Mother* (New York: Sheed and Ward, 1944).
14. ——— *Our Lady's Feasts* (New York: Sheed and Ward, 1945).
15. Doyle, Charles, *Do You Know Jesus?* (Paterson, N. J.: St. Anthony Guild Press, 1942).
16. Heeg, Aloysius, *Jesus and I* (Chicago: Loyola University Press, 1934).
17. ——— *Practical Helps for the Religion Teacher* (St. Louis, Mo.: The Queen's Work, 1944).
18. Hosty, Thos. J., *Small Talks for Small People* (Milwaukee: Bruce, 1943).
19. Hunt, Marigold, *A Life of Our Lord for Children* (New York: Sheed and Ward, 1939).
20. Johnson, George, *The Bible Story* (New York: Benziger Bros., 1931).
21. Jungman, Joseph, *Handing on the Faith* (New York: Herder, 1960). ?.
22. Lloyd, Teresa, *Jesus For Little Folks* (London: Sands and Company, 1934).
23. Lord, Daniel A., *A Catholic Child Believes* (New York: Devotional Pub. Co., 1952).
24. ——— *Jesus, the Hero* (New York: Hirten & Co., Inc., 1944).
25. ——— *The Story of the Blessed Virgin* (New York: Hirten, 1944).
26. ——— *The Story of Christmas* (New York: Hirten & Co., Inc., 1944).
27. ——— *The Story of the Holy Family* (New York: Hirten & Co., Inc., 1944).
28. ——— *When Our Lord Was a Boy* (New York: Hirten, 1945).
29. *Marguerite, Sister Mary, *Their Hearts Are His Garden* (Paterson, N. J.: St. Anthony Guild Press [rev. ed.], 1946).
30. Maria de la Cruz, Sister, H.H.S., Sister Mary Richard, H.H.S., *With Christ to the Father*, Grade I, On Our Way Series (Chicago: Sadlier, Inc., 1958).
31. *Mary, Sister, and Sisters Roberta and Mary Rosary, *The Catholic Mother's Helper* (Paterson, N. J.: St. Anthony Guild Press, 1948).

---

* The starred books are essential to the successful teaching of this religious program.

32. Parsh, Dr. Pius, *The Church's Year of Grace*, Vol. 1–5 (Collegeville, Minn.: Liturgical Press, 1953).
33. *Religion in Life Curriculum*, 1st Grade Manual (Milwaukee: Bruce, 1942).
34. A Religious of the Cenacle, *Stations of the Cross for Children* (New York: Paulist Press, 1936).
35. Schumacher, M. A., *I Teach Catechism*, Vol. I (New York: Benziger Bros., 1946).
36. S.N.D., *Religious Teaching of Young Children* (Westminster, Md.: Newman Bookshop, 1947).
37. Weiser, Francis X., *Religious Customs in the Family* (Collegeville, Minn.: The Liturgical Press, 1956).
38. Westenberger, E. J., and Kleiber, R. J., *God Loves Me* (First Communion Ed.) Our Life With God Religion Series, Grade 1 (Chicago 1, Ill.: Sadlier, Inc.).
39. Windeatt, M. F., *Children of Fatima* (St. Meinrad, Ind.: Benedictine Abbey, 1945).

Poetry

1. Banigan, Sharon, and Pegis, J., *Hear Our Prayer* (Garden City, N. Y.: Garden City Publishing Co., 1946).
2. *Belger, Sister Mary Josita, O.S.F., *Sing a Song of Holy Things* (Milwaukee: Tower Press, 5701 W. Washington Blvd., 1945).
3. Cook, Frederick, *The Way of the Cross for Little Feet* (Paterson, N. J.: St. Anthony Guild Press, 1942).
4. ———— *The Rosary for Little Fingers* (Paterson, N. J.: St. Anthony Guild Press, 1944).
5. Doyle, William, *Religious Poems for Little Children* (Milwaukee: Bruce).
6. Ellis, Constance Turner, *God With Us* (New York: C. Wilderman Co., 1949).
7. *Fitzpatrick, E. A., *Religious Poems for Little Folks* (Milwaukee: Bruce, 1938).
8. Kirby, Anastasia Joan, *A Dream of Christmas Eve* (Paterson, N. J.: St. Anthony Guild, 1937).
9. Lord, Daniel A., *Chants for Children* (St. Louis, Mo.: The Queen's Work, 1946).
10. Moran, *Verses for Tiny Tots* (Milwaukee: Bruce, 1937).
11. School Sisters of Notre Dame, *The Our Father for Little Ones* (St. Paul, Minn.: Catechetical Guild, 1940).
12. S. E., *Poem's for God's Children* (Paterson, N. J.: St. Anthony Guild Press, 1946).
13. Thayer, Mary Dixon, *The Child on His Knees* (New York: Macmillan, 1948).

Music

1. Finn, Wm. J., *Song Wings* (Boston: C. C. Birchard & Co., 1940).
2. Francis, Father, *Around the World in Picture and Song* (Milwaukee: 1501 S. Layton Blvd.).
3. *The Music Hour Series*, Catholic Ed. (Chicago: Silver Burdett Co., 1937).
4. *My First Hymnal* (Cincinnati: World Library of Sacred Music).
5. *The New St. Basil Hymnal* (Cincinnati: Willis Music Co., 1958).

6. *The St. Gregory Hymnal* (Philadelphia: St. Gregory Guild Press, Inc., 1940).

7. School Sisters of Saint Francis, *Our Prayer Songs* (Boston: McLaughlin & Reilly, 1951).

8. *Sing Joyfully* (Lower Grades) (New York: Follett Pub. Co., 1954).

9. *We Sing and Praise Series* (Chicago: Ginn and Company, 1960).

General References

1. Bandas, R., *Religious Instruction and Education* (New York: J. F. Wagner, Inc., 1938).

2. Carroll, James F., *God the Holy Ghost* (New York: P. J. Kenedy & Sons, 1940).

3. Catholic Biblical Association, *A Commentary on the New Testament* (Paterson, N. J.: St. Anthony Guild Press, 1942).

4. Collins, J. B., *Teaching Religion* (Milwaukee: Bruce, 1953).

5. Fouard, Constant, *The Christ: The Son of God,* Vol. I and II (New York: Longmans, Green and Company, 1944).

6. Fuerst, A. N., *The Systematic Teaching of Religion* (New York: Benziger Bros., 1939–1946).

7. Goodier, Alban, S.J., *The Passion and Death of Our Lord Jesus Christ* (New York: P. J. Kenedy and Sons, 1933).

8. ———— *The Public Life of Our Lord Jesus Christ* (New York: P. J. Kenedy and Sons, 1933).

9. *The New Testament* (Confraternity Edition) (Paterson, N. J.: St. Anthony Guild Press).

10. O'Brien, Isidore, *The Life of Christ* (Paterson, N. J.: St. Anthony Guild Press, 1937).

11. Ricciotti, Giuseppe, *The Life of Christ* (Milwaukee: Bruce, 1937).

12. Rosalia, Sister, *Child Psychology and Religion* (New York: P. J. Kenedy and Sons)

13. Russell, Wm. H., *Christ the Leader* (Milwaukee: Bruce, 1937).

14. Strasser, Bernard, *With Christ Through the Year* (Milwaukee: Bruce, 1958).

15. Temple, Patrick J., *Pattern Divine* (St. Louis, Mo.: Herder Book Co., 1950).

16. Willam, Franz, *The Life of Jesus Christ* (St. Louis, Mo.: Herder, 1945).

17. ———— *Mary, The Mother of Jesus* (St. Louis, Mo.: Herder, 1938).

AUDIO-VISUAL MATERIALS

A. Motion Pictures, Slides, Filmstrips

1. Eye Gate House, Inc., 146–01 Archer Ave., Jamaica 35, N. Y.: — *Stations of the Cross; The Mysteries of the Rosary; The Lord's Prayer and Hail Mary; The Catholic Way* (24 filmstrips plus records); *Calendar of the Saints* (10 filmstrips plus record)

2. Catechetical Guild, St. Paul 2, Minn. — *Life of Jesus* (6 filmstrips plus record)

3. St. John University, Jamaica 32, N. Y. — *St. John's Catechism*

4. Encyclopaedia Britannica Films, 1150 Wilmette Avenue, Wilmette, Ill. — *The Holy Mass; New Testament Series* (12 filmstrips)

B. Recordings

1. Catholic Children's Record Club, P.O. 333, Tuckahoe, N. Y. — *The Story of Jesus Christ with Prayers and Hymns*
2. Catholic Educational Recordings, Educational Sales Department, RCA Victor Division, Camden, N. J. — *Lives of the Saints*

C. Pictures

1. Catechetical Guild, Educational Society, 147 E. 5th Street, St. Paul, Minn. — Gouppy Sets: *The Hail Mary; The Our Father; How a Nice Little Girl Spends Her Day; How a Nice Little Boy Spends His Day; The Apostles' Creed; Chi-Rho Cards for Teaching the Mass*
2. Publications for Catholic Youth, 25 Groveland Terrace, Minneapolis, Minn. — *The Sacraments; Bulletin Board Pictures* (Sets A, B, C); *The Commandments*
3. Notre Dame Publishing Co., Inc., 60 Lafayette Street, New York City, N. Y. — *Lord's Prayer; Hail Mary; Stations of the Cross; Apostles' Creed; Mass Pictures*

D. Charts

1. Loyola University Press, Chicago, Ill. — *Jesus and I*
2. Parish Co-op Services, Effingham, Ill. — *The Life of Christ*
3. D. B. Hansen and Sons, 23 N. Franklin Street, Chicago 6, Ill. — *My First Gift*

E. Coloring Books

1. Father Francis, 1501 S. Layton Boulevard, Milwaukee 15, Wis. — *Jesus Our Savior* (Books 1 and 2); *The Catholic Child; Our Mother Mary; The Childhood of Jesus; Jesus is God* (Miracles); *I Follow Jesus* (Stations); *The Holy Rosary*
2. George A. Pflaum Publ. Inc., 38 West Fifth Street, Dayton 2, Ohio — *God's Gifts; Because He Loves Me*
3. Catechetical Guild, St. Paul 2, Minn. — *I Go to Mass; How Jesus Lived; God Is Wonderful; I Want to be Good; The First Story; Christmas Story; Our Father; Creation; Hail Mary; Baby Jesus; Sacred Heart; Guardian Angel; Jimmy and Jane*

F. Magazines, Booklets, Picture Books

1. Catholic Youth Publications, 25 Groveland Terrace, Minneapolis 5, Minn. — *Mine One*
2. Apostolate of the Press Soc. of St. Paul, 2187 Victory Boulevard, Staten Island, N. Y. — *Miki Picture Books; The Children's Seven Corporal Works of Mercy; The Children's Seven Spiritual Works of Mercy; The Our Father; The Hail Mary; The Mysteries of the Rosary*
3. Bruce Publishing Co., 400 North Broadway, Milwaukee 1, Wis. — *Jesus Shows Me the Way*
4. Doubleday and Company, Inc., Garden City, N. Y. — *The Christ Child*
5. Devotional Publishing Company — *The Lord's Prayer and the Beatitudes for Children; The Hail Mary and the Angelus for Children*
6. Catechetical Guild, St. Paul 2, Minn. — *A Child's Book About God; My Prayers; My Mass; The Sacraments; The Rosary; Friends With God*

CPSIA information can be obtained
at www.ICGtesting.com
Printed in the USA
JSHW021231200220
4329JS00002B/11